Empirical Perspectives on the Psychoanalytic Unconscious

Empirical Perspectives on the
Psychoanalytic
Unconscious

Edited by Robert F. Bornstein and Joseph M. Masling

American Psychological Association • Washington, DC

Published by
American Psychological Association
750 First Street, NE
Washington, DC 20002

Copies may be ordered from
APA Order Department
P.O. Box 92984
Washington, DC 20090-2984

In the United Kingdom and Europe, copies may be ordered from
American Psychological Association
3 Henrietta Street
Covent Garden
London WC2E 8LU
England

Typeset in Palatino by EPS Group Inc., Easton, MD

Printer: Data Reproductions Corporation, Auburn Hills, MI
Jacket designer: Berg Design, Albany, NY
Jacket illustrator: Jim Sande, Albany, NY
Technical / production editor: Valerie Montenegro

Volumes 1, 2, and 3 of the series Empirical Studies of Psychoanalytic Theories, edited by Joseph Masling, were published by The Analytic Press, Hillsdale, NJ.

Library of Congress Cataloging-in-Publication Data
Empirical perspectives on the psychoanalytic unconscious / edited by
    Robert F. Bornstein and Joseph M. Masling.—1st ed.
        p.   cm.—(Empirical studies of psychoanalytic theories ; vol. 7)
    Includes bibliographical references and index.
    ISBN 1-55798-463-8 (acid-free paper)
    1. Psychoanalysis.   2. Subconsciousness.   I. Bornstein, Robert F.
II. Masling, Joseph M.   III. Series.
BF175.E47   1998
154.2—dc21   97-37667
                                                                                    CIP

British Library Cataloguing-in-Publication Data
A CIP record is available from the British Library.

Printed in the United States of America
First edition

Contents

Contributors

Robert F. **Bornstein** is Professor of Psychology at Gettysburg College. He has written numerous articles on perception without awareness and has published widely on the dynamics of dependent personality traits. Bornstein wrote *The Dependent Personality* (1993); coedited with Thane Pittman *Perception Without Awareness: Cognitive, Clinical and Social Perspectives* (1992); coedited with Joseph Masling Volumes 4 through 6 in the Empirical Studies of Psychoanalytic Theories series (1993, 1994, 1996); and received the Society for Personality Assessment's 1995 Walter Klopfer Award for Distinguished Contribution to the Literature on Personality Assessment.

Seymour Epstein is Professor Emeritus in the Department of Psychology at the University of Massachusetts at Amherst, where he has been since he received his PhD from the University of Wisconsin in 1953. He is a diplomate in clinical psychology, and he initiated the doctoral program in clinical psychology at the University of Massachusetts, although he is now in the Personality and Social Psychology Division. He has been the recipient of a National Institute of Mental Health (NIMH) research grant for more than 40 years, including a merit award for the past 10 years, and he has received a NIMH Research Scientist Award for 10 years. His major interest is in the development of an integrative theory of personality that retains the virtues of psychoanalytic theory without its limitations.

Daniel Kriegman is a faculty member of the Massachusetts Institute for Psychoanalysis, founder and coeditor of the new psychoanalytic journal, *Self and Other: Critical Debates,* and a founder and on the faculty of The Psychoanalytic Institute for Couple and Family Therapy. He has written numerous articles on the interface of psychoanalysis and evolutionary biology. He is in full-time private practice with individuals and couples in Newton and Cambridge, Massachusetts.

Joseph M. Masling is Emeritus Professor of Psychology at the State University of New York at Buffalo. He has written numerous articles on interpersonal and situational variables influencing projective tests, and he has published widely on the empirical study of psychoanalytic concepts. Masling edited the first three volumes of the Empirical Studies of Psychoanalytic Theories series (1983, 1986, 1990); coedited with Robert F. Bornstein the second three volumes, *Psychoanalytic Perspectives on Psychopathology* (1993), *Empirical Perspectives on Object Relations Theory* (1994), and *Psychoanalytic Perspectives on Developmental Psychology* (1996); and received the Society for Personality Assessment's 1997 Bruno Klopfer Award for Lifetime Achievement in Personality Assessment.

Howard Shevrin is Professor of Psychology in the Departments of Psychiatry and Psychology at the University of Michigan. His primary research interests are in the experimental and clinical study of unconscious processes. He is also a psychoanalyst.

Paul Siegel received his MA in 1997 from the Derner Institute of Advanced Psychological Studies at Adelphi University and is a doctoral student there in clinical psychology. He is also an extern at the New York Psychoanalytic Institute. His interests include the development of rigorous qualitative research methods for studying the psychoanalytic process, the structure of subjectivity, and the nature of unconscious processes. He aspires to become an academic and a clinician.

Jerome L. Singer received his doctorate in clinical psychology from the University of Pennsylvania in 1950 and his certificate in psychoanalysis from the William Alanson White Institute in 1958. He is currently Professor of Psychology at Yale University, where he has also served as director of the Graduate Program in Clinical Psychology and as director of Graduate Studies in Psychology.

Joel Weinberger is a practicing clinical psychologist and Associate Professor at the Derner Institute of Advanced Psychological Studies at Adelphi University. He received his PhD in clinical psychology at the Graduate Faculty of the New School for Social Research and conducted postdoctoral work in human motivation at Harvard University. His areas of specialization include human motivation, unconscious processes, longitudinal personality research, and psychoanalytic and integrative psychotherapy. He is currently writing a book on unconscious processes.

Drew Westen is Associate Professor at Harvard Medical School and chief psychologist at the Cambridge Hospital in Cambridge, Massachusetts. He is the author of numerous articles and two books, including *Self and Society* (1985) and an introductory psychology textbook called *Psychology: Mind, Brain, and Culture* (1996).

Introduction:
The Psychoanalytic Unconscious

Robert F. Bornstein and Joseph M. Masling

Few ideas are as closely linked with Freudian thinking as is the concept of the unconscious. It is the cornerstone of psychoanalytic theory and the thread that connects Freud's earliest writings with the work of those who came years—or even decades—later (Eagle, 1984; Perry & Laurence, 1984). Psychoanalytic theories, neoanalytic models, object relations frameworks, and concepts from self psychology differ in myriad ways, but underlying these differences is a shared emphasis on the critical importance of unconscious mental processes in normal and abnormal development.

The Freudian unconscious is not simply a location where mental processes occur outside of awareness. For Freud (1900/1953, 1926/1959), the unconscious was a dynamic place—a repository for drives, instincts, wishes, and other mental contents so anxiety-laden and full of emotion that they were deliberately kept from awareness (i.e., repressed). Thus, in a now-famous passage from his *General Introduction to Psychoanalysis*, Freud (1920/1956) likened the unconscious to an "ante-room, in which various mental excitations are crowding upon each other, like individual beings. Adjoining this is a second, smaller apartment, a sort of reception-room, in which consciousness resides. But on the threshold between the two there stands a personage with the office of door-keeper, who examines the various mental excitations, censors them, and denies them admittance to the reception-room when he disapproves of them" (p. 305).

For Freud, repressed material represented a kind of double-edged sword, and the process of repression, a necessary evil. Allowed to enter consciousness unaltered, repressed material would be overwhelmingly anxiety-producing, even traumatic. Yet when kept out of consciousness, such material invariably emerged indirectly, resulting in all manner of unrealistic thoughts, troubling dreams, maladaptive behaviors, and psychological symptoms. Moreover, in Freud's view, repression was an energy-consuming process that required eternal vigilance on the part of the ego and diminished the amount of mental energy available for other, more productive endeavors.

Not surprisingly, Freud's concept of the unconscious was controversial from the very beginning. Janet (1905) was harsh in his critique of Freud's hypotheses, noting that "Freud, through his gross exaggeration in this matter of traumatic memory as a cause of nervous disorder, and above all by the way in which he generalizes the theory and applies it to cases in which the patient has no such memories ... suggests to his patients all sorts of notions (sexual for the most part) which are far more likely to be hurtful than helpful" (p. 214). William James (1890) was even more skeptical, declaring that the unconscious "is the sovereign means for believing what one likes in psychology, and of turning what might be a science into a tumbling-ground for whimsies" (pp. 163–164).

Many psychologists viewed Freud's ideas with derision, but not everyone rejected the concept of the unconscious out of hand. In fact, at the same time as William James was dismissing the unconscious as a "tumbling-ground for whimsies," the experimental psychologists C. S. Pierce and Joseph Jastrow were studying unconscious processes in the laboratory and obtaining some promising and provocative results. Attempting to counter the views of early skeptics, Pierce and Jastrow (1884) noted that their findings gave "new reason for believing that we gather what is passing in one another's minds in large measure from sensations so faint that we are not fairly aware of having them, and can give no account of how we reach our conclusions about such matters. The insight of females as well as certain 'telepathic' phenomena may be explained this way. Such faint sensations ought to be fully studied by the psychologist and assiduously cultivated by every man" (p. 83).

Through the years, the concept of the unconscious has remained controversial, and psychologists have continued to hold strong opinions regarding this issue. Until recently, many experimental psychologists remained unconvinced regarding the very existence of unconscious mental processes, utterly resistant to empirical evidence demonstrating that perception, learning, and memory can occur without conscious awareness. Beier (1985) told of his frustrating experience in submitting a subliminal priming study to the *Journal of Experimental Psychology* some years ago, only to have the paper positively reviewed by two associate editors (William Estes and David Grant), but rejected by the journal editor (Arthur Melton) on the grounds that he "just could not believe that critical mental activity could go on without awareness" (p. 248).

Experimental psychologists' skepticism has been surpassed only by the uncritical acceptance of unconscious processes by certain members of the therapeutic community. Consider the views of one contemporary psychotherapist (Fiore, 1989), who asserted with great confidence that "the subconscious mind has a memory bank of everything we ever experienced, exactly as we perceived it. Every thought, emotion, sound of music, word, taste and sight. Everything is faithfully recorded somehow in your mind. Your subconscious mind's memory is perfect, infallible" (p. 17).

Such a passage could be written only by someone who has ignored virtually every published study of human cognition, perception, and memory during the past 40 years. Such a passage would be laughable, except for one thing: It is not all that different from the viewpoint of many practitioners who choose to ignore empirical findings as they formulate clinical theory and make important decisions regarding treatment goals and psychotherapeutic outcomes.

Without question, clinical practice is enhanced when psychologists, psychiatrists, and other mental health professionals are well informed regarding empirical research on unconscious mental processes. The converse is also true: Researchers who study the unconscious empirically are missing a rich source of ideas and hypotheses if they remain uninformed regarding clinical writings on unconscious processes in psychotherapy and if they cannot see for themselves how unconscious thoughts and motivations influence psychotherapeutic process and outcome. In the ensuing chapters, we attempt to bridge this scientist–practitioner gap and to integrate clinical and empirical data on unconscious mental processes in a productive and meaningful way. To put the research programs described in these chapters into the proper perspective, we begin with a brief discussion of the evolution of research on the unconscious during the past 100 years.

The Study of the Unconscious: A Brief History

Research on unconscious mental processes during the twentieth century can be divided into three overlapping phases. For the most part, controversies in this area have centered around the phenomenon of perception without awareness (i.e., implicit perception), the associated phenomena of learning without awareness (i.e., implicit learning), and memory without awareness (i.e., implicit memory). In addition, researchers who study unconscious mental processes have tried to operationalize and study defensive processes (e.g., repression) that occur outside conscious awareness and are revealed only after the fact, oftentimes in a subtle and indirect manner (see Hansen & Hansen, 1988). More recently, researchers have studied the effects of schemas (i.e., mental representations of people, objects, and events, real or imagined; Epstein, 1990) and scripts (i.e., mental agendas that reflect unconscious ideas, ideals, goals, and motivations; Singer & Salovey, 1991). Studies linking social cognitive phenomena with concepts and findings from object relations theory also fall into this important category (Westen, 1991). Other investigators have examined differences between conscious (i.e., explicit or "self-attributed") and unconscious (i.e., implicit) needs and motives (McClelland, Koestner, & Weinberger, 1989).

Early in the twentieth century, research focused on establishing the existence of unconscious mental processes and on demonstrating that these processes could produce measurable effects on motivation, emotion, cognition, and behavior (Dixon, 1971). Poetzl's (1917) classic studies are among the most well-known of these early efforts, but Charles Fisher's (e.g., 1960) classic investigations of subliminal perception and dreaming extended and refined this basic effort. Shevrin's (e.g., Shevrin & Fritzler, 1968) investigations of the effects of stimuli perceived without awareness on primary process thinking and Silverman's (1983; Silverman & Weinberger, 1985) subliminal psychodynamic activation (SPA) studies of the 1960s, 1970s, and 1980s were also concerned to some degree with establishing the existence—and meaningfulness—of unconscious processes in normal and pathological functioning.

The "New Look" perceptual defense and vigilance studies of the 1950s and 1960s ushered in a second phase of research on the unconscious (Greenwald, 1992). These studies produced some striking results that seemed to have important implications for psychodynamic models of repression and other ego defenses. Ultimately, however, these studies turned out to have some noteworthy methodological flaws (Erdelyi, 1974). Disappointing at first, these methodological limitations eventually proved invaluable in alerting researchers to the myriad difficulties inherent in measuring and manipulating unconscious processes. Where measurement issues were once taken for granted, they now moved to center stage and occupied researchers' attention for the next 30 years (Bornstein, 1992).

Controversies surrounding the measurement of unconscious mental processes focused on three major issues. First, researchers attempted to separate the effects of stimulus perception from the effects of memory for previously encountered stimuli (Merikle & Reingold, 1992). Second, researchers tried to minimize the effects of participants' motivations and biases on their willingness to acknowledge subtle stimulus effects (Merikle, 1982). Third, researchers worked to develop measures of stimulus awareness that were sensitive and rigorous enough to satisfy even the most skeptical experimentalists (Masling, 1992).

Holender's (1986) scathing critique of research on subliminal semantic priming prompted researchers to take a long, hard look at the limitations of earlier work in perception, learning, and memory without awareness. By now, however, the paradigmatic tide was beginning to turn; new methods were developed that finally put to rest many of the lingering methodological controversies in this area. By the late 1980s, Jacoby's (e.g., Jacoby, Toth, Lindsay, & Debner, 1992) process dissociation studies and Merikle's (e.g., Merikle & Reingold, 1992) direct/indirect approach to assessing unconscious influences had rendered moot many earlier criticisms. These investigations demonstrated unequivocally that not only do stimuli perceived or remembered without awareness influence behavior, but they also produce effects on responding that are qualitatively different from those produced by stimuli consciously perceived and remembered.

The impact of Jacoby's and Merikle's studies—as well as those of Greenwald (e.g., Greenwald, Klinger, & Liu, 1989), Reber (1989), Schacter (1987), and others (e.g., Kunst-Wilson & Zajonc, 1980)— cannot be overstated. Consider the following: During the 1980s, there were dozens of published papers questioning the existence of unconscious perception and memory. Since 1990, there has not been a single article in a mainstream psychology journal challenging the existence of these phenomena.

The 1990s have seen a major shift in the kinds of questions asked by those who study unconscious processes empirically. Satisfied that such processes exist and that they can be operationalized and measured, researchers are now exploring the dynamics of the unconscious. In this context, many psychologists have focused on the cognition–emotion relationship, attempting to determine whether unconscious preferences and attitudes require extensive cognitive processing in order to develop (Bornstein & D'Agostino, 1994; Murphy & Zajonc, 1993). Cognitive and psychodynamic researchers (e.g., Epstein, 1994; Kihlstrom, 1987) have tried to disentangle the relationship between the cognitive unconscious (which underlies a variety of relatively automatized behaviors, from text comprehension to driving) and the psychoanalytic unconscious (which is typically conceived as motivating behavior as well as directing it).

Some researchers have explored the role of the self-representation in conscious and unconscious perception and memory (Horowitz, 1991; Stern, 1987), whereas others are examining the interaction of implicit and self-attributed needs and motives (Bornstein, Bowers, & Bonner, 1996; McClelland et al., 1989). As these research paradigms become more sophisticated, a new concern has arisen as well: Psychologists are beginning to study the relationships among different forms of unconscious mental processing; examining the mechanisms that underlie implicit perception, implicit learning, and implicit memory; and trying to understand how these mechanisms interact and influence each other (Greenwald & Banaji, 1995; Kurtzman, in press).

The Psychoanalytic Unconscious: Present and Future

Past is prologue, and the key issues being investigated today are rooted in those that came before. We cannot say with certainty what topics will occupy researchers 10 (or even 5) years from now, but on the basis of current trends in this area, we can make some reasonable predictions regarding where the study of the unconscious is headed as the twenty-first century approaches.

The Sociobiology of the Unconscious

Evolutionary theorists posit that unconscious processes predate the beginnings of human consciousness by many millennia (see, e.g., Ornstein, 1986). Moreover, researchers have generated some fascinating hypotheses regarding the adaptive value of unconscious processes in human mental life. Humans' dual processing of internal and external reality is complex and resource-demanding, but it affords many advantages as they adapt to an ever-changing physical and social environment (Slavin & Kriegman, 1992). Sociobiological frameworks are notoriously difficult to test empirically, but work in this area promises to forge new links between psychodynamic thinking and evolutionary theory.

Neuropsychological Correlates of Unconscious Processes

Advances in brain imaging techniques have allowed researchers to observe the neuropsychological correlates of unconscious processes while these processes are occurring (Crick, 1994; Shevrin, Bond, Brakel, Hertel, & Williams, 1996). Implicit memory researchers pioneered work in this area. Now their efforts are being modified and adapted to provide information regarding the neurological un-derpinnings of implicit learning and implicit memory (Joseph, 1992). As unconscious processes are linked to specific brain areas, psychoanalysis in many ways is beginning to come full circle, re-capturing Freud's early efforts to develop a science of psychody-namics rooted firmly in biology.

Testing the Limits of the Unconscious

Freud's conceptualization of the unconscious evolved over time, and it has been modified and updated many times by those who came later. It now appears that the unconscious is "smarter" than first thought, capable of processing complex verbal and visual in-formation and even anticipating (and planning for) future events (Weiss & Sampson, 1986). As the information-processing capabili-ties of the unconscious have been examined in detail, the view of the unconscious has changed as well (Loftus & Klinger, 1992). No longer simply a repository for drives and impulses, the uncon-scious appears to play a role in problem solving, hypothesis test-ing, and creativity (Rothenberg, 1994).

A Life Span Perspective on the Unconscious

People begin life with limited consciousness, and if they are lucky enough to live to old age, they are likely to find that consciousness narrows again at the other end of the life span. Studies of prelin-guistic infants are beginning to provide clues regarding the internal mental states characteristic of the first months of life (see, e.g., Rovee-Collier, 1993). Studies of neuropsychological decline in eld-erly persons and in neurologically impaired individuals provide valuable information regarding the impact of sensory and memory losses on implicit learning and implicit memory (Johnson, Kim, & Risse, 1985).

The Conscious–Unconscious Relationship

Psychology began as the study of consciousness, and as psychol-ogists solve some long-standing questions regarding the uncon-scious, attention has begun to return to consciousness. Researchers are now investigating various dimensions of the conscious–unconscious relationship, exploring the transformations that occur as unconscious material is made conscious (Rakover, 1993; Uleman & Bargh, 1989). Studies in this area are shifting the emphasis of research on the unconscious from content to process—a conceptual shift that began many years ago and is just now beginning to reach fruition.

The Unconscious as a Unifying Concept in Psychology

Once upon a time, only clinical and cognitive psychologists studied unconscious mental processes empirically. Over time, neuropsychologists and social psychologists have joined in what is rapidly becoming an integrative, interdisciplinary exercise (Bornstein & Pittman, 1992). Developmental psychologists are just beginning to study unconscious processes in earnest, but their ideas and findings promise to invigorate the field during the coming years. The study of the unconscious has the potential to become a unifying force in psychology, linking cognition and emotion, infancy and old age, normal and pathological development, brain and psyche.

The Empirical Studies of Psychoanalytic Theories Series

The Empirical Studies of Psychoanalytic Theories book series was begun in 1983 with a single, simple aim: To contribute to the empirical base of psychoanalysis by presenting the best and most current research inspired by psychoanalytic theories. A considerable amount of work has already been completed in this area (see, e.g., S. Fisher & Greenberg, 1996; Kline, 1972; Masling, 1983, 1986, 1990; Masling & Bornstein, 1993, 1994, 1996). Much more remains to be done.

A scientific theory is expected to generate data that will force it to be revised and ultimately discarded (Kuhn, 1962). Psychoanalytic theory has been roundly criticized in this regard (e.g., Crews, 1996; Grunbaum, 1984), although in our view, much of this criticism is unfounded. To be sure, Freud in his later years was a poor empiricist (although the prepsychoanalytic Freud—discoverer of eel testicles and the anaesthetic properties of cocaine—was in fact an accomplished researcher). Compounding the problem, many of Freud's followers have viewed laboratory data with derision (see, e.g., Tansey, 1992). However, many psychoanalytically oriented clinicians are open to empirical findings, provided that these findings are presented in a way that is both accessible and clinically meaningful. Surveys indicate that many practitioners are receptive to empirical data but believe that most studies published in contemporary psychology journals have little relevance for clinical practice (Beutler, Williams, Wakefield, & Entwistle, 1995).

Kurt Lewin (1951) once remarked that "there is nothing so practical as a good theory" (p. 169). This memorable phrase has inspired generations of social psychologists, but it is only partially correct. A theory without data has little practical value, and data cannot help in theory building if those who build the theory ignore them. Psychoanalytic researchers have demonstrated that they are capable of designing studies as methodologically sound as those constructed by experimental psychologists. The goal of psychoanalytic researchers must now be to present these findings in such a way that psychoanalytic psychologists—academic and practitioner alike—find them to be compelling and engaging.

The Empirical Studies of Psychoanalytic Theories series is nearly two decades old. The present volume—the seventh in the series —focuses on empirical research on the psychoanalytic unconscious. Contributors to this volume have approached this topic from many different perspectives, and their contrasting viewpoints, emphases, and methodologies enrich the material presented here. We all agree on the importance of controlled empirical research for theory building and hypothesis testing. Moreover, all contributors to this book have attempted to bring the research findings they discuss to issues of diagnosis and clinical intervention.

The volume opens with Drew Westen's insightful analysis of research on unconscious cognition, affect, and motivation. Westen's integrative review helps link empirical work in three separate domains of experimental psychology, each of which is central to ongoing work on the psychoanalytic unconscious. In addition, Westen's chapter demonstrates how studies from outside psychoanalysis can have important implications for psychodynamic ideas.

Contemporary findings from neuropsychology, social cognition, and implicit memory are surprisingly consistent with some long-standing psychoanalytic hypotheses. Howard Shevrin provides a detailed discussion of the Freud–Rapaport view of consciousness and discusses a number of empirical studies that allow the validity of this important conceptual framework to be assessed and refined. Shevrin's chapter makes explicit the fact that the study of unconscious and conscious experiences are inextricably linked: Studying one set of processes invariably involves scrutinizing the complementary processes as well. Moreover, Shevrin's own research program, wherein evoked brain potentials are used to examine unconscious mental processes that have heretofore eluded close empirical study, represents an innovative, heuristic approach to assessing unconscious conflicts in the laboratory.

Paul Siegel and Joel Weinberger review research on Lloyd Silverman's SPA paradigm and link this work to contemporary research on conscious and unconscious motivation. Siegel and Weinberger's review explores the processes that underlie SPA effects, at the same time demonstrating how these effects are part of a larger set of unconscious (or "implicit") drives and motives. As Siegel and Weinberger show, not only are psychoanalytic theories enhanced by attention to work in other areas of psychology, but also the converse is true: Research in other domains may be enriched when psychodynamic concepts and findings are integrated into ongoing research programs in these areas.

Seymour Epstein's thorough and detailed discussion of cognitive–experiential self-theory has important implications for psychoanalytic models of conscious and unconscious processes, as well as psychodynamic models of the self, transference, and the psychotherapeutic process. Epstein's fascinating and provocative chapter shows how different components of unconscious experience interact to influence normal and pathological adjustment and how these components can be operationalized and studied empirically. Moreover, Epstein's research confirms that psychodynamic clinical work can be enhanced when empirical work on unconscious mental representations and "scripts" are used to facilitate insight and change within the therapeutic milieu.

Jerome Singer's work on daydreams, the stream of consciousness, and self-representations places mental representations of the self and significant others squarely in the center of psychoanalytically informed research on the unconscious. In fact, Singer's work links object relations theory with ideas and findings from a variety of psychodynamic frameworks. By organizing and contrasting various methods for assessing conscious and unconscious experience, Singer not only traces the development of contemporary research on the Freudian unconscious, but he also provides a heuristic framework for exploring aspects of the dynamic unconscious that have yet to be studied.

Daniel Kriegman's challenging, thought-provoking review makes explicit what many psychodynamic theorists and researchers assume but never discuss—that a thorough understanding of unconscious mental processes must involve some attention to biological, evolutionary underpinnings of conscious and unconscious experience. Kriegman describes recent evolutionary work on the dynamic unconscious, and he links this work to the processes that occur in psychodynamic therapy. His analysis goes a long way toward constructing an integrative evolutionary–dynamic conceptualization of the psychoanalytic unconscious.

References

Beier, E. G. (1985). Setting new trends. *American Psychologist, 40*, 248.

Beutler, L. E., Williams, R. E., Wakefield, P. J., & Entwistle, S. R. (1995). Bridging scientist and practitioner perspectives in clinical psychology. *American Psychologist, 50*, 984–994.

Bornstein, R. F. (1992). Perception without awareness: Retrospect and prospect. In R. F. Bornstein & T. S. Pittman (Eds.), *Perception without awareness: Cognitive, clinical, and social perspectives* (pp. 3–13). New York: Guilford Press.

Bornstein, R. F., Bowers, K. S., & Bonner, S. (1996). Effects of induced mood states on objective and projective dependency scores. *Journal of Personality Assessment, 67*, 324–340.

Bornstein, R. F., & D'Agostino, P. R. (1994). The attribution and discounting of perceptual fluency: Preliminary tests of a perceptual fluency/attributional model of the mere exposure effect. *Social Cognition, 12*, 103–128.

Bornstein, R. F., & Pittman, T. S. (Eds.) (1992). *Perception without awareness: Cognitive, clinical, and social perspectives.* New York: Guilford Press.

Crews, F. (1996). The verdict on Freud. *Psychological Science, 7,* 63–68.

Crick, F. (1994). *The astonishing hypothesis: The scientific search for the soul.* New York: Scribner.

Dixon, N. F. (1971). *Subliminal perception: The nature of a controversy.* New York: McGraw-Hill.

Eagle, M. N. (1984). *Recent developments in psychoanalysis.* New York: McGraw-Hill.

Epstein, S. (1990). Cognitive–experiential self theory. In L. Pervin (Ed.), *Handbook of personality: Theory and research* (pp. 165–192). New York: Guilford Press.

Epstein, S. (1994). Integration of the cognitive and the dynamic unconscious. *American Psychologist, 49,* 709–724.

Erdelyi, M. H. (1974). A new look at the "New Look": Perceptual defense and vigilance. *Psychological Review, 81,* 1–25.

Fiore, E. (1989). *Encounters: A psychologist reveals case studies of abductions by extraterrestrials.* New York: Doubleday.

Fisher, C. (1960). Subliminal and supraliminal influences on dreams. *American Journal of Psychiatry, 116,* 1009–1017.

Fisher, S., & Greenberg, R. P. (1996). *Freud scientifically reappraised.* New York: Wiley.

Freud, S. (1953). The interpretation of dreams. *The standard edition of the complete psychological works of Sigmund Freud* (Vols. 4 and 5). London: Hogarth Press. (Original work published 1900)

Freud, S. (1956). A general introduction to psychoanalysis. *The standard edition of the complete psychological works of Sigmund Freud* (Vol. 8). London: Hogarth Press. (Original work published 1920)

Freud, S. (1959). Inhibitions, symptoms, and anxiety. *The standard edition of the complete psychological works of Sigmund Freud* (Vol. 20). London: Hogarth Press. (Original work published 1926)

Greenwald, A. G. (1992). New Look 3: Unconscious cognition reclaimed. *American Psychologist, 47,* 766–779.

Greenwald, A. G., & Banaji, M. R. (1995). Implicit social cognition: Attitudes, self-esteem, and stereotypes. *Psychological Review, 102,* 4–27.

Greenwald, A. G., Klinger, M. R., & Liu, T. J. (1989). Unconscious processing of dichoptically masked words. *Memory and Cognition, 17,* 35–47.

Grunbaum, A. (1984). *The foundations of psychoanalysis.* Berkeley, CA: University of California Press.

Hansen, R. D., & Hansen, C. H. (1988). Repression of emotionally tagged memories: The architecture of less complex emotions. *Journal of Personality and Social Psychology, 55,* 811–818.

Holender, D. (1986). Semantic activation without conscious identification in dichotic listening, parafoveal vision, and visual masking. *Behavioral and Brain Sciences, 9,* 1–66.

Horowitz, M. (Ed.). (1991). *Person schemas and maladaptive interpersonal patterns.* Chicago: University of Chicago Press.

Jacoby, L. L., Toth, J. P., Lindsay, S. D., & Debner, J. A. (1992). Lectures for a layperson: Methods for revealing unconscious processes. In R. F. Bornstein & T. S. Pittman (Eds.), *Perception without awareness: Cognitive, clinical, and social perspectives* (pp. 81–120). New York: Guilford Press.

James, W. (1890). *The principles of psychology* (Vol. 1). New York: Holt.

Janet, P. (1905). *L'Automatisme psychologique.* Paris: Alcan.

Johnson, M. K., Kim, J. K., & Risse, G. (1985). Do alcoholic Korsakoff's syndrome patients acquire affective reactions? *Journal of Experimental Psychology: Learning, Memory and Cognition, 11,* 22–36.

Joseph, R. (1992). The limbic system: Emotion, laterality, and unconscious mind. *Psychoanalytic Review, 79,* 405–456.

Kihlstrom, J. F. (1987). The cognitive unconscious. *Science, 237,* 1145–1152.

Kline, P. (1972). *Fact and fantasy in Freudian theory.* London: Methuen.

Kuhn, T. S. (1962). *The structure of scientific revolutions.* Chicago: University of Chicago Press.

Kunst-Wilson, W. R., & Zajonc, R. B. (1980). Affective discrimination of stimuli that cannot be recognized. *Science, 207,* pp. 557–558.

Kurtzman, H. (Ed.). (in press). *Cognition and psychodynamics: New perspectives.* New York: Oxford University Press.

Lewin, K. (1951). Problems of research in social psychology. In D. Cartwright (Ed.), *Field theory in social science* (pp. 155–169). New York: Harper & Row.

Loftus, E. F., & Klinger, M. R. (1992). Is the unconscious smart or dumb? *American Psychologist, 47,* 761–765.

Masling, J. M. (Ed.). (1983). *Empirical studies of psychoanalytic theories* (Vol. 1). Hillsdale, NJ: Analytic Press.

Masling, J. M. (Ed.). (1986). *Empirical studies of psychoanalytic theories* (Vol. 2). Hillsdale, NJ: Analytic Press.

Masling, J. M. (Ed.). (1990). *Empirical studies of psychoanalytic theories* (Vol. 3). Hillsdale, NJ: Analytic Press.

Masling, J. M. (1992). What does it all mean? In R. F. Bornstein & T. S. Pittman (Eds.), *Perception without awareness: Cognitive, clinical, and social perspectives* (pp. 259–276). New York: Guilford Press.

Masling, J. M., & Bornstein, R. F. (Eds.). (1993). *Empirical studies of psychoanalytic theories: Vol. 4. Psychoanalytic perspectives on psychopathology.* Washington, DC: American Psychological Association.

Masling, J. M., & Bornstein, R. F. (Eds.). (1994). *Empirical studies of psychoanalytic theories: Vol. 5. Empirical perspectives on object relations theory.* Washington, DC: American Psychological Association.

Masling, J. M., & Bornstein, R. F. (Eds.). (1996). *Empirical studies of psychoanalytic theories: Vol. 6. Psychoanalytic perspectives on developmental psychology.* Washington, DC: American Psychological Association.

McClelland, D. C., Koestner, R., & Weinberger, J. (1989). How do implicit and self-attributed motives differ? *Psychological Review, 96,* 690–702.

Merikle, P. M. (1982). Unconscious perception revisited. *Perception and Psychophysics, 31*, 298–301.

Merikle, P. M., & Reingold, E. M. (1992). Measuring unconscious perceptual processes. In R. F. Bornstein & T. S. Pittman (Eds.), *Perception without awareness: Cognitive, clinical, and social perspectives* (pp. 55–80). New York: Guilford Press.

Murphy, S. T., & Zajonc, R. B. (1993). Affect, cognition, and awareness: Affective priming with optimal and suboptimal stimulus exposures. *Journal of Personality and Social Psychology, 64*, 723–739.

Ornstein, R. E. (1986). *The psychology of consciousness.* New York: Penguin.

Perry, C., & Laurence, J. R. (1984). Mental processing outside of awareness: The contributions of Freud and Janet. In K. S. Bowers & D. Meichenbaum (Eds.), *The unconscious reconsidered* (pp. 9–48). New York: Wiley.

Pierce, C. S., & Jastrow, J. (1884). On small differences in sensation. *Memoirs of the National Academy of Science, 3*, 75–83.

Poetzl, O. (1917). The relationship between experimentally induced dream images and indirect vision. *Psychological Issues, 2*, 41–120.

Rakover, S. (1993). Empirical criteria for task susceptibility to introspective awareness and awareness effects. *Philosophical Psychology, 6*, 451–467.

Reber, A. S. (1989). Implicit learning and tacit knowledge. *Journal of Experimental Psychology: General, 118*, 219–235.

Rothenberg, A. (1994). Studies in the creative process: An empirical investigation. In J. M. Masling & R. F. Bornstein (Eds.), *Empirical studies of psychoanalytic theories: Vol. 5. Empirical perspectives on object relations theory* (pp. 195–245). Washington, DC: American Psychological Association.

Rovee-Collier, C. (1993). The capacity for long-term memory in infancy. *Current Directions in Psychological Science, 2*, 130–135.

Schacter, D. L. (1987). Implicit memory: History and current status. *Journal of Experimental Psychology: Learning, Memory and Cognition, 13*, 501–518.

Shevrin, H., Bond, J. A., Brakel, L. A. W., Hertel, R. K., & Williams, W. J. (1996). *Conscious and unconscious processes: Psychodynamic, cognitive, and neurophysiological convergences.* New York: Guilford Press.

Shevrin, H., & Fritzler, D. (1968). Visual evoked response correlates of unconscious mental processes. *Science, 161*, 295–298.

Silverman, L. H. (1983). The subliminal psychodynamic activation method. In J. M. Masling (Ed.), *Empirical studies of psychoanalytic theories* (Vol. 1, pp. 69–100). Hillsdale, NJ: Erlbaum.

Silverman, L. H., & Weinberger, J. (1985). Mommy and I are one: Implications for psychotherapy. *American Psychologist, 40*, 1296–1308.

Singer, J. L., & Salovey, P. (1991). Organized knowledge structures and personality: Person schemas, self schemas, prototypes, and scripts. In M. J. Horowitz (Ed.), *Person schemas and maladaptive interpersonal patterns* (pp. 33–79). Chicago: University of Chicago Press.

Slavin, M. O., & Kriegman, D. (1992). *The adaptive design of the human psyche: Psychoanalysis, evolutionary biology, and the therapeutic process.* New York: Guilford Press.

Stern, R. (Ed.). (1987). *Theories of the unconscious and theories of the self.* New York: Academic Press.

Tansey, M. J. (1992). Countertransference theory, quantitative research, and the problem of therapist–patient sexual abuse. In J. W. Barron, M. N. Eagle, & D. L. Wolitzky (Eds.), *Interface of psychoanalysis and psychology* (pp. 539–557). Washington, DC: American Psychological Association.

Uleman, J. S., & Bargh, J. A. (Eds.). (1989). *Unintended thought.* New York: Guilford Press.

Weiss, J., & Sampson, H. (1986). *The psychoanalytic process: Theory, clinical observation, and empirical research.* New York: Guilford Press.

Westen, D. (1991). Social cognition and object relations. *Psychological Bulletin, 109,* 429–455.

1

Unconscious Thought, Feeling, and Motivation:
The End of a Century-Long Debate

Drew Westen

The notion that much of mental life is unconscious has long distinguished psychoanalytic approaches to personality, psychopathology, psychotherapy, and development from alternative perspectives in psychology. For years, a different epistemology underlay the beliefs of those who either accepted or rejected this central psychoanalytic proposition. Those who accepted it, most of whom were clinicians, tended to find clinical data compelling and to remain uninterested in, or undaunted by, empirical debates about its veracity. Instead, they found the proposition so self-evident from personal and professional experience, and so necessary for making sense of complex events observed or examined in the consulting room, that they took it as axiomatic. Those who rejected the existence of unconscious processes, in contrast, were largely experimentalists, who tended to embrace a positivist–empiricist philosophy of science that views hypothesis testing as the essence of science. They argued that the empirical data either did not exist or did not support the concept of unconscious processes.

Until recently, the debate about unconscious processes has been

The author wishes to thank the editors of this volume for their comments on an earlier draft of this chapter.

1

irresolvable because the two sides have held such vastly different ideas about what constitutes evidence or what would constitute refutation. Today, however, the situation is different. Many clinicians remain relatively uninterested in empirical data (to their peril, and that of their patients, I believe), but the data in support of the concept of unconscious processes generated *from the laboratory alone* are now so overwhelming that I believe the debate is over. The aim of this chapter is to review this evidence by considering empirical data on unconscious thought, feeling, and motivation. I hope to show that even if one were to concede the argument about the utility of clinical data—that is, to assume that clinical observation has no epistemological value—one would still draw the conclusion that the clinically derived proposition about the existence and importance of unconscious processes is now as close to a "fact" as any proposition in contemporary psychology.[1]

Before doing so, however, it is important to note what kind of "unconscious" is being addressed. Today, psychologists often distinguish the "psychoanalytic unconscious" from the "cognitive unconscious." The psychoanalytic unconscious was, in Freud's theory, a sector of the mind isolated by its unacceptability to the

---

[1] I do not, in fact, believe that it is clinically, scientifically, or philosophically sensible to concede that clinical data are epistemologically vacuous. The studies reviewed here demonstrate that clinicians would have been working with their arms tied behind their backs for the past century if they had waited for experimental research to document what was manifestly apparent. The positivist–empiricist philosophy that guides the work of many academic psychologists—which confuses the question of what is (or has been) tested with the question of what is probably true—needs to be reconsidered in light of the belated corroboration of a hypothesis that was pilloried by experimental psychologists since the beginning of the discipline. On the other hand, as argued elsewhere (Westen, in press-b), the data from these studies suggest a number of important revisions in psychoanalytic theory and terminology, such as the use of the term *"the" unconscious*, when experimental data show that unconscious processes do not all share certain crucial properties ascribed to them by Freud. For example, unconscious motives are not all primitive or irrational, and what Freud described as preconscious processes are every bit as associationistic in their operations as what he described as unconscious processes. (For a discussion of the experimental evidence more broadly relating to psychodynamic theories, beyond those related specifically to unconscious processes, see Fisher and Greenberg (1996) and Westen (in press-b).)

censor that guarded consciousness. In the structural model, much of what Freud originally called "the unconscious" became transformed into the id, a seething cauldron of sexual and aggressive drives that were unacceptable to the superego and hence allowed into consciousness only in derivative form by the ego. Like its topographic progenitor (the unconscious), the id was viewed as operating on the basis of primary process (wishful, associative, nonlogical, and imagistic) thought. The ego, like the preconscious and conscious of the topographic model, was more rational, operating on the basis of secondary process thought at least much of the time.

As I have argued elsewhere (Westen, in press-a) and as will become clear in describing experimental investigations of unconscious cognition, affect, and emotion, we would do better to speak of "unconscious processes" (as we usually do in thinking about case material clinically) than of "the unconscious" (as Freud did and as many continue to do theoretically). The reason is that unconscious processes vary on a variety of dimensions and are not so easily described with the same broad brush strokes. Some unconscious processes are wishful. Yet people also have unconscious fears—and many conscious processes are wishful as well. Some unconscious processes operate on the basis of principles of association. However, people can also solve problems unconsciously, as in familiar "aha" experiences. And there is no necessary linkage between thought that is wishful and thought that operates by principles of association. Many associative processes, such as those assessed in cognitive priming studies described below, have little to do with wishes. What these studies suggest is that beneath the veneer of consciousness is a constant flux and flow of associations that produce conscious experience, direct behavior, and produce emotional responses.

Thus, from a psychoanalytic viewpoint, we would do well to move away theoretically from archaic discussions of "the unconscious" inherited from German romanticism and move instead toward the common, everyday clinical usage of the term *unconscious*, which is adjectival, not nominal. That is, when listening to patients, we notice that a thought, feeling, or motive seems to be operating outside of awareness, and we try, in collaboration with our patients, to make progressively closer approximations as to what those processes might be, using all the data at our disposal. In this way, we can help them escape repetitive interpersonal patterns that are unsatisfying or change ways of feeling or responding to feelings (defenses) that may be unpleasant or dysfunctional. Today, when analysts speak of "unconscious fantasies," they are as likely to mean unconscious cognitive constructions—as in a sexually abused patient's belief that she caused the abuse and deserves to be punished for it—as unconscious wishes. The point is that, from a clinical perspective, what is most important today about "the psychoanalytic unconscious" is the hypothesis that wishes, fears, defenses, affects, and beliefs can be unconscious and that in their unconscious state, they can nevertheless have a profound impact on ongoing conscious thought, feeling, and behavior. As will be seen, this is precisely the position supported by experimental data, only a small proportion of which has been conducted by analytically oriented experimentalists.

The cognitive unconscious, in contrast, came onto the scene in the 1980s and was heralded in Kihlstrom's (1987) paper of that title in *Science*. Its explicit roots were in a cognitive–experimental tradition that had happened upon the fact that much of what was going on cognitively was not going on consciously. Researchers studying the cognitive unconscious have generally been careful to steer clear of any discussion of psychoanalytic ideas, and when they do (which is rare), they typically make every kind of disclaimer that their concept has nothing to do with Freud's. In one sense, they are right: Until very recently, studies of the cognitive unconscious had nothing to do with affect and motivation, the primary focus of the psychoanalytic unconscious. Yet studying unconscious cognitive processes has inevitably led down a slippery slope toward affect and motivation. When Descartes proclaimed, "I think, therefore I am," he left out a prior step: "I am, because my parents were sexually attracted to each other." He also left out the fact that what he thinks about largely reflects what he wishes for and fears, that is, what matters to him emotionally and motivationally. Essentially, then, researchers interested in the cognitive unconscious began their work with little interest in affect and motivation. What has become clear as their research has progressed, however, is that what is sauce for the cognitive goose is sauce for the affective and motivational gander: Just as a great deal of cognition occurs through the interaction of hundreds, thousands, or millions of neural circuits activated outside awareness (depending on what one counts as a circuit), so, too, are affective and motivational processes largely processed outside of awareness.

What the proponents of the cognitive unconscious have done, which has never been so clear in the psychoanalytic literature, is to show that this is the way the mind works, regardless of whether a person has a reason to keep a thought, feeling, or motive unconscious. The architecture of the mind is such that a conscious flow of experience is superimposed on an unconscious flow of associations and a dazzlingly complex array of interacting neural circuits that operate in parallel. But what the psychoanalytic point of view—from Freud's earliest papers to the present—adds are (a) a recognition that what is unconscious may also be unconscious for a reason, namely that its access to consciousness would be distressing; (b) a recognition that unconscious processes can be remarkably complex, guiding behavior in very specific directions without ever attaining consciousness; and (c) a method for observing the way people behave that allows the systematic exploration of unconscious networks of association, wishes, fears, and ways of regulating emotion.

As is now obvious, I do not subscribe to the view that the psychoanalytic and the cognitive unconscious are unrelated or incommensurable (see also Epstein, 1994). That they have so appeared largely reflects the limited purview taken by adherents of one or the other. Humans think and feel, and any theory that focuses on one or the other is simply a limited theory. Nor do I believe that empirical and interpretive methods are competing, unrelated, or incommensurable ways of knowing. A century ago, Freud recognized the importance of unconscious processes and built a theory around it. Equally important, he and those who have followed in his tradition have developed a method for interpreting patterns of unconscious activity. This method starts with the raw data of patients' narratives about everyday events, associations, behavior in the consulting room, and so forth, and gradually, through successive approximations, produces hypotheses about patterns of unconscious activity (such as associational networks) that could account for the patterns of observable behavior. This method is empirical in the sense that it begins with data and uses "goodness of fit" to try to account for the data parsimoniously (just as studies of cognitive priming of associational networks do), as clinician and patient together gradually hone more fine-grained hypotheses about the way the patient's mind works. This clinical–interpretive method can provide data that corroborate the notion of unconscious processes, but its major import is the "transformational grammar" it provides for interpreting from psychological surface structure to affective, motivational, and cognitive "deep structure." Experimental investigations, on the other hand, yield much stronger data about the nature, structure, and function of various kinds of unconscious and conscious processes. However, they are less successful at studying complex processes that are difficult to reproduce in the laboratory, and they have a different aim than the construction of grammars of interpretation. As I will show, they have nevertheless begun to describe and refine some of the basic hypotheses underlying a century of interpretive clinical work.[2]

Unconscious Thought and Memory

I will be brief in describing the literature on unconscious cognitive processes, since within the remarkably brief span of a decade or so, the proposition that much of cognition occurs unconsciously has become no longer controversial and the evidence for it has been reviewed elsewhere (Roediger, 1990; Schacter, 1992; Squire, 1987). For years, cognitive psychologists did not specify whether the processes they were describing were conscious or unconscious. The assumption, however, was that cognition had a serial architecture, in which information entered sequential memory stores, was ultimately stored in a single all-purpose long-term memory,

---

[2]Despite the *potential* for integrating psychoanalytic and cognitive, and clinical and experimental, approaches to unconscious processes, I do not believe that we are there, or that getting there will be easy. The major obstacle, I believe, has less to do with issues of theory or method than with the different personality styles of psychologists who tend to pursue one path or the other. People choose to study cognition rather than affect for a reason, and they choose to be clinicians or researchers for a reason. Those reasons tend to be diametrically opposed. Unfortunately, the extremes on each side have too often dominated cognitive science and psychoanalysis, making any rapprochement difficult.

and was retrieved and manipulated in short-term memory (which was equated with consciousness). This standard information processing model has undergone a number of changes over the past 30 years, as researchers have found, for example, that attentional processes guided by information stored in long-term memory influence perception, even when this information has not been retrieved into short-term memory, and that information may be stored in long-term memory without prior storage in short-term memory (see Anderson, 1995). One of the major changes, however, has been the relatively recent discovery of implicit memory.

Implicit Memory

Explicit memory is the kind of memory traditionally studied by memory researchers, involving conscious retrieval of information such as one's prior address, the capital of Egypt, or an event that occurred last year. *Implicit memory*, in contrast, refers to memory that is observable in behavior but is not consciously, explicitly, brought to mind (Roediger, 1990; Schacter, 1992). One kind of implicit memory is procedural memory, or "how-to" knowledge of procedures or skills useful in various activities, such as throwing a ball, behaving toward people of higher status, or playing a complex piece on the piano that had once required considerable conscious attention.

Another kind of implicit memory emerges in priming experiments, in which prior exposure to the same or related information facilitates the processing of new information. Participants show priming effects even when they do not consciously remember being exposed to a prime, such as a semantically related word. For example, Bowers and Schacter (1990) exposed participants to 24 prime words by having them rate each word for its pleasantness or count the number of *t*'s in it. Each word began with a different three-letter stem, which could form the basis of many other words (e.g., the prime *angel* begins with the stem *ang—*, which can be completed with *angel, angle, anger, angst, angry, anglo*, etc.). After participants studied the list, for 10 minutes they completed distracter tasks designed to eliminate the words from short-term memory. Control participants who had not been exposed to these words completed about 12% of the stems with words from the initial list, whereas experimental participants completed about 30% with the primes, replicating the well-known phenomenon of semantic priming.

Of particular import in this study, however, was that neither telling participants that they would later be tested for their memory of the words on the initial list nor informing them that some stems could be completed with study words affected priming, thus demonstrating that priming is not affected by conscious, or explicit, recall. Indeed, other studies using longer delays, such as 1 week, between stimulus presentation and testing for implicit and explicit memory demonstrate that priming effects occur whether or not participants show greater than chance recognition that they have previously seen the primes, a measure of explicit memory (see Ledoux & Hirst, 1986). Priming can in fact occur even when presentation of the initial prime was never conscious. Presenting the word pair *taxi:cab* in the unattended channel using a dichotic listening paradigm renders participants more likely to use the less preferred spelling of the auditorially presented homophone *fare/fair*, even though they have no recognition memory for the word pair (see Nisbett & Wilson, 1977; Schacter, 1992).

Amnesia and the Neural Basis of Implicit Memory

Studies in cognitive neuroscience have now documented that implicit and explicit memory involve different neural mechanisms. The groundwork for this research was actually laid decades ago, in case studies of neurological patients such as Milner's (Milner, Corkin, & Teuber, 1968) celebrated case of H. M., who underwent radical surgery to control intractable seizures. The surgery was intended to remove the locus of the seizures in the temporal cortex, but it also destroyed some underlying neural structures, notably the hippocampus. As a result, H. M. lost the ability to consolidate new explicit memories, such as the recognition of Milner's face, despite his working with her for more than 20 years.

Milner and her colleagues eventually came to realize, however, that he was not incapable of learning. He was able to learn new procedural skills, such as writing words upside-down (evidenced by a normal learning curve, as measured by response speed), even though he had no recognition each time he performed the task that he had ever done so before. Perhaps even more significantly for the discussion of unconscious emotional learning that follows, H. M. also showed some affective learning despite his deficits in explicit memory. For example, following a visit to his mother in the hospital, H. M. remembered nothing of the visit, although he "expressed a vague idea that something might have happened to his mother" (Milner et al., 1968, p. 216). A likely explanation for this dissociation of explicit knowledge and affective knowledge is that the latter involved associative learning—forming a new association between his mother and a feeling—which, like semantic priming, involves automatic activation of unconscious networks of association. Damasio and his colleagues (Bechara et al., 1995) have recently produced evidence for differential deficits in affective associative learning versus conscious declarative memory in patients with lesions in the amygdala and hippocampus, respectively.

Implicit Thought

Various literatures on thinking have similarly come to distinguish implicit and explicit thought processes (Holyoak & Spellman, 1993; Jacoby & Kelly, 1992; Lewicki, 1986; Reber, 1992). As with research on memory, until very recently, psychologists paid little attention to the issue of consciousness when studying mechanisms involved in problem solving, decision making, and other cognitive tasks. In the past few years, this has begun to change. As linguists have known for years, children use a vast number of grammatical rules of which they have no conscious knowledge; the aim of teaching grammar to schoolchildren is to help them refine those rules and automatize the refinements.

Implicit grammars of this sort are involved in nearly every aspect of human cognition, from following culturally constructed grammars of interaction, such as standing the proper distance from another person when speaking, to harmonizing while listening to music on the radio, despite a lack of formal training in tuning the voice a fifth, a third, and so forth, above or below the melody line. Rubin et al. (as cited in Holyoak & Spellman, 1993) demonstrated this phenomenon with respect to ballad construction. Participants asked to compose a ballad after hearing a series of ballads could follow twice as many rules used in their composition than they could consciously articulate. Comparable findings emerge in numerous other domains, converging on the proposition that if people learn information by doing rather than through instruction, they are likely to follow procedural rules of which they have no consciousness (Holyoak & Spellman, 1993).

Unconscious Affective Processes

The existence of unconscious cognitive processes, which were seen as the province of psychoanalysis just a decade ago, is now taken for granted by most cognitive scientists. What remains distinctive about the psychodynamic perspective is the view that affective and motivational processes can be unconscious as well. In fact, several independent lines of research have corroborated this fundamental psychodynamic assertion, suggesting that the cognitive unconscious includes only a subset of unconscious processes, notably those that are most automatic, least intentional, and most comfortable to discuss with one's mother. I will first examine the evidence for unconscious affective processes,[3] including the related literature on defensive processes, and finally examine research relevant to the claim that motives can be unconscious as well.

Before doing so, it is worth noting why the assumption that cognition can be unconscious but affect and motivation must be conscious makes little sense. There is no reason to assume a parallel architecture for cognition but a serial architecture for emotion and motivation. Conscious emotions and motives do not "come out of the blue" any more than conscious thoughts do. They must be activated, and their components assembled, unconsciously. Indeed, to the extent that the subjective experience of emotion often includes interpretive elements (e.g., knowing that one is feeling sad rather than feverish, since the two physiological states can feel experientially similar) motives often include cognitions about feared or wished-for states. Thus, at least the cognitive components of these emotional and motivational processes cannot conform to a serial processing model if cognition has a parallel architecture.

---

[3]This review will not be exhaustive and will emphasize more recent research; for a review of earlier research pertaining to unconscious affect, see Westen, 1985, chapter 2.

Furthermore, from the perspectives of comparative and evolutionary psychology, an organism that had to reflect on every decision—rather than rely frequently on relatively automatic or unconscious emotional and motivational processes—would be at a severe adaptive disadvantage relative to an animal that could rely on prior learning about the affective significance of various stimuli and produce a rapid response. Psychologists do not tend to attribute to other animals the capacity for reflective goal-based behavior. Much as they love their pets, few psychologists really believe that their pets wake up in the morning with plans for the day. Yet Fido may be motivated to pursue all kinds of ends, such as eating, chasing other dogs off his turf, reproducing, getting petted, and retrieving the newspaper. And when a bird is motivated to produce a mating ritual simply by hearing a song of a very particular sort, it presumably does not stop to think, "Hey, I like that tune—I feel like dancing." So if other animals can proceed in goal-directed ways without the kind of consciousness posited in serial processing models in humans, there is no reason to believe that humans cannot do so.

From an evolutionary perspective, consciousness, at least in its human form, appears to be a relatively recent development (Reber, 1992) superimposed on an information-processing system that worked relatively well for millions of years. To assume that consciousness is essential for goal-directed behavior suggests that our non-conscious protohuman ancestors managed to escape extinction for millenia through simple good luck, despite their lack of motivation, until consciousness felicitously evolved. In fact, much of human behavior is motivated simultaneously by multiple goals, which would disrupt goal-directed behavior if they all had to be represented in consciousness because these motives would consume too much working memory. For example, when I speak on the present topic to an audience of psychologists, many of whom may begin with negative attitudes toward Freud, numerous goals are probably active, such as the desire to make a strong case for my argument, to speak grammatically, not to sound foolish, to manage my anxiety, to respond to momentary affective responses of members of the audience that signal whether my message is getting through, to try to keep people interested, to try to seem impressive in order to compensate for feelings that originated in my relationship with my mother (who never loved me enough), and so forth. If I were to attend consciously to even two of these at the same time, I could not simultaneously attend to my content and put together coherent sentences. At the very least, motives must be capable of automatization, and hence, unconscious activation, much as skills are. As I will show, there is now considerable evidence for this last proposition (see Bargh, in press).

Neurological Evidence for Unconscious Emotional Responses

Several lines of empirical evidence suggest that affective processes, like cognitive processes, can be unconscious. One source of data comes from neurology and cognitive neuroscience. Neurological data suggest two routes for affective processing (LeDoux, 1989, 1995). The first is relatively direct and cognitively unsophisticated: Primitive sensory and perceptual information is relayed via the thalamus to the amygdala, which attaches an affective valence to the information. This pathway may be activated by stimuli that innately produce affective responses or by those associated with affect through prior conditioning. The affective response precedes any cortical interpretation and hence any consciousness of the reasons for the affect, at which the person can only guess, demonstrating that affects can be activated without awareness. The second pathway is more indirect and involves cortical processing, in which the thalamus first routes information to the cortex, which evaluates the information more systematically before activating the limbic system. Within this second pathway, some cortical processes may be conscious, whereas others are not, because most appraisal processes, like most processes of judgment and inference, are unconscious.

These neurological data are probably relevant to the argument advanced by Zajonc (1980) that preferences can occur without inferences. For example, Wilson (as cited in Zajonc, 1980) presented tone sequences to participants in the unattended channel in a dichotic listening experiment. Participants showed no recognition memory for tone sequences they had heard as many as five times. However, because of the mere exposure effect (i.e., the tendency to like stimuli that are familiar; Zajonc, 1968), participants reported liking the tone sequences they had heard better than those they had not, demonstrating that they were developing affective preferences outside of awareness—toward stimuli they had never consciously registered. Murphy and Zajonc (1993) similarly found that subliminal presentation of positive or negative faces affected participants' liking or disliking of novel stimuli. Research using subliminal procedures has shown comparable effects on attitudes toward various stimuli, including the self (see Bargh, in press; Eagle, 1959).

Other findings with neurologically impaired patients support the view that affective processes can occur outside of awareness and that they often do so using circuitry involved in implicit, rather than explicit, memory tasks. As noted earlier, H. M., who lost the capacity to consolidate new explicit declarative memories because of hippocampal damage, was nevertheless able to *feel* in some vague way that something had happened to his mother. Johnson, Kim, and Risse (1985) reported similar findings with Korsakoff's patients. In one experiment, the patients showed a preference for melodies they had heard 5 minutes earlier, reflecting the mere exposure effect, even though they were highly impaired relative to controls in conscious recognition memory for the melodies. In a second experiment, Korsakoff's patients read biographical material on two fictional characters, one who was "good" and the other, "bad." Approximately 20 days later, they had difficulty recalling any of the information about the characters, but they preferred the "good" one. These studies suggest that the neural circuitry for affective associative learning is distinct from that for conscious, declarative memory.

Damasio and his colleagues (Bechara et al., 1995) have recently shown that patients with bilateral hippocampal lesions, who have difficulty with explicit memory, show no impairment in emotional conditioning as measured by skin conductance response (SCR). In other words, for these individuals, a conditioned stimulus can evoke fear or other conditioned responses if repeatedly paired with an aversive unconditioned stimulus; however, these patients cannot consciously learn to connect the two events. In contrast, individuals with an intact hippocampus who have bilateral lesions to the amygdala show deficits in emotional conditioning, even though they are conscious of the link between the conditioned and unconditioned stimulus. That is, explicit memory is intact, but implicit affective learning is impaired. The investigators found that individuals with bilateral damage to the amygdala were able to tell which colored objects were followed by a loud horn, but they could not develop a startle response to objects of that color.

Other research has found that individuals with prosopagnosia, who have lost the capacity to discriminate faces consciously (a form of explicit knowledge), may nevertheless show differential electrophysiological responses to familiar versus unfamiliar faces (Bruyer, 1991). Research with split-brain patients similarly has documented that individuals presented with affectively evocative visual stimuli to the right hemisphere may show appropriate affective responses but be unable to offer any verbal explanation for them (Gazzaniga, 1985).

Conditioning and Unconscious Affect

A second, related source of data on unconscious affect comes, paradoxically, from research using conditioning paradigms. In a classic study, Lazarus and McCleary (1951) paired nonsense syllables with a mild electric shock and subsequently presented the conditioned stimuli to participants subliminally. The nonsense syllables (in contrast to control syllables not previously associated with shock) reliably elicited a galvanic skin response (GSR) below the threshold of conscious recognition of them, demonstrating an unconscious affective response. Moray (as cited in Shevrin & Dickman, 1980) found that conditioned stimuli (words) paired with electric shocks reliably elicited a GSR when presented in the unattended channel in a dichotic listening task, even though participants had no recognition that they had heard them. Thus, a conditioned stimulus can elicit affect, as assessed electrophysiologically, even when presented subliminally. Numerous other studies have produced similar results (see, e.g., Ohman, 1994; Weinberger, in press; Wong, Shevrin, & Williams, 1994), using dependent variables ranging from skin conductance to evoked–related brain potentials (ERPs).

Other studies have shown that classically conditioned emotional responses can be not only elicited but *acquired* without consciousness (e.g., Bunce, Bernat, Wong, & Shevrin, 1995; Esteves, Dimberg,

& Ohman, 1994). For example, studies from Shevrin's laboratory on unconscious processes (Bunce et al., 1995; Wong et al., 1994) have paired subliminally presented stimuli with mild electric shocks. The investigators have found evidence of classically conditioned emotional responses to these conditioned stimuli, assessed by dependent variables such as facial electromyograms (EMGs; which measure facial muscle indicators of emotion) and brain ERPs indicating a preparatory response. Weinberg, Gold, and Sternberg (1984) showed that a conditioned auditory stimulus paired with electric shock while rats were unconscious (anesthetized) produced a conditioned response 10 days later. Garcia and Rusiniak (1980) produced a conditioned taste aversion by associating a food eaten while animals were conscious with nausea induced while the animals were subsequently anesthetized. A similar phenomenon has been reported in humans by Hutchins and Reynold (cited in Leventhal & Everhart, 1979), who found evidence of affective learning while dental patients were anesthetized with nitrous oxide but not with Novocain; the former apparently blocked consciousness of pain but did not block implicit memory for the experience.

Other research from the behaviorist tradition demonstrates "desynchrony" between the behavioral, physiological, and subjective experience of emotions such as fear (Rachman, 1978). People can learn to suppress one aspect of an emotion, such as its subjective experience, while still showing signs of it electrophysiologically. For example, behavior therapy researchers in the 1970s who believed they had "cured" homosexuality in male patients subsequently discovered, using genital plethysmography (which measures sexual arousal in males by essentially measuring degree of erection), that their patients had suppressed the conscious response while remaining physiologically aroused by pictures of naked men (McConaghy, 1976).

Unconscious Affect and Attitudes

Social psychologists studying attitudes and prejudice now recognize the importance of distinguishing between conscious and unconscious attitudes (see Greenwald & Banaji, 1995) and in so doing have documented unconscious affective and motivational processes. Fazio (1990) has found that when people are consciously focusing on their attitudes, these attitudes heavily influence their behavior. When they are not focusing on their attitudes, only highly accessible (i.e., chronically activated and often automatic and unconscious) attitudes do so. This finding directly parallels a similar finding in the motivation literature, to be reviewed shortly, that conscious motives guide consciously chosen behavior, whereas implicit or unconscious motives guide behavior over the long run, when consciousness is not directly focused on goals (McClelland, Koestner, & Weinberger, 1989).

Social psychologists have traditionally defined attitudes as including both a cognitive and an affective–evaluative component. (Some also include a behavioral tendency.) This means that unconscious attitudes include unconscious affective dispositions, which can be activated automatically and without conscious awareness. Petty and Cacioppo's (1986) work on attitude change distinguishes between a central route to attitude change involving conscious attention to reasoned arguments and a peripheral route typically based on heuristics, automatic processes, affective appeals, and primitive evaluative processes that require minimal attention and effort. The fact that attitude models have begun to converge with psychodynamic models is in some respects not surprising, because some prominent models of attitudes (e.g., Devine, 1989; Fazio, 1990) are based on the distinction between controlled and automatic information processing (Schneider & Shiffrin, 1977). This distinction is very similar to Freud's (1900/1953) distinction between secondary and primary process thought (i.e., rational and conscious vs. associational and unconscious).

Some of the most convincing research on unconscious affect comes from studies of prejudice (Devine, 1989; Dovidio & Gaertner, 1993; Katz & Hass, 1988). These studies demonstrate that people in the United States who consider themselves nonracist often have two conflicting sets of attitudes that influence their behavior. Their conscious attitudes are generally egalitarian and positive toward minority groups, whereas their unconscious attitudes are more negative. Devine (1989) demonstrated the subtle and pervasive nature of automatic, unconscious stereotypes by priming White participants with words related to stereotypes of Black people and then assessing their attributions to a fictitious person of unspecified race. She found that simply activating stereotypes related to Black people led subjects to rate the character as more hostile. Even people who have consciously positive attitudes toward minority group members may harbor unconscious negative feelings toward them. These feelings emerge in their behavior when their attention is not focused on their conscious attitudes, as when they check their wallet after a Black man has passed on the subway. Considerable research suggests that the conflict between these conscious and unconscious attitudes can lead to defensive efforts to justify either one set of feelings or the other, depending on the circumstance (Katz, 1981).

Fazio and his colleagues (Fazio, Jackson, Dunton, & Williams, 1995) have recently measured individual differences in unconscious negative racial attitudes and have found them to be uncorrelated with individual differences in conscious racial attitudes. To measure implicit attitudes, Fazio and his colleagues presented a series of Black and White faces followed by either a positive or negative adjective about which the participant had to press a key indicating its affective connotation ("good" or "bad"). Because negative attitudes toward Black people should facilitate (prime) responses to negative adjectives, response latency to negative words following priming with a Black face can be used as a measure of the affective quality of unconscious attitudes. The investigators found that this measure of individual differences in implicit attitudes predicted an implicit behavioral index—the extent to which a Black confederate of the experimenters rated participants as friendly and interested in their interaction with her when she debriefed them about the study—but not their conscious attitudes when asked to respond to some questions about the Rodney King beating and the ensuing riots in Los Angeles. In contrast, a measure of conscious racism predicted participants' responses to these conscious attitude questions but not their behavior with the Black confederate. Banaji and Hardin (1996) produced similar findings with respect to gender stereotypes: Implicit and explicit attitudes toward gender were uncorrelated.

To what extent negative unconscious attitudes toward various groups are found among members of those groups themselves is not yet known, because until recently, the only measures available of racial attitudes assessed conscious feelings and beliefs. Among the participants in the study by Fazio et al. were eight Black students, for whom Black faces facilitated responses to positive, rather than negative adjectives. However, in this study, the stimuli were not, strictly speaking, subliminal. Hunter and Mackie (1996), in contrast, found a very different pattern of findings with Hispanic and Asian American participants when primes were presented subliminally. The experimenters briefly presented participants with the word *White, Hispanic,* or *Asian* followed by a masking stimulus. Following the primes were positive or negative words, as in the Fazio et al. study. Presenting White participants with the word *White* facilitated responses to positive words and increased response latency to negative words, as one would expect, given in-group positivity biases. However, Asian American and Hispanic participants showed the opposite pattern with respect to their in-group—decreased response latency for negative words and increased for positive—suggesting unconscious negative associations to their own ethnic in-group. Steele (1997) has similarly found that simply asking Black students to indicate their race at the beginning of an examination that they expect to find difficult activates negative stereotypes and diminishes performance substantially. This suggests that regardless of their conscious attitudes, these students have internalized negative attitudes toward the competence of members of their racial group.

Other Studies Documenting Unconscious Emotional Processes

Other literatures document unconscious affective processes as well. Morokoff (1985) assessed sexual arousal in women using self-report and genital plethysmography while participants viewed an erotic videotape. She found that women high in self-reported sexual guilt reported *less* arousal but showed *greater* physiological arousal than those low in sexual guilt. This suggests that their self-reports were influenced by their defense against their guilt. (I will discuss alternative self-presentation hypotheses later.) Research on hypnotic analgesia often finds that physiological indices of pain show persistence of pain despite conscious self-reports and consciously controlled behavior (e.g., keeping a hand immersed in ice water) indicative of minimal pain (Hilgard, 1979). Zillmann (1978) found that following vigorous exercise, participants gradually lose awareness of their arousal as its most manifest indicators (e.g., heavy breathing) disappear, even though they still show covert signs of physiological arousal. When presented with anger-arousing or erotic stimuli during this postawareness phase, they respond with increased aggression or sexual excitement (depending on the stimulus), demonstrating that they are acting at least in part on arousal of which they are unaware.

McGinnies (1949) demonstrated, in a classic New Look study that not only replicated but proved robust in the face of numerous rival hypotheses (see Broadbent, 1977; Dixon, 1971, 1981; Erdelyi, 1985), that neutral words are more readily perceived than taboo words when presented briefly on a screen, and that participants show higher SCRs for the taboo words prior to conscious recognition of them. This suggests a preconscious stage of processing in which information is evaluated for its affective content, a position similarly arrived at by Bargh (in press). Blum (1954) used a similar procedure to test the hypothesis that unconscious identification of a threatening stimulus leads to vigilance toward and subsequent defense against it. To test the hypothesis, he tachistoscopically presented participants with either threatening or nonthreatening pictures (chosen on the basis of psychoanalytic theory) well below the threshold for conscious perception and simply asked them which pictures appeared to "stand out" the most, even though they could not identify them. He then presented them at longer durations to assess conscious recognition threshold. As predicted, anxiety-provoking pictures were rated as standing out the most but showed the highest recognition thresholds, suggesting that participants were vigilant to them but then defended against them. As described below, Wegner (1992) has produced similar findings by instructing participants to try to suppress thoughts consciously.

Other researchers (as cited in Shevrin & Dickman, 1980) have discovered differences in amplitude of brain ERPs in response to emotional versus neutral words presented subliminally. Heinemann and Emrich (1970) presented neutral and emotional words that were originally imperceptible with gradually increasing intensity. They found that emotional words evoked more alpha waves as assessed by an electroencephalogram than did neutral words—and did so prior to conscious recognition. This suggests that the emotional content was processed prior to conscious recognition. More recently, using an idiographic empirical method matching stimulus words to patients' specific hypothesized unconscious conflicts, Shevrin and his colleagues (Shevrin, Bond, Brakel, Hertel, & Williams, 1996) have been using brain wave activity to examine the impact of subliminal presentation of words selected by a team of clinicians (based on extensive interview and projective data) as relevant to patients' symptoms.

Silverman and his colleagues (Silverman & Weinberger, 1985; Weinberger, in press; Weinberger & Hardaway, 1990) have demonstrated that subliminal presentation of stimuli hypothesized to be psychodynamically meaningful can affect a wide range of behavior. A meta-analysis of more than 100 studies documented a modest but robust effect of subliminal stimulation of this sort; supraliminal stimulation often does not produce the same effect. For example, male participants presented subliminally with the stimulus "Beating dad is OK" tend to show better performance on a competitive dart-throwing task than do those presented with control stimuli matched on relevant qualities such as length and word similarity (e.g., "Being a doctor is OK"). Studies such as these demonstrate that people can process relatively complex, affectively meaningful information unconsciously and that this affects their behavior.

Unconscious Affect and Defensive Processes

A discussion of unconscious affect invariably leads to literatures pertaining to psychological defense, because the function of defensive processes is to protect the person from experiencing unpleasant emotional states such as anxiety and guilt. This literature thus provides a segue into the discussion of unconscious motivation, because defenses are processes that people use, without consciousness, to control their emotional states, and efforts at control suggest motivation.

The most important research in this area has been conducted by Vaillant, who adapted Haan's (1977) defense Q-sort to study numerous longitudinal samples (Roston, Lee, & Vaillant, 1992). Beginning with a sample of Harvard students followed up from the 1940s to the present (Vaillant, 1977), Vaillant has shown that reliably scored defenses, arranged according to four levels of adaptiveness—from psychotic and reality-distorting defenses such as gross denial, through neurotic defenses such as repression, to mature defenses such as humor—have a number of predictable correlates longitudinally as well as at a single time. For example, Vaillant and Drake (1985) found strong associations between level of defense maturity and independently rated measures of psychological health/sickness and presence of a personality disorder.

Other researchers have tried to operationalize defense mechanisms empirically as well (see, e.g., Paulhus, Fridhandler, & Hayes, 1997; Perry & Cooper, 1987), with the highest interrater reliability typically found in studies using Q-sort methodology. For example, using a new Q-sort procedure, Davidson and MacGregor (1995) found, as predicted, that overall degree of defensiveness moderates the discrepancy between self-reported and informant-reported neuroticism. The correlation between self- and informant-reports for low-defensiveness participants was moderately positive, whereas the correlation for high-defensiveness participants was strongly negative.

Westen, Muderrisoglu, Fowler, Shedler, and Koren (1997) assessed the reliability and validity of a Q-sort measure of affect regulation that includes unconscious defensive and conscious coping strategies. Factor analysis of clinician descriptions of 90 patients yielded three affect regulation factors. The first, labeled *reality-focused regulation*, is defined by the poles of *active coping* and *acting impulsively*. People high on this dimension tend to use active coping strategies such as anticipating problems and seeking out information, whereas people low on this dimension use maladaptive defenses and behaviors, such as dissociating and using drugs and alcohol. The second factor, *externalizing defenses*, is defined by the poles of *blaming others* and *blaming the self*. Individuals high on this factor deny responsibility for their own problems and brag or dwell on their successes to bolster flagging self-esteem, whereas those who are low on this factor have difficulty expressing or acknowledging anger, tend to feel bad or unworthy instead of feeling appropriately angry at others, and remain passive in the face of distress. The third factor, *avoidant defenses*, is defined by the poles of *avoiding consciousness of unpleasant affect* and *containing affective leakage*. People who are high on this factor tend to avoid thinking

about distressing experiences consciously and to think in intellec-
tualized or abstract terms about emotion-laden events, whereas
people low on this factor find themselves constantly trying to contain breakthroughs of distress, vacillating between clinging to others and pushing them away, expressing distress in the form of
physical symptoms, and ruminating when distressed. Interrater reliability from clinical research interviews is relatively high ($r = .78$),
and factor scores predict behavior such as capacity to maintain
employment, history of psychiatric hospitalization, history of sui-
cidality, and diagnosis and clinician ratings of adjustment.

Perry and Cooper (1989) have used a complex rating procedure
to assess defenses in process during interviews. Although interrater reliability is lower than in most Q-sort studies, they have obtained some important results, such as differentiation of patterns
in patients with different personality disorders in terms of level of
defense—similar to Vaillant's hierarchy, which proceeds from
reality-distorting to mature defenses. They have also produced
considerable evidence of validity, such as correlation of level of
defense with Global Assessment of Functioning (American Psychiatric Association, 1994). Other researchers have developed self-
report measures of defense (Bond et al., 1983; Ihilevich & Gleser,
1986) that have shown a mix of positive and negative results (e.g.,
a failure to correlate with observer-based measures such as Vaillant's), which is not surprising, because asking individuals to self-
report on processes that are by definition inaccessible to consciousness is probably not an appropriate measurement strategy.

A number of studies have added to the literature on defensive
processes considerably by using experimental rather than solely
correlational methods. Paulhus and Levitt (1987) produced an increase in positivity of participants' self-descriptions following a
threat manipulation, suggesting defensive alteration of conscious
self-representations. Cramer (1996) has developed a Thematic Apperception Test (TAT) measure of three defenses—projection, denial, and identification. In one experimental study (Cramer, 1991),
she found that experimentally inducing anger led to increases in
projection and identification. A different projective measure of defense was used by Hedegard (1969), who experimentally manipulated anxiety using hypnosis and found that more intense anxiety
predictably evokes less mature defenses, as predicted by theories

that view defenses as hierarchically organized (A. Freud, 1936; Vaillant, 1977). Other researchers have used cognitive or perceptual tasks to measure defensive processes experimentally (see Smith & Westerlundh, 1980).

Several social–psychological literatures document defensive processes as well (see Westen, 1994). Particularly relevant is the literature on self-serving biases and more recent empirical outgrowths of it on narcissism. For years, researchers have documented numerous self-serving biases, such as the tendency to see oneself as above average on positive characteristics such as intelligence (when, of course, not everyone can be above average), to overrate one's role in group projects with positive outcomes, and so forth (see Epstein, 1992; Greenwald & Pratkanis, 1984). More recent research has begun to track down individual differences in the tendency to see oneself differently than others do and has found, as clinical observation suggests, that narcissistic people tend to hold defensively grandiose views of themselves and their accomplishments, and that this has substantial personal and interpersonal costs.

John and Robins (1994) asked 11 psychologists to provide Q-sort assessments of MBA students after observing them for a weekend. Observers also ranked students' contributions on a task involving a group discussion with five other individuals, realistically simulating a corporate decision-making meeting. At the end, students ranked themselves and their peers on their performance, from *one* to *six*. Students' rankings of their peers were remarkably consistent with the psychologists' rankings (about $r = .50$). In contrast, their self-rankings correlated with peer and psychologist rankings of them at only about $r = .30$, and 60% overestimated their own performance, suggesting a self-serving bias. Most students did rank themselves within one rank of peer and psychologist rankings; however, the one third who overestimated themselves by two or more ranks were significantly more narcissistic by both observer- and self-report. Indeed, the tendency of the students to self-enhance in this study correlated at about .50 with psychologists' ratings of their narcissism. The study thus suggests that most people wear mildly rose-tinted glasses when they look in the mirror but that narcissistic people keep a pair of opaque spectacles on hand to hide the blemishes.

In a longitudinal study, Robins and Beer (1996) compared two groups of college freshmen who were matched in level of ability based on high school grades and Student Aptitude Test scores: (a) those who were strongly self-enhancing, whose perceived, or self-reported, level of academic competence was much greater than their actual past performance (based on records in the admissions office) and (b) those who were relatively accurate in their assessments of their own abilities. At the end of their sophomore year, the self-enhancers, who had expected much greater academic success than they had achieved, nevertheless reported significantly higher subjective well-being. A behavioral measure, however, suggested otherwise: They were 32% more likely to have dropped out of school.

Colvin, Block, and Funder (1995) have recently shown that people whose views of themselves are overly favorable relative to those of independent observers or peer informants show numerous psychological and social difficulties, both longitudinally and cross-sectionally. In two studies using the Block and Block longitudinal data set, the investigators measured self-enhancement by comparing the favorability of observer- and self-administered Q-sorts and calculating the discrepancy between z-transformed scores. They used these scores to predict observer Q-sort ratings of the participants 5 years before and 5 years after. The data were quite consistent with the hypothesis that people who self-enhance to a significant degree—that is, those who are narcissistic—pay the price socially and do not appear healthy psychologically. For example, men who were highly self-enhancing at age 18 were described by observer Q-sorts at age 23 as having fluctuating moods, being deceitful and distrustful, and having brittle defenses. Low self-enhancers, in comparison, were described as cheerful, straightforward and forthright, and dependable. In a third study, self-enhancement was operationalized as the difference in favorability between self- and peer-descriptions using a Q-sort. Participants were then described by observers using a different Q-sort that assessed their social behavior in the laboratory. Similar findings emerged. For example, self-enhancing women were described in the laboratory as seeking reassurance from their interaction partners, irritable, awkward, cynical, fearful, hostile, insecure, and anxious. Low self-enhancing women were described as having good social skills, genuinely enjoying the interaction with their partner in the laboratory study, and relaxed and comfortable.

Defense Against Unpleasant Emotions and Its Physiological Correlates

Several other literatures bear on psychological defense, particularly on the hypothesis that people can prevent themselves from consciously experiencing affect as a way of trying to manage unpleasant feeling states. Wegner (summarized in Wegner, 1992) has conducted an impressive program of research on suppression, a conscious process, but has found that it involves both controlled and automatic (unconscious) components. In a variety of studies, often using the simple manipulation of instructing participants not to think about a white bear, Wegner has demonstrated that the act of suppression instigates a conscious control process, in which participants actively search for distracters, as well as an automatic, unconscious search process aimed at detection of the word to be suppressed. When the automatic process detects the target word— for example, while participants are asked to think aloud or complete a word-association task—it activates the conscious distracter process. The automatic search process, however, has the unintended effect of keeping the to-be-suppressed thought activated unconsciously.

Experimental evidence for this unconscious activation comes from two types of studies (Wegner, 1992). One shows that under conditions of high cognitive load, when conscious attention is diverted from its distracter mission, a suppressed thought (e.g., a white bear) is more likely to enter consciousness in participants who have been instructed to suppress it than in control subjects— even more than in participants instructed to *think about* it—because the automatic search process remains active and hence primes the suppressed thought and related associations. Other research, particularly germane to the study of defenses and their psychophysiological correlates, has found that when people are instructed to suppress an exciting thought about sex, they remain psychophysiologically aroused even while the thought is outside awareness (Wegner, Shortt, Blake, & Page, 1990). In fact, participants in the thought suppression condition remain just as aroused as those instructed to think about the sexual thought. The only difference is that they do not habituate to it; that is, when it returns to their consciousness, they show physiological arousal again, unlike participants who have kept a sexual thought in consciousness long enough for it to lose its passionate appeal. This suggests, much as Freud suggested throughout his career, that affect-laden thoughts kept from consciousness may continue to have an affective press.

Adult attachment research has demonstrated that people may inhibit conscious access to representations of the self, others, and relationships based on their affective qualities. Adults with secure attachment styles speak freely and openly about their relationships with their parents. People with ambivalent styles appear preoccupied with, and ambivalent about, their parents. Avoidant adults dismiss the importance of attachment relationships or offer idealized generalizations about their parents while being unable to back them up with specific examples (Main, Kaplan, & Cassidy, 1985). Remarkably, classifications of adults based on inferences about their representational styles from narrative accounts of their attachment relationships strongly predict their infants' patterns of attachment with them (von IZjendoorn, 1995).

Dozier and Kobak (1992) have produced physiological evidence of the discordance between what avoidant adults know and feel consciously and unconsciously. The investigators monitored electrodermal response while participants were asked to recall memories involving separation, rejection, and threat from their parents. Avoidant adults, like avoidant infants, are hypothesized to shut off or deactivate attachment-related feelings as a way of coping with them. In fact, the more individuals showed avoidant, deactivating strategies by disavowing feelings, the more physiological reactivity they manifested while answering affectively evocative questions about separations, rejections, and parental threats (the correlation was in the range of .40). This disjunction between reported concerns and physiologically expressed affect appeared only while participants were responding to probes that were theoretically expected to draw this kind of defensive strategy (e.g., rejections) and did not emerge on affectively neutral items.

Two entirely different lines of research have produced parallel findings. Shedler, Mayman, and Manis (1993) examined participants in two studies who self-reported a relative absence of psychological distress and symptomatology but whose descriptions of their early memories—a projective measure—were rated as showing signs of psychological disturbance. Participants underwent a mildly stressful procedure that can be disturbing to someone who is highly defensive (e.g., reading aloud, performing a phrase association test, or providing projective stories). Those individuals who viewed themselves as healthy but who showed unconscious evidence of distress in their early memories were significantly more reactive on a measure of cardiac reactivity related to heart disease than were those who were either low or high on both measures of distress. They also showed more indirect signs of anxiety (e.g., stammering, sighing, and avoiding the content of the stimulus) while declaring themselves to be the *least* anxious during these tasks.

Research on repressive coping styles—which refers not to the use of repression but to a tendency to avoid feeling emotions as a way of managing distress, more akin to intellectualization, isolation of affect, and obsessive style in psychoanalytic theory—has documented a direct link between defensive disavowal of affect, particularly anger, and physical illness (Schwartz, 1990; Weinberger, 1990, 1992). Respondents characterized by this style report low anxiety but have high scores on the Marlowe-Crowne scale (Crowne & Marlow, 1960), which appears to measure some combination of defensiveness, social desirability, and overcontrol of affect. Several studies have documented the impact of repressive personality styles on information processing of, for instance, memory for unpleasant events; people characterized by this style are less able to recall unpleasant memories (Davis & Schwartz, 1987). Repressors, like the participants with illusory mental health in the studies by Shedler and colleagues (1993) and the avoidants in the Dozier and Kobak study (1992), report low levels of anxiety while demonstrating marked physiological reactivity. Weinberger (1990) has demonstrated a link between repressive coping, particularly suppression of aggressive or angry feelings, and both cholesterol levels and asthma. Other research has uncovered an association between repressive strategies and vulnerability to cancer (Jensen, 1987; Weinberger, 1992). Apparently, inhibiting conscious access to one's emotions places the body, and particularly the heart and the immune system, under considerable stress.

These studies are important because they demonstrate the existence not only of unconscious affective and motivational processes but of what Freud (1915/1957) referred to as *dynamically* unconscious processes, that is, those that are kept unconscious for a reason. These various findings converge with a literature that has existed for many years documenting a negative correlation between emotional expressiveness and physiological reactivity (see Gross & Levenson, 1993). In a sample of several thousand medical patients, for example, Schwartz, Krupp, and Byrne (1971) found that patients who minimize their conscious feelings of anxiety report more organic problems, whereas those who focus on them report more psychological problems.

More recent research by Pennebaker (1989) has demonstrated that simply writing about or discussing painful experiences (such as job loss) produces increases in immune functioning, physical health, and adaptive behavior (such as getting a new job). In recent research, Pennebaker and his colleagues (Hughes, Uhlmann, & Pennebaker, 1994) have been studying the moment-to-moment psychophysiological changes that occur as participants write about painful or traumatic events that they have previously not discussed at length with anyone; the researchers record somatic changes that occur as the participants type each new word or phrase. Their most relevant finding to date is that skin conductance increased when participants used words expressing unpleasant emotion—but also precisely when their words were rated as evidencing denial or defensiveness. Pennebaker has found that in the short run, expressing unpleasant emotion leads to a momentary increase in arousal, but over the long run, doing so decreases arousal. In contrast, keeping oneself unaware of what one really feels appears to maintain arousal continuously. Relevant to these findings is a study in which women with advanced breast cancer who participated in group psychotherapy lived an average of 18 months longer than control patients matched for stage of the illness (Spiegel, Bloom, Kraemer, & Gottheil, 1989).

At this point, I believe that the data on unconscious affect are incontrovertible. Considerable affective processing occurs unconsciously in daily life, whether or not a person is responding defensively. Conscious affective experience, like conscious cognition, appears to be assembled through the action of multiple neural modules operating in parallel. The capacity to respond with automatic affective responses, some of which occur in the absence of conscious recognition of a stimulus, is highly adaptive and, in evolutionary terms, likely guided human ancestors long before they developed the kind of reflective self-awareness characteristic of contemporary humans. Furthermore, people can keep thoughts and feelings out of consciousness or distort their conscious cognitions as a way of attempting to minimize unpleasant affect, although many defenses, such as narcissistic self-aggrandizement and externalization of blame, are associated with poor social and mental health outcomes. Blocking conscious emotional experience also carries a cost, because people who chronically keep themselves unaware of their feelings are more likely to suffer from physical disorders such as heart disease. Readers who remain unconvinced should probably consult their cardiologists.

Unconscious Motivation

As noted earlier, data on defensive processes provide evidence simultaneously for the existence of unconscious motivational processes, because a defense is by definition a motivated unconscious effort to minimize painful or maximize pleasurable emotion. Increasing evidence from other quarters, however, speaks even more directly to the phenomenon of unconscious motivation, suggesting that the distinction between implicit and explicit processes applies not only to cognition and affect but to motivation as well.

Some of the best evidence for unconscious motivational processes comes from research comparing the correlates of self-report and projective measures of motives (McClelland et al., 1989). The correlation between these two types of measures typically hovers around zero; for example, self-reported and projective assessments of the need for power tend to show no relation to each other, leading adherents of each method to proclaim that the other is obviously invalid. In fact, however, each type of measure predicts different kinds of behavior. The correlates of each are highly predictable if one views consciousness as an override mechanism or as a special lens for examining information and choosing courses of action when unconscious standard operating procedures require monitoring. For example, over the long run, assessment of motives from TAT stories predicts entrepreneurial or managerial success much better than do self-report measures of need for achievement or power, which tend to have little predictive validity. Tell people that they need to achieve on a particular task, however, and their self-reported achievement motivation will predict their effort and performance much better than motives assessed from TAT responses.

When conscious motives are activated, they guide behavior. When they are not—which is much of the time as people muddle through their lives—unconscious motives guide behavior. This should be no surprise to people who have ever broken New Year's resolutions. Most psychologists today accept a similar phenomenon regarding cognition: Controlled information processing operates when people are focusing attention on a problem or task, whereas automatic information processing—including associative memory, activation of procedural skills, and activation of schemas—guides thought, emotion, and behavior in the absence of consciously focused attention (see Schneider & Shiffrin, 1977).

Bornstein's (1995) meta-analysis of objective and projective studies of dependency led to similar conclusions. In addition, Bornstein found substantial, and predictable, gender differences. On objective measures, females consistently show higher dependency scores, which makes sense, given the greater cultural acceptability of dependency for females. On projective tests, however, such as the Rorschach and the TAT, men tended to show slightly higher dependency scores, and the gender difference increased with age. Bornstein and his colleagues have found that objective dependency measures are better predictors of diagnosis of dependent personality disorder, whereas projective measures are better predictors of observed behavior among psychiatric and medical patients, such as compliance with therapeutic regimens. This makes sense, because Axis II diagnoses are currently made via self-reports and interviews, which tap explicit knowledge, whereas everyday behavior is likely to be guided by standard operating procedures that are implicit.

Peterson and Ulrey (1993) may have uncovered a similar phenomenon with respect to explanatory style (the tendency to attribute negative events globally, stably, and internally). They administered four TAT cards, a self-report measure of explanatory style, and the Beck Depression Inventory (BDI; Beck, 1974) to undergraduate students and coded globality and stability from TAT responses. (Internality could not be assessed because respondents may or may not identify with the protagonist.) Although both of the implicit (TAT) measures (stability and globality) and both of the explicit (self-report) variables correlated significantly, albeit weakly, with the BDI (in the range .25), implicit and explicit measures of explanatory style did not correlate strongly with each other; for example, the correlation between stability measured by TAT and by self-report was only .10. Using multiple regression, the investigators found that TAT stability and self-reported stability both contributed significantly to BDI variance, as did TAT globality and self-reported globality. This suggests that individuals may be pessimistic consciously, unconsciously, or both. The differences between these two types of depressed people may be quite substantial. This finding also has potential implications for outcome measures in studies of the efficacy of cognitive therapies for depression, which may produce misleading findings because the treatment is, among other things, a training procedure for altering or disavowing negative cognitions about the self.

Bargh (in press; Bargh & Barndollar, 1996) has produced another, quite different line of research on unconscious motivation, documenting the existence of unconscious motivational processes experimentally. Bargh has extended the literature on automatization of cognitive processes (Anderson, 1995) to motives, arguing that well-learned goals can be activated by environmental stimuli—and attendant behavioral plans can run their course—even without conscious awareness. Bargh draws on principles of association, notably Hebb's (1948) principle that frequent coactivation of more than one representation leads to an associative link between them, to argue that "if an individual frequently and consistently chooses the same goal within a given situation, that goal will come to be activated by the features of that situation, and serve to guide behavior, without the individual consciously intending or choosing or even aware of the operation" (Bargh & Barndollar, 1996, p. 8).

Bargh takes issue with the conception of unconscious processes prevalent in cognitive psychology (e.g., Greenwald, 1992) as simple and irrational. He contends instead that the history of a person's learning in a given situation that is embodied in habitual, automatic motives is often a better guide to behavior than conscious, presumably "rational" analysis of a single, current instance, which may be ignorant of base rates and prior automatic actions. This supposition fits well with some of Wilson's work (e.g., Wilson & Schooler, 1991; Wilson et al., 1993), which demonstrates that people's "gut level" feelings are often more effective guides to action and lead to more subsequent satisfaction than do their reasoned reflections, which can interfere with emotion-based judgments. Damasio and colleagues (Bechara, Tranel, Damasio, & Damasio, in press) have obtained parallel findings with patients with ventromedial prefrontal damage, whose reasoning processes are largely intact but who cannot use prior affective associative learning to guide their responses adaptively.

Bargh suggests that priming procedures that have been shown to influence the way people subsequently categorize or make inferences should be equally capable of influencing their motives and cites evidence from his own and others' laboratories to support this supposition. For example, Chaiken, Giner-Sorolla, and Chen (as cited in Bargh & Barndollar, 1996) presented participants with scenarios in which a protagonist was interested in either accurately assessing a situation or making a good impression. Then, in a "second study" that appeared to be independent of the first, participants were asked to discuss their opinions about a topic with a partner after being told what the partner's attitudes toward it were. Participants who had been primed in the first "study" with the impression management story were more likely to align their attitude with that of their partner, whereas those in the accuracy condition were unswayed by their partner's alleged position. Thus, simply activating *thoughts* about two different kinds of motives actually primed the motives. Bator and Cialdini (as cited in Bargh, in press) similarly found that surreptitiously activating consistency motives influenced dissonance-reduction motivation in a subsequent task. In a similar experiment, Bargh and his colleagues (as cited in Bargh, in press) unobtrusively primed respondents with achievement-related words and then observed their behavior when asked to take a test of "language ability." Respondents in the priming condition were considerably more likely to continue the task beyond the time limit when they thought they were not being observed than were those in the control condition.

In an important series of studies paralleling the work of McClelland et al. (1989), Bargh and his colleagues (as cited in Bargh, in press) primed respondents with words related to either achievement (e.g., *strive*) or affiliation (e.g., *friend*) in an allegedly unrelated first task. Next, they placed participants in a situation of motivational conflict: Participants worked with an incompetent partner on a puzzle task at which they could either succeed—and hence presumably make their partner feel humiliated and stupid—or not be so successful but protect the confederate's self-esteem. As predicted, participants who had been primed with achievement words outperformed those primed with affiliation words (and control participants), even though upon debriefing they were, not surprisingly, unaware of the potential influence of the primes. In a second study, the same findings occurred, but the manipulation wore off after the first few trials. A variable that *then* predicted success was participants' need for achievement as assessed by the TAT. In other words, after recent activation effects decayed, chronically active motives "kicked in" to control behavior. Similar findings occurred in the previously cited studies by Chaiken and colleagues and Bator and Cialdini. Collectively, these studies show that many of the same processes found in research on unconscious cognitive processes—such as the impact of both recently and chronically activated mental processes on thought and behavior (Higgins, 1990)—apply to motivation as well.

Further data on unconscious motives come from a variety of other sources. For example, Lewicki (1985) demonstrated a phenomenon akin to response generalization outside awareness that influenced motivation. Participants avoided a person whose physical appearance resembled an experimenter with whom they had had a single, brief, unfriendly encounter, essentially generalizing a conditioned emotional response, which in turn motivated avoidance behavior. Participants who did not have an unfriendly encounter with the experimenter did not avoid the confederate. When the investigators asked participants who avoided the confederate why they did so, almost all replied that their choice was random. This suggests that motivational learning can occur outside awareness.

Research with neurologically impaired patients has also documented unconscious motivational processes. An early demonstration occurred almost a century ago, when Claparede (described in Cowey, 1991) shook hands with a patient suffering from Korsakoff's disorder. Claparede had concealed a pin between his fingers, which pricked the patient as their hands clasped. Upon meeting again, the patient, because of her amnesia for recent events, was unable to recognize Claparede but was nonetheless unwilling to shake his hand, despite being unable to explain why. Gazzaniga (as cited in Bargh, in press) has similarly described the behavior of split-brain patients who can carry out instructions to produce some action presented to their right hemisphere. When subsequently asked what they are doing, they offer seemingly sensible but incorrect rationalizations for their behavior, because the motivation is inaccessible to their right hemisphere.

Similar hypnotic demonstrations, in which participants given a suggestion for posthypnotic amnesia carried out an action and then tried to explain it, were precisely the kind of data that led Freud to his hypotheses about unconscious motivational processes. He was also impressed that hysterical symptoms could be created hypnotically, leaving their bearers as unable to explain them as were true hysterics, and that true hysterical symptoms could sometimes be temporarily relieved by hypnotic suggestion (see Erdelyi, 1985). That such hypnotic cures tended to fade may not be unrelated to the fading of priming effects and the ultimate resurgence of unconscious influences on behavior.

Phenomena such as these are not limited to neurological patients, hypnotized individuals, or hysterics. Nisbett and Wilson (1977) reviewed a wide array of studies demonstrating that when people act on the basis of motives or preferences for which they cannot access reasons, they tend to "tell more than they know," making up sensible explanations based on their intuitive theories of themselves and of psychological causality that are entirely post-facto and often incorrect. In more recent research, Wilson (e.g., Wilson & Schooler, 1991; Wilson et al., 1993) has shown that when people subsequently act on the basis of such reasons, or when they try to think about why they might prefer one option over another before expressing their preference, they often make worse choices, and the original affective preference ultimately returns.

Conclusion

I have, because of space considerations, clearly done an injustice to earlier work from the New Look tradition that is highly relevant to current research on unconscious processes (see Dixon, 1971, 1981; Erdelyi, 1974, 1985; Weinberger, in press), and I have undoubtedly omitted mention of numerous other contemporary studies that would further document the central argument of this section. I believe, however, that the point is sufficiently clear: The notion of unconscious processes is not psychoanalytic voodoo, and it is not the fantasy of fuzzy, muddle-headed clinicians. It is not only clinically indispensable, but it is good science. At this point, I believe that the question of whether unconscious cognitive, affective, and motivational processes exist is no longer interesting or informative and that we would do better to turn our attention to the *implications* of their existence and the mechanisms by which they influence information processing and behavior.

Elsewhere (Westen, in press-b), I have explored in greater depth the implications for psychoanalytic theory and technique of the research reviewed in this chapter, and I will not repeat those arguments here. The take-home point from this chapter, however, is the following: Some of Freud's metapsychology may have been—as all first approximations are—inadequate, such as his attempt to describe a *system* unconscious in *The Interpretation of Dreams* (Freud, 1900/1953), characterized by certain qualities that are not in fact true of all unconscious processes. Yet his most important contributions—the recognition of the existence and pervasive influence of these processes, the categorization and systematization of various types of unconscious events (Freud, 1915/1957), the recognition that unconsciousness is often motivated and not just incidental, and the development of grammars that allow a clinician to move from manifest to latent content—represent the kind of legacy that few in psychology, or in all of intellectual history, can ever hope to attain.

References

American Psychiatric Association. (1994). *Diagnostic and statistical manual of mental disorders* (4th ed.). Washington, DC: Author.

Anderson, J. R. (1995). *Learning and memory: An integrated approach.* New York: Wiley.

Banaji, M., & Hardin, C. D. (1996). Automatic stereotyping. *Psychological Science, 7,* 136–141.

Bargh, J. (in press). The automaticity of everyday life. In J. S. Wyer, Jr. (Ed.), *Advances in social cognition* (Vol. 10). Hillsdale, NJ: Erlbaum.

Bargh, J., & Barndollar, K. (1996). Automaticity in action: The unconscious as repository of chronic goals and motives. In P. M. Gollwitzer & J. Bargh (Eds.), *The psychology of action* (pp. 457–481). New York: Guilford Press.

Bechara, A., Tranel, D., Damasio, H., & Damasio, A. (in press). Failure to respond autonomically to anticipated future outcomes following damage to prefrontal cortex. *Cerebral Cortex.*

Bechara, A., Tranel, D., Damasio, H., Adolphs, R., Rockland, C., & Damasio, A. (1995). Double dissociation of conditioning and declarative knowledge relative to the amygdala and hippocampus in humans. *Science, 29,* 1115–1118.

Beck, A. (1974). The development of depression: A cognitive model. In R. J. Friedman & M. M. Katz (Eds.), *The psychology of depression: Contemporary theory and research.* Washington, DC: V. H. Winston & Sons.

Blum, G. S. (1954). An experimental reunion of psychoanalytic theory with perceptual vigilance and defense. *Journal of Abnormal and Social Psychology, 49,* 94–98.

Bond, M., Gardner, S. T., Christian, J., et al. (1983). Empirical study of self-rated defense styles. *Archives of General Psychiatry, 40,* 333–338.

Bornstein, R. F. (1995). Sex differences in objective and projective dependency tests: A meta-analytic review. *Assessment, 2,* 319–331.

Bowers, J. S., & Schacter, D. L. (1990). Implicit memory and test awareness. *Journal of Experimental Psychology: Learning, Memory, and Cognition, 16,* 404–416.

Broadbent, D. E. (1977). The hidden preattentive processes. *American Psychologist, 32,* 109–118.

Bruyer, R. (1991). Covert face recognition in prosopagnosia: A review. *Brain and Cognition, 15,* 223–235.

Bunce, S., Bernat, E., Wong, P., & Shevrin, H. (1995, August). *Event-related potential and facial EMG indicators of emotion-relevant unconscious learning.* Paper presented at the 103rd annual convention of the American Psychological Association, New York.

Colvin, R., Block, J., & Funder, D. (1995). Overly positive self-evaluations and personality: Negative implications for mental health. *Journal of Personality and Social Psychology, 68,* 1152–1162.

Cowey, A. (1991). Grasping the essentials. *Nature, 349,* 102–103.

Cramer, P. (1991). Anger and the use of defense mechanisms in college students. *Journal of Personality, 59,* 39–55.

Cramer, P. (1996). *Story-telling, narrative, and the Thematic Apperception Test.* New York: Guilford Press.

Crowne, D. P., & Marlowe, A. (1960). A new scale of social desirability independent of psychopathology. *Journal of Consulting Psychology, 24,* 349–354.

Davidson, K., & MacGregor, B. A. (1995, August). *Clinically judged defensiveness as a moderator of self–friend neuroticism consensus.* Paper presented at the 103rd annual convention of the American Psychological Association, New York.

Davis, P., & Schwartz, G. (1987). Repression and the inaccessibility of affective memories. *Journal of Personality and Social Psychology, 52,* 155–162.

Devine, P. (1989). Stereotypes and prejudice: Their automatic and controlled components. *Journal of Personality and Social Psychology, 56,* 5–18.

Dixon, N. F. (1971). *Subliminal perception: The nature of a controversy.* New York: McGraw-Hill.

Dixon, N. F. (1981). *Preconscious processing.* New York: Wiley.

Dovidio, J., & Gaertner, S. (1993). Stereotypes and evaluative intergroup bias. In D. Mackie & D. Hamilton (Eds.), *Affect, cognition, and stereotyping: Interactive processes in group perception* (pp. 167–193). San Diego: Academic Press.

Dozier, M., & Kobak, R. (1992). Psychophysiology in attachment interviews: Converging evidence for deactivating strategies. *Child Development, 63,* 1473–1480.

Eagle, M. (1959). The effects of subliminal stimuli of aggressive content upon conscious cognition. *Journal of Personality, 27,* 678–688.

Epstein, S. (1992). Coping ability, negative self-evaluation, and overgeneralization: Experiment and theory. *Journal of Personality and Social Psychology, 62,* 826–836.

Epstein, S. (1994). Integration of the cognitive and the psychodynamic unconscious. *American Psychologist, 49,* 709–724.

Erdelyi, M. (1974). A new look at the New Look: Perceptual defense and vigilance. *Psychological Review, 81,* 1–25.

Erdelyi, M. (1985). *Psychoanalysis: Freud's cognitive psychology.* San Francisco: Freeman.

Esteves, F., Dimberg, U., & Ohman, A. (1994). Automatically elicited fear: Conditioned skin conductance responses to masked facial expressions. *Cognition and Emotion, 8,* 393–413.

Fazio, R. (1990). Multiple processes by which attitudes guide behavior: The MODE model as an integrative framework. *Advances in Experimental Social Psychology, 23,* 75–109.

Fazio, R., Jackson, J. R., Dunton, B., & Williams, C. J. (1995). Variability in automatic activation as an unobtrusive measure of racial attitudes: A bona fide pipeline? *Journal of Personality and Social Psychology, 69,* 1013–1027.

Fisher, S., & Greenberg, R. P. (1996). *Freud scientifically reappraised: Testing the theories and therapy.* New York: Wiley.

Freud, A. (1936). *The ego and the mechanisms of defense.* New York: International Universities Press.

Freud, S. (1953). The interpretation of dreams. In J. Strachey (Ed. and Trans.), *The standard edition of the complete psychological works of Sigmund Freud* (Vol. 4, pp. 1–338). London: Hogarth Press. (Original work published 1900)

Freud, S. (1957). The unconscious. In J. Strachey (Ed. and Trans.), *The standard edition of the complete psychological works of Sigmund Freud* (Vol. 14, pp. 159–214). London: Hogarth Press. (Original work published 1915)

Garcia, J., & Rusiniak, K. W. (1980). What the nose learns from the mouth. In D. Muller-Schwarz & R. M. Silverstein (Eds.), *Chemical signals.* New York: Plenum.

Gazzaniga, M. S. (1985). *The social brain: Discovering the networks of the mind.* New York: Basic Books.

Greenwald, A. (1992). New look 3: Unconscious cognition reclaimed. *American Psychologist, 47,* 766–779.

Greenwald, A. G., & Banaji, M. (1995). Implicit social cognition: Attitudes, self-esteem, and stereotypes. *Psychological Review, 102,* 4–27.

Greenwald, A., & Pratkanis, A. (1984). The self. In R. Wyer & T. Srull (Eds.), *Handbook of social cognition* (Vol. 3, pp. 129–178). Hillsdale, NJ: Erlbaum.

Gross, J. J., & Levenson, R. (1993). Emotional suppression: Physiology, self-report, and expressive behavior. *Journal of Personality and Social Psychology, 64,* 970–986.

Haan, N. (1977). *Coping and defending: Processes of self-environment organization.* San Diego, CA: Academic Press.

Hebb, D. O. (1948). *Organization of behavior.* New York: Wiley.

Hedegard, S. (1969). *A molecular analysis of psychological defenses.* Unpublished doctoral dissertation, University of Michigan, Ann Arbor.

Heinemann, L., & Emrich, H. (1970). Alpha activity during inhibitory brain processes. *Psychophysiology, 7,* 442–450.

Higgins, E. T. (1990). Personality, social psychology, and person-situation relations: Standards and knowledge activation as a common language. In L. Pervin (Ed.), *Handbook of personality: Theory and research* (pp. 301–338). New York: Guilford Press.

Hilgard, E. (1979). Divided consciousness in hypnosis: The implications of the hidden observer. In E. Fromm & R. E. Shor (Eds.), *Hypnosis: Developments in research and new perspectives* (2nd ed.). New York: Aldine.

Holyoak, K., & Spellman, B. (1993). Thinking. *Annual Review of Psychology,* *44,* 265–315.

Hughes, C., Uhlmann, C., & Pennebaker, J. (1994). The body's response to processing emotional trauma: Linking verbal text with autonomic activity. *Journal of Personality, 62,* 565–585.

Hunter, S. B., & Mackie, D. (1996, April). *In-group bias among ethnic majority and minority group members.* Paper presented at the annual convention of the Western Psychological Association, San Jose, CA.

Ihilevich, D., & Gleser, G. (1986). *Defense mechanisms: Their classification, correlates, and masurement with the Defense Mechanisms Inventory.* Owosso: DMI Associates.

Jacoby, L., & Kelly, C. M. (1992). A process-dissociation framework for investigating unconscious influences: Freudian slips, projective tests, subliminal perception, and signal detection theory. *Current Directions in Psychological Science, 1,* 174–179.

Jensen, M. R. (1987). Psychobiological factors predicting the course of breast cancer. *Journal of Personality, 55,* 317–342.

John, O., & Robins, R. W. (1994). Accuracy and bias in self-perception: Individual differences in self-enhancement and the role of narcissism. *Journal of Personality and Social Psychology, 66,* 206–219.

Johnson, M. K., Kim, J. K., & Risse, G. (1985). Do alcoholic Korsakoff's syndrome patients acquire affective reactions? *Journal of Experimental Psychology: Learning, Memory, and Cognition, 11,* 22–36.

Katz, I. (1981). *Stigma: A social psychological analysis.* Hillsdale, NJ: Erlbaum.

Katz, I., & Hass, R. (1988). Racial ambivalence and American value conflict: Correlational and priming studies of dual cognitive structures. *Journal of Personality and Social Psychology, 55,* 893–905.

Kihlstrom, J. (1987). The cognitive unconscious. *Science, 237,* 1445–1452.

Lazarus, R. S., & McCleary, R. A. (1951). Autonomic discrimination without awareness: A study of subception. *Psychological Review, 58,* 113–122.

LeDoux, J. (1989). Cognitive–emotional interactions in the brain. *Cognition and Emotion, 3,* 267–289.

LeDoux, J. (1995). Emotion: Clues from the brain. *Annual Review of Psychology, 46,* 209–235.

LeDoux, J., & Hirst, W. (Eds.). (1986). *Mind and brain: Dialogues in cognitive neuroscience.* Cambridge, England: Cambridge University Press.

Leventhal, H., & Everhart, D. (1979). Emotion, pain, and physical illness. In C. E. Izard (Ed.), *Emotion in personality and psychopathology.* New York: Plenum.

Lewicki, P. (1985). Nonconscious biasing effects of single instances on subsequent judgments. *Journal of Personality and Social Psychology, 48,* 563–574.

Lewicki, P. (1986). *Nonconscious social information processing.* San Diego, CA: Academic Press.

Main, M., Kaplan, N., & Cassidy, J. (1985). Security in infancy, childhood, and adulthood: A move to the level of representation. In I. Bretherton & E. Waters (Eds.), Growing points of attachment theory and research. *Monographs of the Society for Research in Child Development, 50* (1–2; pp. 67–104).

McClelland, D. C., Koestner, R., & Weinberger, J. (1989). How do self-attributed and implicit motives differ? *Psychological Review, 96,* 690–702.

McConaghy, N. (1976). Is a homosexual orientation reversible? *British Journal of Psychiatry, 129,* 556–563.

McGinnies, E. (1949). Emotionality and perceptual defense. *Psychological Review, 56,* 244–251.

Milner, B., Corkin, S., & Teuber, H. L. (1968). Further analysis of the hippocampal amnesic syndrome: Fourteen year follow-up study of H. M. *Neuropsychologia, 6,* 215–234.

Morokoff, P. J. (1985). Effects of sex guilt, repression, sexual "arousability," and sexual experience on female sexual arousal during erotica and fantasy. *Journal of Personality and Social Psychology, 49,* 177–187.

Murphy, S. T., & Zajonc, R. (1993). Affect, cognition, and awareness: Affective priming with optimal and suboptimal stimulus exposures. *Journal of Personality and Social Psychology, 64,* 723–739.

Nisbett, R., & Wilson, T. (1977). Telling more than we can know: Verbal reports on mental processes. *Psychological Review, 84,* 231–259.

Ohman, A. (1994). "Unconscious anxiety": Phobic responses to masked stimuli. *Journal of Abnormal Psychology, 103,* 231–240.

Paulhus, D., Fridhandler, B., & Hayes, S. (1997). Psychological defense: Contemporary theory and research. In R. Hogan, J. Johnson, & S. R. Briggs (Eds.), *Handbook of personality psychology* (pp. 544–580). San Diego, CA: Academic Press.

Paulhus, D., & Levitt, K. (1987). Desirable responding triggered by affect: Automatic egotism? *Journal of Personality and Social Psychology, 52,* 245–259.

Pennebaker, J. (1989). Stream of consciousness and stress: Levels of thinking. In J. S. Uleman & J. A. Bargh (Eds.), *Unintended thought* (pp. 327–350). New York: Guilford Press.

Perry, J. C., & Cooper, S. H. (1987). Empirical studies of psychological defense mechanisms. In R. Michels & J. O. Cavenar, Jr. (Eds.), *Psychiatry.* Philadelphia: Lippincott.

Perry, J. C., & Cooper, S. (1989). An empirical study of defense mechanisms: I. Clinical interview and life vignette ratings. *Archives of General Psychiatry, 46,* 444–460.

Peterson, C., & Ulrey, L. (1993). Can explanatory style be scored from TAT protocols? *Personality and Social Psychology Bulletin, 20,* 102–106.

Petty, R. E., & Cacioppo, J. T. (1986). The elaboration likelihood model of persuasion. In L. Berkowitz (Ed.), *Advances in Experimental Social Psychology, 19,* 123–205.

Rachman, S. J. (1978). *Fear and courage*. San Francisco: Freeman.

Reber, A. (1992). The cognitive unconscious: An evolutionary perspective. *Consciousness and Cognition, 1*, 93–133.

Robins, R. W., & Beer, J. S. (1996). *A longitudinal study of the adaptive and maladaptive consequences of positive illusions about the self*. Unpublished manuscript, University of California, Berkeley.

Roediger, H. L. (1990). Implicit memory: Retention without remembering. *American Psychologist, 45*(9), 1043–1056.

Roston, D., Lee, K., & Vaillant, G. (1992). A Q-sort approach to identifying defenses. In G. Vaillant (Ed.), *Ego mechanisms of defense: A guide for clinicians and researchers* (pp. 217–233). Washington, DC: American Psychiatric Association.

Schacter, D. L. (1992). Understanding implicit memory: A cognitive neuroscience approach. *American Psychologist, 47*, 559–569.

Schneider, W., & Shiffrin, R. (1977). Controlled and automatic human information processing: I. Detection, search, and attention. *Psychological Review, 84*, 402–411.

Schwartz, G., Krupp, N., & Byrne, D. (1971). Repression-sensitization and medical diagnosis. *Journal of Abnormal Psychology, 78*, 286–291.

Schwartz, G. E. (1990). Psychobiology of repression and health: A systems perspective. In J. J. Singer (Ed.), *Repression and dissociation: Defense mechanisms and personality styles: Current theory and research* (pp. 405–434). Chicago: University of Chicago Press.

Shedler, J., Mayman, M., & Manis, M. (1993). The illusion of mental health. *American Psychologist, 48*, 1117–1131.

Shevrin, H., Bond, J., Brakel, L., Hertel, R., & Williams, W. J. (1996). *Conscious and unconscious processes: Psychodynamic, cognitive, and neurophysiological convergences*. New York: Guilford Press.

Shevrin, H., & Dickman, S. (1980). The psychological unconscious: A necessary assumption for all psychological theory? *American Psychologist, 35*, 421–434.

Silverman, L., & Weinberger, J. (1985). Mommy and I are one: Implications for psychotherapy. *American Psychologist, 12*, 1296–1308.

Smith, G. J. W., & Westerlundh, B. (1980). Perceptogenesis: A process perspective on perception-personality. In L. Wheeler (Ed.), *Review of personality and social psychology* (pp. 94–124). Beverly Hills, CA: Sage.

Spiegel, D., Bloom, J. H., Kraemer, H. C., & Gottheil, E. (1989). Effect of psychosocial treatment on survival of patients with metastatic breast cancer. *Lancet, 11*, 888–891.

Squire, L. R. (1987). *Memory and brain*. New York: Oxford University Press.

Steele, C. M. (1997). A threat in the air: How stereotypes shape intellectual identity and performance. *American Psychologist, 52*, 613–629.

Vaillant, G. (1977). *Adaptation to life*. Boston: Little, Brown.

Vaillant, G., & Drake, R. (1985). Maturity of defenses in relation to DSM–III Axis II personality disorders. *Archives of General Psychiatry, 42*, 597–601.

von IZjendoorn, M. (1995). Adult attachment representations, parental responsiveness, and infant attachment: A meta-analysis on the predictive validity of the Adult Attachment Interview. *Psychological Bulletin, 117,* 387–403.

Wegner, D. (1992). You can't always think what you want: Problems in the suppression of unwanted thoughts. *Advances in Experimental Social Psychology, 25,* 193–225.

Wegner, D., Shortt, J., Blake, A. W., & Page, M. S. (1990). The suppression of exciting thoughts. *Journal of Personality and Social Psychology, 58,* 409–418.

Weinberg, N. M., Gold, P. E., & Sternberg, D. B. (1984). Epinephrine enables Pavlovian fear conditioning under anesthesia. *Science, 223,* 605–607.

Weinberger, D. (1990). The construct validity of the repressive coping style. In J. Singer (Ed.), *Repression and dissociation* (pp. 337–386). Chicago: University of Chicago Press.

Weinberger, D. (1992, August). Not *worrying yourself sick: The health consequences of repressive coping.* Paper presented at the annual convention of the American Psychological Association, Washington, DC.

Weinberger, J. (in press). *The unconscious.* New York: Guilford Press.

Weinberger, J., & Hardaway, R. (1990). Subliminal separating science from myth in subliminal psychodynamic activation. *Clinical Psychology Review, 10,* 727–756.

Westen, D. (1985). *Self and society: Narcissism, collectivism, and the development of morals.* Cambridge, England: Cambridge University Press.

Westen, D. (1994). Toward an integrative model of affect regulation: Applications to social–psychological research. *Journal of Personality, 62,* 641–647.

Westen, D. (in press-a). The scientific legacy of Sigmund Freud: Toward a psychodynamically informed psychological science. *Psychological Bulletin.*

Westen, D. (in press-b). The scientific status of unconscious processes: Is Freud really dead? *Journal of the American Psychoanalytic Association.*

Westen, D., Muderrisoglu, S., Fowler, C., Shedler, J., & Koren, D. (1997). Affect regulation and affective experience: Individual differences, group differences, and measurement using a Q-sort procedure. *Journal of Consulting and Clinical Psychology, 65,* 429–439.

Wilson, T. D., & Schooler, J. W. (1991). Thinking too much: Introspection can reduce the quality of preferences and decisions. *Journal of Personality and Social Psychology, 60,* 181–192.

Wilson, T. D., Lisle, D., Schooler, J., Hodges, S. D., Klaaren, K., & LaFleur, S. (1993). Introspecting about reasons can reduce post-choice satisfaction. *Personality and Social Psychology Bulletin, 19,* 331–339.

Wong, P., Shevrin, H., & Williams, W. J. (1994). Conscious and nonconscious processes: An ERP index of an anticipatory response in a con-

ditioning paradigm using visually masked stimuli. *Psychophysiology,*
31, 87–101.

Zajonc, R. B. (1968). The attitudinal effects of mere exposure. *Journal of*
Personality and Social Psychology, 9, 1–27.

Zajonc, R. (1980). Feeling and thinking: Preferences need no inferences.
American Psychologist, 35, 151–175.

Zillmann, D. (1978). Attribution and misattribution of excitatory reactions.
In J. H. Harvey, W. Ickes, & R. F. Kidd (Eds.), *New directions in attri-*
bution research (Vol. 2). Hillsdale, NJ: Erlbaum.

The Freud–Rapaport Theory of Consciousness

Howard Shevrin

In recent years, consciousness as an important, even fashionable, topic has returned to psychology with a vengeance. Where are the doubters of yesteryear for whom an interest in consciousness was only one step removed from an interest in the unconscious, that true behaviorist bugbear? From even a cursory look at the literature on consciousness, one is struck by the fact that the topic has surfaced in psychology largely under the auspices of philosophers such as Searle (1992), Dennett (1995), Flanagan (1992), and others. As with no other issue, discussion of consciousness in the psychological literature is interwoven with philosophical references perhaps because in philosophy, concern with the nature and function of consciousness never disappeared. Neither did consciousness disappear from the minds of psychoanalysts who have had to deal with the pathology of consciousness on a daily basis.

What has largely disappeared in psychoanalysis, however, is a serious theoretical and conceptual consideration of the nature and function of consciousness, both as a general condition of mind and as a specific factor in psychopathology and treatment. Most recent thinking in psychoanalysis has been preoccupied with the *content* of the mind rather than with its various forms. What is generally taken for granted is the way in which consciousness and the unconscious, each with its own distinctive properties, affect the particular content. As a result, critical questions remain infrequently addressed: What are the means through which something unconscious becomes conscious? Conversely, what are the means through which something conscious becomes unconscious? How and why does one become aware at all? And what is awareness as such?

I will undertake to show in this chapter that Freud from the start of his career attempted to address these questions, albeit sporadically, and was convinced of their importance to psychoanalysis and to any science of the mind. It was Rapaport (1960/1967) who, as the only serious systematizer of psychoanalytic thought, brought together Freud's thinking on the subject in the form of a series of propositions that I will examine below. Rapaport made the point that during the early decades of the twentieth century, while psychology was in the thralls of Watson's behaviorist revolution against the nineteenth-century psychology of consciousness and its reliance on introspection, Freud was developing a theory of consciousness that took into account the limitations of naive introspectionism and boldly speculated on the "apparatus of consciousness," or the means through which consciousness emerges and is sustained—a matter of general importance as well as of clinical relevance.

In fact, without a theory of consciousness and its relationship to the unconscious, psychoanalysis cannot account for treatment change, whether from a structural, object relations, self psychological constructivist, or intersubjective point of view, because each conceives of change as involving shifts in the relationship between consciousness and the unconscious, albeit with respect to different contents or representations. In short, all these theories can offer at best is a necessary but not sufficient account of treatment change and, by extension, of development. Is successful treatment change largely silent, that is, unconscious? If so, what role does consciousness play, for example, in the apprehension and understanding of interpretations? The problem can also be placed in the larger context of learning: What role do conscious and unconscious processes play in the development of any new psychological structure, whether it is a significant shift in compromise formations, object relations, self-regulation, or intersubjective experience?

Once the problems related to consciousness (and its companion concept, the unconscious) are separated from any particular clinical theory, the issue becomes a consideration of mind in its most general sense. On that plane, other theories of mind that explain the same phenomena in different ways must be addressed. I will try to show that one strength possessed by psychoanalysis, compared with other approaches, is that it does not leave out important dimensions of experience. Unlike much cognitive science, psychoanalysis includes affects, motives, conflicts, fantasies, dreams, and the whole range of psychopathology. By the same token, by opening its theoretical grasp wide, it runs the risk of vagueness and ambiguity so that the particulars elude its hold.

The balance of this chapter will be organized as follows: (a) a brief historical account of Freud's theory of consciousness, (b) a discussion of Rapaport's systematization and extension of Freud's theory, and (c) a presentation of new implications of the theory derived from recent research on conscious and unconscious processes.

Freud's Theory of Consciousness: A Preliminary Sketch

Insofar as Rapaport undertook the only known systematic reworking of Freud's theory of consciousness, I will leave the fuller exegesis of Freud's theory until the next section, which deals with the Rapaport effort in some detail. What follows is a brief introduction that stresses the strengths of Freud's approach and points to one of its weaknesses.

First, it is essential to stress that Freud carefully distinguished between consciousness as a *term* describing the phenomenon of subjective awareness and consciousness as a *concept* referring to hypothesized functions (Freud, 1915/1955). In the earliest topographic model, he simply described an idea as being *conscious* (present in subjective awareness), *preconscious* (readily capable of entering subjective awareness), and *unconscious* (in a state of repression and not readily available to consciousness; Breuer & Freud, 1893/1955). Consciousness in this sense is adjectival and not substantive; it modifies the status of an idea that might otherwise be preconscious or unconscious. In his later systems theory, he used the term *consciousness* as a noun and referred to the system

Cs. and in complementary fashion, to the systems *Pcs.* and *Unc.* (Freud, 1900/1953). In this systems theory, he was talking about more than the sheer quality of subjective awareness but was attributing a wealth of distinguishing characteristics to each of these systems.

For the purposes of this chapter, however, I will focus on consciousness in the adjectival, phenomenal subjective awareness sense. Consciousness in this sense need not be linked to any particular system or content characteristics. It can be as present for a perception as for a memory, thought, feeling, fantasy, or desire; it can be found in a variety of states such as waking and dreaming; and it can be associated with a variety of pathologies—fugues, multiple personalities, obsessions, delusions, and hallucinations. With respect to each of these mental contents, states, and pathological conditions, consciousness as subjective awareness is present. Consciousness as subjective awareness is a pervasive condition of mind that may cease only in deep comas and slow-wave sleep. As Freud (1915/1957) stated in his paper on the unconscious, "the attribute of being conscious, which is the only characteristic of psychichal processes directly presented to us, is in no way suited to serve as a criterion for the differentiation of systems" (p. 192).

This last quotation may strike the reader as contradicting Freud's own systems theory designating the *Cs.*, *Pcs.*, and *Unc.* systems, in which consciousness appears to be a function of only one system. Indeed it does, especially since he had to maintain on the basis of clinical observations that although repressed ideas can become conscious, the mere fact of their being conscious reveals nothing about their origin in the unconscious. A similar confounding is evident among cognitive psychologists. Posner and others, for example, designated consciousness to be a single channel system in contrast to multiple parallel unconscious processes (Mandler, 1975; Posner & Boies, 1971). The Shiffren and Schneider (1977) distinction between controlled processes that are conscious and automatic processes that are unconscious is subject to the same confounding. The problem arises when the adjectival and substantive uses of consciousness are confounded. Fortunately, Freud also attempted to account for the purely subjective nature of consciousness, although as I will show, he did not altogether escape the confusion.

Perhaps his most interesting attempt can be found in his intriguing paper, "A Note Upon the 'Mystic Writing Pad' " (Freud, 1925/ 1961), in which a commonplace device provided a model for the relationship between consciousness, perception, and memory. As early as "The Interpretation of Dreams," Freud (1900/1953) had speculated that the mind has to have a means to be receptive to new perceptions while retaining some record of these perceptions. These had to be separate functions. As I will try to make clear in the third section of this chapter, the relationship between perception and memory is crucial to an understanding of consciousness as subjective experience. Freud put his finger on the importance of this relationship as early as 1900. It was the mystic writing pad, however, that fortuitously offered him a way to concretize the relationship between perception and memory and the role consciousness plays in that relationship.

As every child knows, what is "mystic" about the mystic writing pad is that what one inscribes on its plastic cover magically disappears when the cover is raised. When the plastic sheet is replaced, one can write on it all over again. This, said Freud, is like the function of perception. One can perceive different things in immediate succession without "using up" the perceptual "space." However, Freud pointed out, if one inspects the bottom wax board on which the plastic sheet rests, one can easily make out the writing in the telltale depressions in the wax; thus, the wax board is analogous to memory.

Freud then drew another and most interesting analogy. He likened "the appearance and disappearance of the writing" with the "flickering-up and passing-away of consciousness in the process of perception" (Freud, 1925/1961, p. 231). But what was the mental counterpart of raising and replacing the plastic sheet? Because his answer is of crucial importance to understanding his theory of consciousness, I will quote it in full. For the reader unacquainted with psychoanalytic theory, two terms used by Freud need to be explained in advance. When Freud talked about "cathectic innervations," he was using a concept in function not too different from the concept of activation in contemporary cognitive psychology. A semantic network, for example, is *activated* by a stimulus, resulting in *activation* spreading through the network and ending in a response. The other term is *Pcpt.-Cs*, by which Freud referred to a close link between perception and consciousness, a link that has not stood the test of time in the light of the growing body of sub-liminal research (see the section Consciousness, Subliminal Perception, and Repression). It is another example of confounding con-sciousness as subjective awareness with consciousness as linked to a particular system. Now for the quote:

> My theory was that cathectic innervations are sent out and with-drawn in rapid periodic impulses from within into the com-pletely pervious system *Pcpt.-Cs.* So long as that system is ca-thected in this manner, it receives perceptions (which are accom-panied by consciousness) and passes the excitation on to the unconscious mnemic systems; but as soon as the cathexis is withdrawn, consciousness is extinguished and the functioning of the system comes to a standstill. It is as though the uncon-scious stretches out feelers, through the medium of the system *Pcpt.-Cs.*, towards the external world and hastily withdraws them as soon as they have sampled the excitations coming from it. Thus the interruptions, which in the case of the Mystic Pad have an external origin, were attributed by my hypothesis to the discontinuity in the current of innervation; and the actual breaking of contact which occurs in the Mystic Pad was replaced in my theory by the periodic non-excitability of the perceptual system. (Freud, 1925/1961, p. 231)

The notion of "rapid periodic impulses" being sent out and withdrawn, resulting in consciousness or its absence, is remarkably parallel to a recent theory proposed by the neurophysiologist Lli-nas (Pare & Llinas, 1995) who posited that there is a scanning fre-quency emanating from the thalamus that sweeps across the brain some 40 times per second, producing consciousness.

There is, however, a significant difference between the two the-ories as well. For Freud, in the absence of cathectic innervation from within, the perceptual system falls silent; no external activa-tion can occur. Not so for Llinas. The thalamic scanning frequency interacts with only those sensory regions that have already been activated, in this way acting like a TV channel selector. If the sta-tion is broadcasting, the selector will pick it up and activate the screen; if the station is not broadcasting, nothing will appear on the screen for that channel. As the scanning frequency sweeps across the entire brain, it will render conscious whatever brain regions have been activated by incoming stimuli. Here it is apparent how Freud's confounding of subjective consciousness with system properties gets him into trouble. The perceptual system in Freud's theory is too closely tied to consciousness (i.e., *Pcpt.-Cs.*), making it theoretically impossible for perceptual activation to occur without consciousness. Yet clinical observation supplies many instances in which individuals respond to cues without any awareness of doing so, and certainly the rapidly growing body of subliminal research attests to the existence of perception without awareness (see the section Consciousness, Subliminal Perception, and Repression).

There is, however, a further parallel between Freud and Llinas of considerable importance. Both the corresponding innervations resulting in consciousness are indifferent to what has been perceptually activated. Perceptual activation and conscious innervation are independent of each other. Only in this way can consciousness provide, in Freud's terminology, "indications of reality." If consciousness as a subjective given were intrinsically biased, then the information received from outside and inside would not be experienced for what it is. Distortions and defensive activity across a broad spectrum may in fact supervene (as may perceptual illusions), but these will become conscious with the same completeness as any undistorted perception; otherwise, consciousness itself would contribute to an endless, tangled skein of distortion that could never be unraveled; external and internal reality in any shape or form would never be known. Consciousness as subjective experience "tells it like it is," warts and all, including the warts of defensive distortions, avoidances, and of built-in perceptual limitations.

Now I will turn to examine Rapaport's systematizing of Freud's theory quite briefly sketched above.

The Freud–Rapaport Theory of Consciousness

Rapaport's (1960/1967) main effort at systematizing Freud's theory of consciousness occurred in his paper, "On the Psychoanalytic Theory of Motivation." He took pains to point out that Freud not only addressed consciousness as subjective experience apart from the systematic role of consciousness in *Pcpt.-Cs.*, but he also developed a theory for the "apparatus of consciousness." I have already provided evidence that Freud did not altogether divest himself of the confusion between the subjective and substantive character of consciousness. The claim that he developed an apparatus of consciousness is important to evaluate, however, and to see how Rapaport then uses Freud's theory in this regard.

I take Rapaport to mean by an apparatus of consciousness that it constitutes an account of how consciousness as subjective experience works and how it comes about. Rapaport formulated the essence of Freud's apparatus of consciousness in 14 briefly stated propositions. Again, it is useful to point out that Rapaport, like Freud, postulated the existence of an energy taking the form of attention cathexis that functions conceptually in a way similar to the cognitive science concept of activation. I make this point in order to counteract the tendency in psychoanalysis to dismiss any thinking involving an energy concept. Without something like activation or attention cathexis, one cannot account for how mental processes are initiated, maintained, and ended. With this proviso in mind, I quote Rapaport's 14 propositions below in full:

1. Subjective conscious experience is determined by the distribution of a limited quantity of mental energy termed attention cathexis.
2. Changes in the distribution of attention cathexis are conceptualized as the function of the apparatus of consciousness.
3. Attention cathexis is part of the energy of the system *Pcpt.-Cs.* (in present day terminology, the ego) which is termed hypercathexis.
4. Excitations within the mental apparatus (internal) or on the receptor organs (external) attract attention cathexis proportionately to their intensity.
5. Attention cathexis, if so attracted and if exceeding a certain amount (threshold), gives rise to the conscious experience of the excitation.
6. Simultaneous or contiguous excitations compete for limited quantity of attention cathexis.
7. When an external excitation is congruent with or related to a representation of the internal representation

which is simultaneous or contiguous with it, then there is no competition, but rather both excitations attract attention cathexis to the common representation.

8. Internal excitations may be defended against in such a way (e.g., by repression) that they cannot attract attention cathexis.

9. Defenses, and other processes utilizing great amounts of hypercathexis diminish the quantity of attention cathexis available.

10. When an excitation of short duration ceases, the attention cathexis it attracted becomes available to other excitations.

11. An excitation of long duration attracts cathexis proportionate to its duration as well as intensity.

12. Attention cathexis attracted by an excitation in a sufficient amount and for a sufficient duration gives rise to a structure (e.g., memory trace).

13. Structures so built retain only a small quantity of the attention cathexes that were needed to give rise to them. The condition of these cathexes is termed *bound*, and the process is *binding*.

14. Once structure building is completed, the attention cathexis used in the process—except for those which become bound in the structure—become available to other excitations.[1]

These 14 propositions are meant to be the foundations not only for a theory of consciousness but also for a theory of learning (structure formation), which, as Rapaport believed, psychoanalysis lacked, and thus lacked a theory of treatment change and individual development. Notably, Rapaport (and Freud) further believed that consciousness as subjective experience play an important role in both.

There is one important difference between Rapaport's formulations and that of Freud's as previously described which corrects a difficulty in the position taken by Freud in the Mystic Pad paper: In the fourth proposition, Rapaport *separated* excitations, internal or external, from attention cathexis; indeed, he asserted that the

---

[1]From *The Collected Papers of David Rapaport* (Rapaport, 1960/1967), pp. 898–899. Reprinted with permission.

amount of attention cathexis attracted is proportional to the intensity of the excitation, thus making the amount of attention cathexis dependent on the intensity of the excitation. This appears to be different from Freud's assertion that without attention cathexis priming the sense organs, no excitation would occur. Rapaport's reformulation instead makes it possible to consider that a process of excitation, both internal and external, can occur in the absence of consciousness. This is further supported by the fifth proposition in which a *threshold* for attention cathexis must be exceeded before a conscious experience of an excitation can occur. If one puts the fourth and fifth propositions together, it becomes possible to imagine an excitation of low intensity that would not attract sufficient attention cathexis to exceed the threshold for consciousness but would nevertheless have attracted *some* attention cathexis, thus initiating an ongoing mental process. This would be a way to account for subliminal stimuli and their effects.

Implicit in the Freud–Rapaport theory are three characteristics of attention cathexis: (a) it is nonconscious; (b) it is in itself nonmotivational, although its activity may be variously affected by motivations; and (c) it is an activator of mental processes. Attention cathexis emerges in this model as a nonconscious, nonmotivational activator of mental processes.

Nonconscious in Rapaport's frame of reference refers to a mental process that is not represented either consciously or unconsciously. Mental *processes* are nonconscious and unrepresented; mental *contents* are representational and can be either conscious or unconscious. The distribution of attention cathexes is a psychologically silent process lacking in a phenomenal, subjectively experienced counterpart. The *consequences* of this distribution, however, are very much represented and experienced either consciously or unconsciously (more of this later), but not the process itself. (For a fuller discussion of this issue, see chap. 12, pp. 264–266, in Shevrin, Bond, Brakel, Hertel, & Williams, 1996).

The nonmotivational nature of attention cathexis is centrally important to any understanding of the role of consciousness as subjective experience. It recalls the previous point concerning the *unbiased* nature of consciousness as subjective experience. The biases as such are intrinsic to the underlying mental processes and are inherent in the contents made conscious but are not caused by the conscious experience itself. Otherwise, consciousness as subjective experience would not provide indications of reality, its main function. The external reality it indicates may already be selectively responded to because of the limitations of sensory and perceptual apparatus and is distorted by *their* built-in biases. For example, illusions may be experienced that can be undone only by inference and reflection but not by consciousness itself. Even after one understands why the two lines appear different in length in the Muller-Lyer illusion, they still look different. When above-threshold strength attention cathexis is invested in the perceptual activation initiated by the Muller-Lyer figures, it can only make conscious what is perceptually given, no matter how much one's insight confirms that the lines are the same. The desire (motivation), based on superior knowledge, to correct conscious perception cannot directly influence what attention cathexis causes to become conscious.

Finally, it is necessary to explain what the Freud–Rapaport theory means by cathexis itself, or that which *activates*. Stimuli from without and from within produce *excitations* of various kinds. Unless these excitations are cathected, however, they will soon cease and not achieve conscious or unconscious representational status; they will simply disappear, which is probably the fate of most external stimuli impinging on the sense organs. The sense organs will respond with their own variety of excitation, but unless cathected with some minimum amount of subthreshold attention cathexis, they will disappear like vanishing fireworks.

There are, of course, significant differences between external and internal stimuli. External stimuli may be adventitious, brief, and sporadic; internal stimuli such as instinctual demands are persistent, or at the least, cyclic. It is thus highly likely that at one time or another some attention cathexis has been invested in these instinctual excitations, resulting in memory trace formation and representational status. When attention cathexis is subthreshold, they remain unconscious; when the attention cathexis is above threshold, they become conscious. Repression would then be a special case in which the defensive process kept an otherwise powerful instinctual excitation from receiving sufficient attention cathexis to become conscious. But it would need to be posited that the instinctual excitation still retained enough subthreshold attention cathexis to maintain its representational status.

Those acquainted with Rapaport's metapsychological thinking will note that I have replaced the concept of drive cathexis with the concept of excitation and have defined an instinct as an internal stimulus (or excitation) on the same footing with respect to attention cathexis as an external stimulus. What is gained by this reconceptualization? For one thing, it is more in keeping with Freud's view of an instinct as making a demand on the mind for work (Freud, 1915/1957). In this sense, an instinct is as external to the workings of the mind as is an external stimulus. The demand it makes on the mind is the excitation of its internal organs of perception so that attention cathexis is attracted in some determinable amount, representation is achieved, and a mental process is begun that may or may not lead to consciousness. The particular nature of the excitement will depend on both the nature of the instinct *and* the nature of the organs of internal perception. Those instincts that have no internal organs of perception will remain silent and unrepresented in the workings of the mind, although they may have significant effects on well-being. The instinctual need for a certain electrolyte balance may be an example of an important instinctual requirement that is unrepresented in the mind, although imbalance will have deleterious consequences on both physical and mental well-being. The sexual instinct, on the other hand, would be supposed to have a highly sensitive internal organ of perception and therefore result in excitation and the subsequent attraction of attention cathexis.

The term *perceptual organ* is in need of clarification. Could it not be argued that an electrolyte imbalance is also detected by some internal perceptual organ that then entrains homeostatic mechanisms to correct the imbalance? One must then suppose that there is some built-in difference between classes of internal detectors so that some attract attention cathexis and others do not.

I believe that one can recast Freud's assumption that some instincts start with a representative in the mind, the so-called instinctual representative (Freud, 1915/1957), and posit instead that these instincts (i.e., sex, hunger) can excite from the start already existing internal perceptual organs of a special class described previously, attract attention cathexis, and achieve representation. In other words, from the very first instinctual excitation, an internal perception occurs and is cathected. It would also be possible to reconcile these two views if it were assumed that the first instinctual excitations occur in utero, are invested with subthreshold attention cathexis, and thus achieve representation before birth. In the light of the growing body of research demonstrating that the near-term fetus is capable of some perception that carries over to postbirth experience, this formulation is not beyond possibility.

I believe that by treating instincts as internal stimuli, a more parsimonious conceptualization becomes possible in which there is only one kind of cathexis, attention cathexis, and one kind of excitation, perceptual excitation. It is a cathected, instinctual, internal perceptual excitation that the neonate experiences as an intense craving, a concept I have taken up in greater detail elsewhere (Shevrin, in press). Whether this craving is conscious or unconscious depends on the amount of attention cathexis directed to the instinctual excitation. It is entirely possible that at the very beginning of life (and immediately before birth), the reservoir of attention cathexis may be severely limited and only subthreshold attention cathexis can be directed to the instinctual excitations, in which case infantile cravings may be intense, result in much motor activity including crying, and be altogether unconscious. If this were the case, then there would be fateful consequences for the infant's early mental organization, which I address in the following section that deals with those other two great classes of significant unconscious mental events, subliminal perception and the repressed.

First, however, I must comment on the later propositions in the Freud–Rapaport model dealing with structure formation, or learning. Since it is not the main purpose of this chapter to discuss the nature of structure formation, I will comment only that if attention cathexis is necessary for representation of an excitation to occur, then it has already created a structure. An instructive case in point is provided by the increasing knowledge of how visual perception works. It is known that when retinal excitation produced by a visual stimulus reaches the occipital lobe, some 30 subsystems are activated, each responsive to a particular feature of the stimulus. This feature-by-feature excitation is still not a perceived object, however. These features must be "bound" together before the object is perceived. For this to occur, the excitation from the previous feature analyzers must proceed toward the temporal lobe and be further processed in the hippocampus, at which point it becomes possible to perceive an object. I would analogize (it may in fact be a case in point) that attention cathexis of the feature-by-feature excitation is what appears to take place in the hippocampus. The previous feature-by-feature excitations are not experienced, that is, they are not represented because they have not been cathected. What I am suggesting is similar to what Treisman (Treisman & Gelade, 1980), within a cognitive science framework, has proposed for the role of attention, which in her view serves to bind into a unitary whole the initial piecemeal visual processing. The view I have described has the advantage of placing this explanation of visual perception in a larger theoretical framework.

Consciousness, Subliminal Perception, and Repression

In this section I will explore implications of the theory previously sketched for understanding the function of consciousness as subjective experience, the nature of subliminal perception as brought to light by recent empirical research, and how repression works and what it does. I emphasize here the verb *explore*. Clearly, on such difficult matters no final word can be claimed, only a suggestion for a different perspective and a consideration of new possibilities.

In the position taken earlier on the unbiased nature of consciousness as subjective awareness, the important implication was that consciousness as subjective awareness could provide the mind with what Freud (1895/1950) first described in his *Project for a Scientific Psychology* as indications of reality. Primarily, Freud had in mind the indications of *external* reality. However, there are at least two important extensions that logically follow from his position and the Freud–Rapaport theory of consciousness. Consciousness as subjective awareness must also provide indications of reality for *internal* as well as external reality. In fact, the two need to be coordinated if the individual is to gratify instinctual demands adaptively. Rapaport's seventh proposition makes the interesting point that when external and internal excitation are congruent, there is no competition for attention cathexis, and a "common representation" is cathected. I assume that the common representation is some ideational representation of the means for adaptive gratification.

The mind quickly develops beyond a mere instinctual level as may prevail in the early days of infancy, however. Once instinctual excitations have been cathected, representations formed, experience with the environment acquired, memories laid down, and a variety of internal experiences made possible, the need for indications of reality becomes all the more important. By "varieties of internal experience," I refer to the different forms that the same mental content can assume. The same content can appear in a dream, an image, a perception, a memory, a daydream, a fantasy, or a thought. It is of the greatest importance to know which of these is the case. A person dreamed about must not be confounded with the same person perceived. I have proposed elsewhere (Shevrin, 1992) that consciousness as subjective awareness serves the function of "fixing" mental contents in the form initially experienced in subjective awareness. I intended that hypothesis to explain why participants in a subliminal experiment who recover elements of a subliminal stimulus in a dream or image cannot then identify these elements as belonging to the subliminal stimulus, that is, to the memory of a perception. I suggested that because the subliminal stimulus was never conscious in subjective awareness, it was not fixed as a percept although its content was unconsciously perceived and could influence later mental processes such as dreams and images. Now I can restate that hypothesis in a more general form: Because consciousness as subjective awareness is not able to provide indications of reality (in this instance, that of a perception) for the subliminal stimulus but is able to provide indications of reality for the dream or image, the recovered stimulus contents can be experienced only as belonging to the image or dream in which they first appeared in subjective awareness.

By providing indications of reality for all the different mental forms, as contrasted with mental contents, consciousness as subjective awareness performs perhaps its most important role. When different mental forms are confounded as occurs in schizophrenia, this is identified as "thought disorder." However, it is, of course, much more general than a disorder of thought only; it is fundamentally a disorder of consciousness as subjective awareness, and the ability of consciousness to provide indicators of reality has been compromised. As a result, the schizophrenic perceives as an external reality what is in fact a memory or a thought, an experience described as a hallucination. When a patient in psychoanalysis treats the analyst as if the analyst were *really* a parent from the past, a so-called psychotic transference, at the very least, a memory is being experienced as a perception. Again, consciousness as subjective experience is failing to provide appropriate indications of reality.

Rapaport (1957/1967) in his paper on cognitive structures described in detail a self-experiment in which he followed during the course of a night how a particular intention—to stay awake and record his experiences—was represented in different mental forms: waking, image, reverie, and dream. At times, a confounding of these different mental forms occurred, as when waking and dreaming were confused, presumably as a result of excessive fatigue that affected the availability of adequate attention cathexis. In this same paper he also described the widespread confounding of "frames of reference" that occurs in schizophrenia as well as in certain organic psychoses such as Korsakoff syndrome.

In short, once consciousness as subjective awareness is conceptualized as having a potent and essential function, then disorders of that function that appear to occur in transference psychoses, fullblown psychoses, certain organic psychoses, and conditions of excessive fatigue can begin to be identified. Three other important instances need to be considered in which indications of reality are compromised: (a) implicit memory, (b) subliminal perception, and (c) repression.

Much recent cognitive memory research (Squire, 1992) has focused on the distinction between explicit and implicit memory. It is possible to demonstrate, especially with organic amnesiac persons, that what is initially learned (e.g., a list of words) can be neither recalled nor recognized at some later time; in fact, amnesiacs fail to remember having even learned the list originally (Squire, 1992). However, if asked to complete certain word stems or to fill in missing letters in a word, they will do so with words from the original list at a better than chance frequency, showing that a memory trace has been formed and retained.

However, there is a significant difference between *knowing* that you have recalled or recognized a previous word and simply filling in an earlier word with no awareness that it is from the previous list. Cognitive psychologists refer to recall and recognition as *explicit memory*, and the unaware completion of words as *implicit memory*. I suggest that in case of implicit memory, consciousness as subjective awareness has failed to provide a significant indicator of reality; when the word stem, for example, elicits the correct completion unaccompanied by recognition or recall, consciousness has failed in its fixing function at some point along the way. As a result, a mental content appears in consciousness without its appropriate "tag" as a particular mental form—in this instance, as a memory.

One might speculate that people suffering from amnesia are affected by an impairment in this tagging function of consciousness, which is very likely to have occurred at the time the memory was laid down. In the case of persons with amnesia, a hippocampal organic lesion is thought to have interfered with the laying down of explicit memories (Squire, 1992), suggesting that this impairment in consciousness could be associated with a hippocampal function. I emphasize that the problem is in this fixing function of consciousness because the evidence suggests that sufficient attention cathexis must have been initially invested in the words, resulting in a conscious perception of them and the formation of memory traces; otherwise, no above-chance results would have been obtained in later tests of implicit memory. Nevertheless, the words could not be retrieved *as a memory*. How might the Freud–Rapaport theory as amended to include the generalized fixing function of consciousness explain this failure?

There are five tasks that first need to be identified: (a) the initial exposure to the word list, (b) efforts at unassisted recall, (c) efforts at recognition, (d) efforts at completing the word stems or fragments with a *recalled* word, and (e) efforts at completing the word stems or fragments with *"the first word that comes to mind"* (the usual instruction used in this condition). In the case of people with amnesia, only the final task meets with success. Why? I will look at each task separately.

In the first task, the words are sufficiently cathected so that they are at least momentarily in consciousness as a perception and a memory trace of them is formed. It is at this crucial point that the fixing function fails so that the memory trace is no longer retrievable *as a memory* of a previous perception because the percept *initially* had not been tagged as a perception. Thus, the percept can have no mental home; it is a mental content without a mental form. As we shall see later, what an organic lesion causes in people with amnesia, subliminal presentations cause in "normal" persons and repression causes in neurosis.

In the second task when participants are asked to *recall* the list, they are unable to recathect the memory trace because there is, in effect, no tagged memory to recall. In the third recognition task, an interesting circumstance is created in which there is a perception of the correct word—which would presumably activate memory traces of itself and related words, including the memory trace of its previous exposure on the word list—but this activation does not succeed because the activated correct memory trace has not been tagged as a memory; it has no advantage in this respect over any other activated trace. The fourth task is really a degraded recognition task that fails for the same reason the previous recognition task fails.

It is the fifth task, succeeding where the others had failed apparently because of an interesting change in instruction, that challenges explanation. The word stem (or fragment) is perceived, and its letters activate a number of word completions including the correct word as in the full recognition task—but why this time is the correct word given as the completion at a better than chance rate? What gives the correct word a better chance than the other activated alternatives? Precisely because it is *not* a memory task yet does have the advantage of recent activation, which the other activated traces do not. In the absence of a memory tag, a memory task is at best confusing; at the same time, the recently activated memory trace (which acts as an excitation) attracts attention cathexis and enters consciousness as a word able to complete the required task without creating any awareness that it is the correct word. The distinction between a memory of a perception and a free association that has the same content has been lost as a result of an impairment of the fixing function of consciousness.

Now, what of subliminal perception? The ensuing discussion will benefit from citing a curious and provocative finding from a series of experiments showing that participants who prefer to look hard at the tachistoscopic flash and try to discern what was there display a fascinating response when they are instructed to use a quite different strategy of simply letting the flashed word pop into mind (Shevrin & Snodgrass, 1997; Snodgrass & Shevrin, 1997a, 1997b; Snodgrass, Shevrin, & Kopka, 1993a, 1993b). These participants do *worse* than chance in guessing the subliminal word under the "pop" condition. The finding is remarkably stable; we have found it in four experiments, and it has been replicated independently by Van Selst and Merikle (1993). Both men and women show the same effect.

The experimental procedure is straightforward: The participants are told in advance that one of four words (e.g., *pleasure, fighting, pain, rose*) will be flashed so quickly (at 1 ms, 10 footlamberts) that it will be very hard to see but that they will be asked to say which word it was. Participants are then told that there are two different ways of enhancing correct identification: the "look" and "pop" strategies. Participants are given the opportunity to use each strategy in the course of the experiment and to determine which they prefer. (It is also possible to obtain the same results by asking participants to announce their preferred strategy in advance of the experiment so that any influence of the experiment itself is eliminated.)

If the finding is valid, as the evidence so far strongly suggests, then these look-preference participants when attempting to use the pop strategy must be *rejecting* correct responses without being aware of so doing. Only by this rejection can they perform below chance. From a detection procedure administered at the end of the experiment it can be determined that neither the look- nor the pop-preferring participants can consciously see the stimuli under the experimental conditions, so consciousness of the stimulus can be ruled out. Aside from its intrinsic interest in understanding the effects of subliminal stimuli, the finding may be an analog of what happens during defensive activity when an anxiety-arousing unconscious content is denied access to consciousness. It is possible that it is more than an analog and that actual defensive activity might be involved. In any case, how can this below-chance finding be explained by the Freud–Rapaport theory of consciousness?

It is first necessary to describe in theoretical terms what must happen during subliminal stimulation. First, the participant is asked to look into a viewing box, the tachistoscope, and to fixate a dot in the middle of a rectangular, moderately illuminated field. The participant is told to be alert and "pay attention"; following a prearranged signal, the stimulus is flashed (at 1 ms) and excites the receptor organs of vision. According to Rapaport's fourth proposition positing that excitations in the receptor organs will attract attention cathexis proportionate to their intensity, the briefly flashed stimulus would attract minimal attention cathexis. This minimal amount of attention cathexis would be below the amount necessary to bring the excitation above the threshold of consciousness as required by the fifth proposition.

I have also posited by generalizing the indications of reality function that without consciousness, the subliminal excitation cannot be experienced as a perception. What then is its status in the mind? It is simply a mental content that has achieved representational status because of the attention cathexis invested in it and has formed a mental trace, but has not been tagged as to its mental form. A subliminal mental content is a representation without a mental home. What an organic lesion produces in amnesia, subthreshold excitation produces in "normal" functioning.

Nevertheless, the participant's conscious task is to guess what the word is. The first step in guessing would be to cathect the memory traces of all four words. One of those four memory traces has already recently been cathected as a result of the subliminal excitation (similar to the recent cathexis of the correct words on the list in cases of amnesia). There are thus simultaneously present two sources of attention cathexis for the correct word: (a) the cathexis of the memory trace that can readily become conscious as a memory, for these words have been consciously perceived before; and (b) the subthreshold cathexis of the subliminal excitation rapidly dissipating (see Proposition 10). As the correct word makes its way toward consciousness as a result of its *above*-threshold cathexis as a memory, it brings with it the rapidly dissipating *below*-threshold cathexis of its recent subliminal excitation. The incorrect words, on the other hand, enter consciousness solely as recathected memory traces of previous conscious perceptions. The participant's task is then to guess which of the four words had just been flashed. The personal inclination of the look-preference participants is to look hard to see, that is, to perceive, what is actually there in the flash; they are instructed, however, to do the opposite, to follow the pop strategy and just let a word pop into mind. But what they have actually seen consciously is nothing; the indications of reality point to no stimulus at all. Nevertheless, they are to disregard the evidence of their conscious experience and to act as if they had seen a word. One word, the correct word, carries with it more attention cathexis than the other three; it somehow is different, but it still contains no indications of reality as a perception. It has not really been seen, and yet there is something different about it (the additional cathexis of the recent subliminal excitation). The looker-preference participant might thus be expected to be attracted to the word as a good guess, but there is precisely the problem. The attraction itself cannot be justified for one dedicated to act solely on the basis of the indications of reality. In fact, the attraction to the correct word, which must go on entirely unconsciously, may give rise to a feeling of uncanniness. As Freud (1919/1955) described in his paper on the uncanny, "an uncanny effect is often and easily produced when the distinction between imagination and reality is effaced, as when something that we have hitherto regarded as imaginary appears before us as reality" (p. 244). One can hypothesize that it is exactly this sense on the part of the look-preference participants that a significant distinction between memory and perception is in danger of being violated that results in their rejecting the correct word more often than the incorrect words for which there is no such danger. Their responses are simply guesses and no more, posing no threat to reality testing; they do not create the conditions for the experience of uncanniness.

Previously I have cited the memory findings for participants with organic amnesia as an example of a pathology of consciousness. The foregoing analysis of the subliminal inhibition finding suggests further that there are pathologies of consciousness related to its important function of providing indications of reality for both internal and external stimuli. Given that it is highly unlikely that for the look-preference participants, deeper repressed unconscious conflicts are stirred by the task, or even by the specific words, it is my contention that a conflict over indications of reality can create its own anxieties and is likely related to the earliest dilemma faced by the infant, which is how to learn to distinguish between a reexperienced memory and a perception. Perhaps it is precisely this developmental achievement that is made possible by the appearance of consciousness as subjective awareness with its capacity to provide indications of reality (see Opatow, in press for a thorough theoretical exegesis of this developmental turning point). Only then can the infant distinguish between a revived memory of previous gratification and a perception of gratification. If these thoughts are correct, then either the infant is not conscious in the subjectively aware sense before that development, or the consciousness that the infant experiences has not as yet developed its unique function. If the infant is in fact unconscious in the sense described, then he or she is still experiencing and behaving, but on an entirely unconscious level.

It is possible to think of the look-preference participants' rejection of the correct word as a defense against violating categories of inner and outer reality. The consequence is to keep from conscious awareness a correct guess that would create distress (the sense of the uncanny) if it were to become conscious, and in this respect it could be considered a variety of repression. This possibility raises the more general question of the relationship between the function of consciousness as subjective awareness and repression. Although it is not the purpose of this chapter to discuss repression in all of its complexity, there is one contribution to the subject that these considerations can make. One of the consequences of repression is to undo the indications of reality provided by consciousness as subjective awareness. Once a perception, thought, image, or fantasy has been repressed, its mental content loses its mental home, and in the unconscious it is cast loose from its temporal and spatial moorings; in contemporary cognitive terms, it becomes implicit. In Freudian terms, dynamic unconscious representations are timeless insofar as mental contents cannot be experienced as referring back to some previously experienced conscious mental form. From this standpoint, in the unconscious one is returned to the state of the young infant who cannot as yet distinguish between a perception and a memory. The attention cathexis of instinctual excitations in a state of repression must at the very least remain below the threshold for consciousness (see Proposition 8), much as is the case for subliminal excitations but for an entirely different reason. However, because the instinctual excitations of repressed mental representations are great and would normally attract considerable attention cathexis (see

Proposition 4), there must be some mental process that blocks access to the flow of attention cathexis or diverts it to other less anxiety-arousing representations.

Although in this chapter I have not discussed the particular mechanisms involved, displacements and derivatives of repressed contents that appear in consciousness cannot be referred back or experienced consciously as belonging to their correct previous mental home. As in subliminal experiments, when the mental contents from the subliminal stimulus appear in subsequent responses—dreams, images, or free associations—they cannot be identified as to their true source. In the case of subliminal stimulation, it is a function of too little cathexis due to stimulus duration, whereas in the case of repression, it is due to the repressive undoing of mental categories. Finally, in the case of organic amnesia, it is a function of an organic insult.

It might be instructive to consider in a little more detail some of the clinical implications of the theory. There are, of course, self-evident pathologies of consciousness as occur in dissociative and fugue states. When, for example, a child responds to abuse with defensive dissociation and numbing, one consequence may be that the function of consciousness as an indicator of reality is functionally impaired so that the perceptions experienced at the time are not tagged, resulting in subsequent difficulty in remembering. Instead, the events may appear in dreams, enactments, and affect states, but cannot be identified as memories. Psychic traumas in general may involve the temporary loss of this function of consciousness. If this were in fact the case, then it would follow that memories as such are irretrievable and must be reconstructed and independent evidence adduced. At the same time, it is essential to bear in mind that many traumas may occur without the loss of this function, in which case one would be dealing with repression that entails a *secondary* loss of tagging so that with the undoing of repression, the original memories as memories can be retrieved. How to distinguish between these two possibilities has to be left in the hands of the sensitive clinician.

Psychotic states and states of intoxication may also involve this pathology of consciousness so that different mental forms are confounded, producing hallucinations in which perception and memory are confounded, and delusions in which perception and judgment are confounded.

Insofar as it is a fundamental theorem of the psychoanalytic theory of neurosis that wishes as the mental representatives of instinctual excitations always strive for fulfillment by the most direct route, everyone lives in danger of treating memories of satisfaction as perceptions. As a result, we fall in love with the wrong people, or hate people for the wrong reasons, retreat into fantasy, or experience therapists as parents. Fortunately, the pathology of consciousness involved is usually circumscribed and potentially reversible.

How early in development this function of consciousness develops and achieves stability become an important question from the standpoint of this theory. It could be argued that stability is not achieved until the child can consistently distinguish between fantasy and reality and between dream hallucination and waking perception, which would place the achievement of stability at about 3 to 5 years of age.

As a final word, I propose that the Freud–Rapaport theory of consciousness as I have tried to exposit and extend it offers a way to understand why consciousness as subjective awareness is of such paramount importance to reality testing and why it has to play a vital role in treatment. The theory also conceptualizes how consciousness might be related to the mechanism of attention; how it might be applied to explaining subliminal perception, the nature of repression, and its crucial place in development; and how implicit memory functions in persons with amnesia. Finally, it is also necessary to stress that these hypotheses are all provisional and require considerably more theoretical clarification and empirical support.

References

Breuer, J., & Freud, S. (1955). Studies on hysteria. In J. Strachey (Ed. and Trans.), *The standard edition of the complete psychological works of Sig-*

mund Freud (Vol. 2, pp. 1–335). London: Hogarth Press. (Original work published 1893)

Dennett, D. (1995). *Consciousness explained*. New York: Basic Books.

Flanagan, O. (1992). *Consciousness reconsidered*. Cambridge, MA: MIT Press.

Freud, S. (1950). Project for a scientific psychology. In J. Strachey (Ed. and Trans.), *The standard edition of the complete psychological works of Sigmund Freud* (Vol. 2, pp. 281–347). London: Hogarth Press. (Original work published 1895)

Freud, S. (1953). The interpretation of dreams. In J. Strachey (Ed. and Trans.), *The standard edition of the complete psychological works of Sigmund Freud* (Vol. 5, pp. 1–630). London: Hogarth Press. (Original work published 1900)

Freud, S. (1955). The 'uncanny.' in J. Strachey (Ed. and Trans.), *The standard edition of the complete psychological works of Sigmund Freud* (Vol. 17, pp. 217–256). London: Hogarth Press. (Original work published 1919)

Freud, S. (1955). The unconscious. In J. Strachey (Ed. and Trans.), *The standard edition of the complete psychological works of Sigmund Freud* (Vol. 14, pp. 159–216). London: Hogarth Press. (Original work published 1915)

Freud, S. (1957). Instincts and their vicissitudes. In J. Strachey (Ed. and Trans.), *The standard edition of the complete psychological works of Sigmund Freud* (Vol. 14, pp. 109–140). London: Hogarth Press. (Original work published 1915)

Freud, S. (1961). A note upon the 'mystic writing pad.' In J. Strachey (Ed. and Trans.), *The standard edition of the complete psychological works of Sigmund Freud* (Vol. 19, pp. 227–234). London: Hogarth Press. (Original work published 1925)

Mandler, G. (1975). Consciousness: Respectable, useful and probably necessary. In R. Solsos (Ed.), *Information processing and cognition: The Loyola Symposium* (pp. 229–254). Hillsdale, NJ: Erlbaum.

Opatow, B. (in press). The distinctiveness of the psychoanalytic unconscious. *Journal of American Psychoanalytic Association*.

Pare, D., & Llinas, P. (1995). Conscious and preconscious processes as seen from the standpoint of sleep-walking cycle neurophysiology. [Special issue: The biology and neuropsychology of consciousness]. *Neuropsychology, 33*(a), 1155–1168.

Posner, M. I., & Boies, S. L. (1971). Components of attention. *Psychological Review, 78*, 391–408.

Rapaport, D. (1967). Cognitive structures. In M. M. Gill (Ed.), *The collected papers of David Rapaport* (pp. 631–664). New York: Basic Books. (Original work published 1957)

Rapaport, D. (1967). On the psychoanalytic theory of motivation. In M. M. Gill (Ed.), *The collected papers of David Rapaport* (pp. 853–915). New York: Basic Books. (Original work published 1960)

Searle, J. R. (1992). *The rediscovery of mind*. Cambridge, MA: MIT Press.

Shevrin, H. (1992). Subliminal perception, memory and consciousness:

Cognitive and dynamic perspectives. In R. F. Bornstein & T. S. Pittman (Eds.), *Perception without awareness* (pp. 123–142). New York: Guilford Press.

Shevrin, H. (in press). Psychoanalysis as the patient: Low in energy, high in feeling. *Journal of the American Psychoanalytic Association.*

Shevrin, H., Bond, J. A., Brakel, L. A., Hertel, R. K., & Williams, W. J. (1996). *Conscious and unconscious processes: Psychodynamic, cognitive, and neurophysiological convergences.* [Monograph]. New York: Guilford Press.

Shevrin, H., & Snodgrass, J. M. (1997). *ERP indicators of subliminal inhibition.* Manuscript in preparation.

Shiffrin, R. M., & Schneider, W. (1977). Controlled and automatic human information processing: II. Perceptual learning, automatic attending, and a general theory. *Psychological Review, 84,* 127–190.

Snodgrass, M., & Shevrin, H. (1997a, May). *The inhibition of subliminal perceptions: Evidence for unconscious defensive processes.* Paper presented at the American Psychological Society Conference, Washington, DC.

Snodgrass, M., & Shevrin, H. (1997b). *Replicable unconscious inhibition of subliminal perceptions: Unconscious defense?* Manuscript submitted for publication.

Snodgrass, M., Shevrin, H., & Kopka, M. (1993a). Absolute inhibition is incompatible with conscious perception. *Consciousness and Cognition, 2*(3), 204–209.

Snodgrass, M., & Shevrin, H., & Kopka, M. (1993b). The mediation of intentional judgments by unconscious perceptions: The influences of task strategy, task preference, word meaning, and motivation. *Consciousness and Cognition, 2,* 169–193.

Squire, L. R. (1992). Declarative and non-declarative memory: Multiple brain systems supporting learning and memory. [Special issue: Memory systems]. *Journal of Cognitive Neuroscience, 4*(3), 232–243.

Treisman, A. M., & Gelade, G. (1980). A feature–integration theory of attention. *Cognitive Psychology, 12,* 97–136.

Van Selst, M., & Merikle, P. (1993). Perception below the objective threshold? *Consciousness and Cognition, 2*(3), 194–203.

3

Capturing the "Mommy and I Are One" Merger Fantasy:
The Oneness Motive

Paul Siegel and Joel Weinberger

Storytelling provides the basic material of psychoanalysis. The basic rule of psychoanalysis, free association, is after all a means of inducing the patient to tell stories that are emblematic of his or her personality and ways of construing the world. An early psychoanalytic researcher who grasped the power of this simple idea was Henry Murray (1938/1962), whose staff at the Harvard Psychological Clinic conducted intensive studies of healthy individuals by having them tell stories about evocative stimulus pictures. What grew out of this work was not only an important clinical tool that would become part of the standard psychological test battery, the Thematic Apperception Test (TAT; Morgan & Murray, 1935; Murray, 1943), but also Murray's enabling clinical and research idea of the *thema* (Demorest, 1995). Drawing on Freud's (1912/1963) canonical notion of the *stereotype plate* or *complex*, as well as on Jung's (1936/1969) discussion of complexes, this construct was conceived of as the distinctive and consistent patterns that define an individual's personality. A thema was defined as a compound unit comprised of a "need" (i.e., a force within individuals that propels them to change an unsatisfying situation) and a

Preparation of this chapter was supported by National Institute of Mental Health First Award Grant 1 R29 MH48955-01A1 to Joel Weinberger.

"press" (i.e., a force in the environment that facilitates or impedes the satisfaction of a need).

The need concept, which also drew on the seminal idea in classical psychoanalysis of the "wish," thereafter rose to prominence in the work of McClelland and Atkinson and their colleagues. These investigators focused their research on three of Murray's original taxonomy of 20 needs: achievement, power, and affiliation (Atkinson & Birch, 1970; McClelland, 1951, 1985; McClelland & Winter, 1969; Winter, 1973). (McAdams, 1988, later introduced the intimacy motive, which is related to affiliation.) Their research program, spanning almost 50 years, has been dedicated to investigating the place of these universal human motives in people's lives. They have found that, consistent with psychoanalytic theorizing and clinical experience, these needs are centrally affective and function largely outside of moment-to-moment conscious awareness. Because of this latter characteristic, they have come to be referred to as "implicit motives" (McClelland, Koestner, & Weinberger, 1989; Weinberger & McClelland, 1990).

In this chapter, we posit the existence of another primary dimension of the human motivational system, a motive that was not included in Murray's (1938/1962; Morgan & Murray, 1935) original taxonomy of needs. Rather, its source lies in the work of other psychoanalytic theorists (e.g., Limentani, 1956; Searles, 1979) who contended that people harbor wishes for oneness or merger with what was termed "the good mother of early childhood" (i.e., mother when she was experienced early in life as comforting, protective, and nurturing). These thinkers averred that some form of gratification of these wishes in the patient's experience of the analytical relationship often leads to a better outcome. Experimental research conducted by Silverman and his associates (Silverman, Lachmann, & Milich, 1982; Silverman & Weinberger, 1985) supports this proposition. We conceptualize this motive as a drive to become part of, at one with, or belong to, a larger whole. We call it the *oneness motive* (OM).

People are not normally aware of the OM and its operation. It is therefore an implicit motive like achievement, power, affiliation, and intimacy. Like those motives, it influences a variety of adaptive and maladaptive behaviors. It is most clearly manifest in interpersonal relationships and has been recognized in that arena since ancient times.

> The intense yearning which each of them had for the other does not appear to be the desire of lover's intercourse, but of something else which the soul of either evidently desires and cannot tell and of which she has only a dark and doubtful presentiment. Suppose Hephaestus, with his instruments, [was] to come to the pair who are lying side by side and said to them . . . "do you desire to be wholly one: always day and night to be in one another's company? For if this is what you desire I am ready to melt you into one and let you grow together." . . . There is not a man . . . who when he heard the proposal would deny that this meeting and melting into one another, this becoming one instead of two, was the very expression of his ancient needs. (Plato, cited in Bergmann, 1971, p. 192)

The experience is also common in psychotherapy. A musician (Sylvia), who was a patient of the second author (JW), was making little progress on her complaint that she was unable to feel genuine intimacy. During one session, she described what it was like for her to perform musical solos. She would become so involved in playing the music that she forgot about her audience. She was almost surprised to discover them before her when she was done. This can be understood as a symbiotic-like, or oneness, experience. The therapist noted that it occurred only when Sylvia played solos, not when she played as a member of the orchestra. Indicating her inability to experience intimacy, she could have such experiences only when not involved with others. Her need to have intimacy was expressed in the oneness experience; her private fears did not permit it to take place in connection with others. Thus, her intrapersonal oneness experience could be seen as a compromise formation. To highlight what he felt was the healthy aspect of this experience, the therapist asked Sylvia whether she felt almost literally connected to the music, so that it seemed as though she were not merely playing it but was actually part of it. She was moved by this interpretation. She decided that, to understand her experience so deeply, the therapist must also be a musician. She felt that he could understand her better now because they shared this experience. This was a healthy symbiotic-like, or oneness, experience with another person and so represented an advance. She then went on to discuss similar experiences in her past. As a child, she had had experiences of this sort with toys. This was directly analogous to her experience with the music (i.e., a oneness experience without people). She also spoke of the few similar experiences she had with her husband (also a musician); this was analogous to the adaptation-enhancing experience she had just had with me and reinforced the adaptive aspect of the motive. She wished that she could have had such experiences of connectedness with her parents, who were generally distant and critical. This sequence of associations led to recollections and working through of early experiences that had heretofore been unavailable to her which were linked to her current social inhibitions.

The OM is not restricted to interpersonal relations. People also may seek to become one with or part of more abstract entities such as organizations, teams, political parties, religions, and so on. It also plays a part in some mystical experiences:

> In mystic states we . . . become one with the Absolute. . . . This is the everlasting and triumphant mystical tradition, hardly altered by differences of clime and creed. . . . The me and . . . the thou are not (separate). . . . In the One, there can be no distinction. (James, 1902, pp. 410–411)

Silverman et al. (1982) provided many more literary and anecdotal examples of the operation of the OM. Searles (1979) devoted many chapters of his book to the salutary effects of symbiosis in psychotherapy. The tenacity with which individuals seek to attain and maintain these affiliations, as well as the disorientation and distress they experience when such connections are threatened or severed, bear witness to the power of these attachments.

Early Empirical Investigations of OMs: The Work of Lloyd Silverman

Silverman and Silverman (1964) developed an innovative experimental strategy for testing dynamic psychoanalytic propositions. It involved presenting psychoanalytically inspired messages via a tachistoscope at a speed and illumination level that ensured that observers could not report seeing them. That is, the messages were presented subliminally. In this way, Silverman and Silverman reasoned, the messages would be perceived and processed unconsciously. Psychoanalytic theory makes much of unconscious processes, positing that they differ qualitatively from conscious processes and that they influence much of human thinking, feeling, and behavior (see, e.g., Westen, 1990). Silverman and Silverman hoped to trigger such processes and determine whether they would generate the kinds of effects predicted by psychoanalytic theory. They termed this experimental paradigm *subliminal psychodynamic activation* (SPA; see Silverman, 1976, 1983, for more on the SPA method).

Early SPA research focused on stirring up conflicts held by many psychoanalytic theorists to be characteristic of certain clinical and nonclinical populations. Activating these conflicts was predicted to lead to distinctive defensive and even maladaptive behaviors. Silverman summarized much of this early work more than 20 (Silverman, 1976) and again 14 (Silverman, 1983) years ago. More recent research has focused on triggering or arousing the oneness fantasies that are the object of this chapter to determine whether they generate the kinds of adaptation-enhancing effects that the aforementioned psychoanalysts (e.g., Limentani, 1956; Searles, 1979) have associated with them. The subliminal stimulus used in the SPA studies designed to trigger these symbiotic-like fantasies was the verbal message "Mommy and I are one" (MIO), sometimes accompanied by a congruent picture. A second, neutral message (usually "people are walking" [PAW]), was used as a control message for purposes of comparison.

Initial experiments with the MIO stimulus were conducted with patients with schizophrenia. Results indicated that the MIO stimulation could temporarily diminish what was termed *schizophrenic ego pathology* but only in the patients who were relatively well differentiated from their mother (see Mendelsohn & Silverman, 1982, for a review of this research).

Subsequent researchers explored the effects of MIO stimulation on other populations. In a remarkable series of studies, researchers reported relatively long-term effects in nonschizophrenic clinical populations (e.g., Linehan & O'Toole, 1982; Palmatier & Bornstein,

1980). In these investigations, the MIO stimulus served as an adjunct to proved psychotherapeutic treatments. The effectiveness of these treatments was found to be enhanced when sessions were preceded by the MIO rather than the PAW stimulus. Another series of studies showed that nonclinical populations also could be positively affected by the MIO stimulus (e.g., Ariam & Siller, 1982; Parker, 1982). These investigations showed increases in school grades when classes were preceded by the MIO rather than the PAW stimulus. (See Silverman et al., 1982, Silverman & Weinberger, 1985, and Weinberger & Silverman, 1987, for more comprehensive reviews of both types of research.)

SPA work generally and MIO work in particular became and, to some degree, remain controversial (Weinberger, 1992). Some critics simply did not believe the results, and some argued that they had not been adequately replicated (e.g., Balay & Shevrin, 1988; however, see Weinberger, 1989, for a rejoinder). Hardaway (1990) addressed these concerns with a comprehensive meta-analysis. His meta-analysis of all MIO studies yielded an effect size of .41. This is a respectable effect in psychology; it falls between a small and a medium effect, as Cohen (1977) defined power. Weinberger and Hardaway (1990) reported more fine-grained analyses that determined that the effect sizes of investigations associated with Silverman's laboratory were equivalent to those conducted independently of Silverman. They also found that the effect sizes of published, peer-reviewed MIO studies were virtually identical to the effect sizes of unpublished studies. Moreover, they conducted what Rosenthal (1979) termed a "file-drawer analysis." Such an analysis determined how many null (and presumably unreported) findings would be needed to obviate the number of reported positive findings. Their analysis revealed that there would have to be 2,287 null findings to annul the known MIO results, establishing MIO studies as robust.

These meta-analyses speak to the reality of MIO effects. However, they tell nothing of how or why MIO stimulation generates such effects (cf. Weinberger, 1992). Weinberger suggested that the MIO message may generate positive affect (Silverman & Weinberger, 1985; Weinberger, 1992; Weinberger, Kelner, & McClelland, in press) and that this might mediate the reported effects. There is considerable evidence that affect and mood can have powerful effects on behavior, cognition, and even physical health (Salovey & Birnbaum, 1989; Salovey & Rosenhan, 1989; see Weinberger, 1992, and Weinberger, Siegel, & DeCamello, in press, for more information on this).

To determine whether MIO stimulation did induce positive mood, Weinberger, Kelner, et al. (in press) conducted two experiments in which they assessed mood using self-report and free-response mood measures after subliminal stimulation. Awareness was assessed using signal-detection analyses. Randomly selected participants were presented with 100 discrimination trials, and d' (a statistical measure of detectability) was calculated. Results indicated that the stimuli were not consciously detected (i.e., they were subliminal). The self-report measure was the State version of the Profile of Mood States (POMS; McNair, Lorr, & Droppleman, 1971/1981), as modified by McClelland and Meterko (1983) to be more sensitive to positive mood. The free-response measure involved the rating of early memories. Respondents were allowed a few minutes to write brief descriptions (phrases or single sentences) of any incidents they could recall having occurred to them before 14 years of age. They then rated these memories for quality (positive or negative) and intensity (1 through 7) of affect. It was hypothesized that the MIO effects would be more evident in free-response, implicit mood than in self-report, explicit mood (see Weinberger, 1992, for a detailed description of the reasoning behind this prediction).

In the first experiment, respondents were presented with either subliminal MIO or PAW stimulation. There were no differences between these two groups on POMS scores, but there were large differences on the early-memories measure. The MIO group evidenced more positive memories and a higher overall positive affective score. Thus, MIO stimulation had affected only implicit positive mood.

The second experiment both confirmed and added to these findings. Three groups were run. The first two were exactly as just described; the third was presented with the subliminal message "Mommy is gone" (MIG). This message was chosen because it had words and structure in common with MIO but had a totally different meaning. Thus, both messages contained the word *mommy*. Both also had the word *one*, although it was embedded in *gone* in the MIG message. Results replicated those of the first experiment in that the MIO group exhibited significantly more positive memories as well as more positive mood on the early-memories task than did either of the other two groups. Once again, there were no differences on the POMS. Furthermore, a linear mood effect was obtained on the overall scores. The MIO group showed the most positive affect, the MIG the least, and the PAW group scored right in the middle. This directly paralleled the affective valence of the meaning of the messages.

How Does MIO Stimulation Affect Mood? The Origin of the Oneness Motive Scoring System

The meta-analyses of Hardaway (1990) and Weinberger and Hardaway (1990) indicated that MIO effects are real. The mood study of Weinberger, Kelner, et al. (in press) suggested that mood changes accompany and may underlie these effects. However, what is it about MIO stimulation that leads to changes in mood? Recall that Silverman et al. (1982) and Silverman and Weinberger (1985) posited that the subliminal MIO stimulus triggers a symbiotic-like, or oneness, fantasy. As Bornstein and Masling (1984) pointed out, however, Silverman and colleagues presented no direct evidence for the existence of such a mediating fantasy. Cognitivists (e.g., Bower 1981; Gilligan & Bower, 1984) might suggest that MIO stimulation activates a schema, habitually learned under and therefore linked to positive mood. Silverman and colleagues presented no evidence for such a schema either, however.

In this section, we describe efforts to capture this mediating schema or fantasy. These endeavors were based on the motive measurement paradigm innovated by McClelland and his colleagues (McClelland, 1985; Smith, 1992). The experimental strategy involves arousing a motive, having participants write stories to TAT cards in their aroused state, and comparing these stories with those written by unaroused control participants. Observed differences between the two sets of stories, in combination with theoretical considerations, become the basis for devising a scoring system that captures the relevant dimensions of the motive.

In a study described by Weinberger (1992), TAT-type stories were collected from individuals who had undergone subliminal MIO, PAW, and MIG stimulation. (Subliminality was determined as described above.) Differences were apparent in the stories written by the three groups. A scoring system was devised to capture the dimensions that underlie these differences, structurally patterned after those designed by McClelland and Atkinson for measuring other motives. This system could not be used to measure differences between the aforementioned three conditions because it had been derived from them. Projective stories therefore were collected from two other sets of individuals (one subliminally stimulated with MIO and the other with PAW) and blindly scored. The MIO group was found to have significantly higher scores than the PAW group ($t = 2.26$, $N = 18$, $p < .05$, $d = 1.17$, $r = .50$). Thus, the system was able to differentiate an aroused from an unaroused condition.

At first, what the system measured was referred to as the "need to belong" (Weinberger & McLeod, 1989). It is now called the *oneness motive* (Weinberger, 1992), and the scoring system is titled the *Oneness Motive Scoring System* (OMSS; Weinberger, Stefanou, Scroppo, & Siegel, 1996). In this system, "oneness" refers to an experience of being part of something larger than or beyond the self while preserving an autonomous (stable, intact), coherent sense of self. A story must have one or more of the following themes to be scored for the presence of OM imagery:

1. *Emotionally close interpersonal relationship*: An ongoing positive and emotionally close interpersonal relationship (e.g., "These two people love one another").
2. *Oneness attainment*: A character or force that, while retaining its own bounded identity, is explicitly described as joining with another person or entity to form a unity or larger whole (e.g., "The two work as a unit, as if they were one being").
3. *Merger or flow experience*: A nonaversive softening of boundaries between a character and the outside world (e.g., "The music flowed through his fingers").

If any of these categories appear in a story, it is said to have *basic oneness imagery*. A single point is awarded for the occurrence of each of these categories. A story can therefore earn 0 to 3 points on basic imagery. If a story cannot qualify for any of these categories, it receives no points and no further ratings are done. Stories that contain oneness imagery but that also refer to a loss of self are termed *spoiled oneness imagery* (OM−). Such a story is evidenced by a character described as "brainwashed" or converted into a mindless automaton. Murder, suicide, or the eventual loss of a oneness experience also are considered losses of self and are labeled *OM−*. OM− stories receive a score of zero just like stories that do not score at all. We are flagging such occurrences for possible future investigations.

If basic imagery is scored, the story is examined for the presence of additional subcategories. These include the following: (a) *wish* —a stated hope, need, desire, or wish related to any oneness imagery; (b) *focus*—strong concentration on oneness imagery or a purposeful narrowing of the field of attention so that the oneness imagery dominates that field; (c) *block*—explicit concern about obstacles to the fulfillment of oneness; (d) *fulfillment*—an experience of a pleasurable, homeostatic end state of inner peace or satisfaction, or of being recharged or refueled, as a result of a oneness experience; and (e) *thema*—the story qualifies for more than one basic imagery category or the entire story concerns a oneness experience or is saturated with oneness imagery (oneness is the leitmotif of the story).

A single point is awarded for the occurrence of each of the subcategories that appears in the story. The subcategories can therefore add 0 to 5 points to a story's basic imagery score. This means that overall totals can range from 0 to 8. For a more detailed discussion of the system, which includes rules for making scoring decisions and practice stories for becoming reliable, see the scoring manual (Weinberger et al., 1996).

Reliability and Validity of the OMSS

Reliability

The next step in this research program was to determine whether the OMSS would have any utility. First, we assessed reliability. If a measure is not reliable, it cannot be valid. Projective measures of the sort we are describing here have long been held to be unreliable (e.g., Entwisle, 1972). We therefore examined interrater and test–retest reliability for the OM measure.

In one early assessment of reliability (Weinberger & McLeod, 1989), respondents were presented with four TAT pictures from the standard six typically used by motivational researchers in the McClelland tradition. The volunteers were participants in a behavioral medicine treatment lasting 8 weeks. (This treatment is described in more detail later in this chapter in our review of OM validity studies.) Two raters, trained using the OMSS manual, independently scored the stories for OM. Interrater reliability, when adjusted via the Spearman–Brown correction formula, was .88 ($p < .001$; $N = 120$).

The participants in this study were assessed twice at a 3-month interval (when they signed up for the treatment and at its conclusion), giving us an opportunity to get our first measurement of test–retest reliability. The overall test–retest reliability was .42 ($p < .01$; $n = 51$). A more fine-grained analysis revealed an interesting aspect to this finding. Our assessment of test–retest reliability combined two groups: One received the treatment (which was predicted to alter OM), and the other was a waiting-list control. The treated group showed poor test–retest reliability, presumably because the treatment altered their score on the OM measure ($r = .26$, ns; $n = 35$); the control group demonstrated good test–retest reliability ($r = .67$, $p < .01$; $n = 17$). The test–retest reliability obtained in this study was only suggestive, however, because it was based on a relatively small sample, especially after participants were divided into treated and untreated groups. This study demonstrated good interrater reliability, however.

We recently completed another, more extensive reliability assessment. Eighty undergraduates (41 women and 39 men, aged 19–26 years) were administered four TAT cards from the set used by Weinberger (1992). The same four cards were administered to the same participants about a week later. We independently scored all stories written over the two administrations, which were put in random order to avoid biasing ratings due to sample size. Two measures of interrater reliability were then calculated. One was a more liberal measure based on the raters' total OM scores (the sum of scores across a participant's set of four stories). Using this type of rater agreement, we found the raw interrater reliability to be .81 ($p < .001$; $n = 75$). When this was corrected using the Spearman–Brown correction formula, reliability was .91. The other assessment of interrater reliability was McClelland's more conservative method (see Smith, 1992) of dividing the total number of scoring agreements by the total number of scoring instances. Under the protocol for this method, an agreed-on score of zero for any category is not counted as an agreement. It is ignored, and only positive scoring decisions are examined. Interrater reliability using this highly conservative percentage agreement-type system was .95.

To assess test–retest reliability, we averaged the raters' total OM scores for each participant (as justified by adequate interrater reliability) for each week, and we determined the consistency of these scores from one week to the next. The consistency of a respondent's total score, rather than the individual scores of stories written in response to the same picture, was determined because oneness construct concerns a person's general tendency, or underlying motivation, for oneness. Thus, although respondents' scores for any of the four stories might vary from one week to the next (and they did; the content of stories also often changed from week to week), their total score should be roughly the same (cf. Smith 1992; Weinberger & McClelland, 1990). Test–retest reliability was .80 ($p < .001$; $n = 75$). Results of this study confirm the interrater reliability found by Weinberger and McLeod (1989) and add solid evidence for test–retest reliability using a large enough sample.

Validity

The OMSS seems to capture a stable psychological phenomenon. To be valid, individual differences in OM should relate to other measures in a theoretically meaningful manner. According to Silverman et al. (1982) and Silverman and Weinberger (1985), the MIO fantasy ought to be related to variables such as treatment outcome and measures of psychological health. Weinberger, Scroppo, McLeod, Santorelli, and Kabat-Zinn (1991) tested this hypothesis. Volunteers for this study participated in a stress reduction and relaxation program at the Stress Reduction Clinic of the University of Massachusetts Medical Center in Worcester. The participants all suffered from diseases and disorders that are potentially deadly (e.g., cancer, heart disease, AIDS) or, although not life threatening, are difficult to arrest and control and are chronically painful (e.g., chronic headaches, digestive problems, arthritis).

The program is a hospital-based, intensive 8-week treatment. Patients are referred by their physicians to learn how to cope with the stresses associated with their illnesses. Treatment involves learning a set of mindfulness meditation techniques.[1] The participants meet weekly for 2 hr with a group leader who instructs them in these techniques. They also are asked to complete an additional 45 min of meditation per day, on their own, at home. To aid them in this, they are given instructional audiotapes. Eventually, they dispense with the tapes and meditate entirely on their own.

Weinberger et al. (1991) were interested in this treatment because Kabat-Zinn (1990) had suggested that the central mutative agent in mindfulness meditation practice is achieving a sense of "wholeness" and "connectedness." Through such practice, individuals no longer identify with their particular physical or emotional pain, but instead experience a feeling of at-one-ment with it, and possibly eventually with the external world. That is, the meditators often eventually experience an attendant sense of connection to the world. Kabat-Zinn related this experience to the experience of oneness or attunement that infants have with their mother.

Weinberger et al. (1991) hypothesized that this behavioral medicine treatment would successfully reduce psychological distress. They further predicted that OM would be negatively related to psychological distress and positively related to psychological health in their sample. They also predicted that OM would increase in the course of treatment. Finally, they predicted that, at the end of treatment, OM would be related to the maintenance of gains. That is, if the treatment works by enhancing a sense of wholeness, connectedness, or oneness, then OM should be affected by the treatment and should be related to clinical measures of positive outcomes. This would parallel the SPA findings (e.g., Silverman et

---

[1]These techniques have their roots in Buddhist meditative traditions but are not presented in any philosophical or spiritual context. Participants are simply encouraged to develop moment-to-moment awareness of self and environment.

al., 1982) that subliminal MIO stimulation results in a better treatment outcome.

To assess treatment efficacy, Weinberger et al. (1991) measured mood, psychological symptomatology, and physical symptomatology. They measured these variables before and after treatment and at a 2-year follow-up (to examine possible relapse). TATs were administered before and after treatment (3 months apart) and scored blindly for OM. A measure of a sense of coherence (Antonovsky, 1984) and the Stress-Hardiness Scale (Kobassa, 1977) also were administered before and after treatment. These are thought to assess a health-related personality structure.

Results indicated that the stress reduction and relaxation program was an effective treatment. Physical symptoms decreased over the course of the treatment, both as assessed by the Medical Symptom Check List (Overall: $F = 9.33$, $N = 22$, $p < .001$, $\eta = .55$, $f = .67$; pre- vs. posttreatment: $F = 10.72$, $N = 22$, $p < .004$, $\eta = .59$, $f = .73$) and SCL-90-R (Overall: $F = 16.12$, $N = 22$, $p < .001$, $\eta = .67$, $f = .90$; pre- vs. posttreatment: $F = 18.4$, $p < .001$, $N = 22$, $\eta = .70$, $f = .98$). Mood also improved, both as assessed by the Positivity Scale (Overall: $F = 12.1$, $N = 25$, $p < .001$, $\eta = .58$, $f = .71$; pre- vs. posttreatment: $F = 14.14$, $N = 25$, $p < .001$, $\eta = .62$, $f = .78$) and Negativity Scale (Overall: $F = 12.8$, $N = 25$, $p < .001$, $\eta = .58$, $f = .72$; pre- vs. posttreatment: $F = 12.4$, $N = 25$, $p < .002$, $\eta = .58$, $f = .72$) of the POMS. Moreover, these gains were maintained at the 2-year follow-up (Medical Symptom Check List: $F = 6.38$, $N = 22$, $p < .02$, $\eta = .49$, $f = .56$; SCL-90-R: $F = 9.35$, $N = 22$, $p < .006$, $\eta = .57$, $f = .70$; Positivity: $F = 9.45$, $N = 25$, $p < .005$, $\eta = .54$, $f = .64$); Negativity: $F = 13.8$, $N = 25$, $p < .001$, $\eta = .60$, $f = .76$). These gains endured even though patients did not receive any additional training beyond the 8-week program; they were on their own once the program ended.

Additionally, OM scores were related to stress and psychological health, as predicted. This pattern of correlations is shown in Table 1.

As Table 1 shows, OM correlated negatively with most of the subscales of the SCL-90-R, a commonly used symptom checklist (Derogatis, 1983). That is, OM negatively correlated with symptomatology. Oneness also was negatively correlated with the Medical Symptom Check List devised by Kabat-Zinn (1990) especially for

Table 1

Correlations of Oneness Motive With Personality and Clinical
Measures in the Behavioral Medicine Study

Variable	r
Personality	
Stress-hardiness (*n* = 40)	.39**
Sense of coherence (*n* = 43)	.30*
Clinical (SCL-90-R; *n* = 43)	
Somatization	−.31**
Obsessive–compulsive	−.37**
Interpersonal sensitivity	−.34**
Depression	−.32**
Anxiety	−.33**
Hostility	−.46***
Phobic anxiety	*ns*
Paranoid anxiety	−.46***
Psychoticism	−.33**
General Severity Index	−.38**
Medical Symptom Check List (*n* = 43)	−.38**
Mood (Modified POMS; *n* = 50)	
Anger-hostility	−.32**
Loved-friendly	.48***
Resourceful	.29**

Note. From Weinberger, Scroppo, McLeod, Santorelli, and Kabat-Zinn (1991). Correlations include all of the individuals who began the treatment.
*$p < .10$.   **$p < .05$.   ***$p < .01$.

the stress reduction and relaxation program. This check list assesses physical symptomatology. OM thus was negatively related to reports of physical discomfort. Oneness was also correlated with feelings of being resourceful and loved-friendly as assessed by the modified POMS. It was negatively related to anger and hostility on this measure. Finally, OM was positively related to the personality measures of stress and hardiness (Kobassa, 1977) and a sense of coherence (Antonovsky, 1984), both of which have been related to positive health outcomes. Thus, OM correlated with a healthy personality structure.

Table 2

Correlations of the Oneness Motive at Posttreatment With Outcome Variables at the 2-Year Follow-Up

Variable	r
Clinical (SCL-90-R; $n = 27$)	
Somatization	−.34*
Interpersonal sensitivity	−.35*
Anxiety	ns
Obsessive–compulsive	−.45**
Depression	ns
Hostility	ns
Phobia	−.37*
Paranoia	−.43**
Psychoticism	ns
Medical Symptom Check List ($n = 27$)	ns
Mood (Modified POMS; $n = 26$)	
Loved-friendly	ns
Tense	−.40**
Depressed	ns
Resourceful	ns
Anger-hostility	−.47**
Fatigue	ns
Confused	ns
Positivity	ns
Negativity	−.39**

Note. From Weinberger, Scroppo, McLeod, Santorelli, and Kabat-Zinn (1991). Measures of stress-hardiness and a sense of coherence were not administered at follow-up. POMS = Profile of Mood States.
*$p < .10$. **$p < .05$.

Next, as predicted, OM scores increased over the course of the treatment ($t = 2.81$, $N = 32$, $p < .01$, $d = 1.00$, $r = .45$).

Finally, Table 2 shows the correlations between OM at the end of treatment and the outcome measures at the 2-year follow-up.

In Tables 1 and 2, the correlations between OM and the SCL-90-R subscales are of a similar magnitude, but fewer achieved statistical significance, possibly because of diminished power (i.e., a smaller sample size). Nonetheless, 2 of the 10 subscales were significant at the .05 level, three showed trends at the .10 level, and all correlations were in the predicted direction. This is much more than would be expected by chance. The Medical Symptom Check List was no longer significantly correlated with OM, although this correlation, too, was in the expected direction. The mood results supported our predictions. OM was negatively related to 2 subscales measuring negative mood and to overall negative mood. The correlations with the rest of the subscales were of the same order as shown in Table 1, and all were in the expected direction, but none reached statistical significance, possibly because of low power. A replication with a larger sample would be needed to address this issue. Nonetheless, the overall pattern of findings depicted in Table 2 suggests that OM at treatment termination is related to continued positive outcome 2 years later.

Taken together, these findings support the validity of the OMSS and of OM as a psychological construct. They also parallel the SPA findings, described earlier (Silverman et al., 1982; Silverman & Weinberger, 1985), that subliminal MIO stimulation enhances therapeutic effectiveness. In this behavioral medicine study, OM was negatively related to symptomatology and positively to a healthy personality; it increased over the course of treatment; and it correlated somewhat with a positive outcome at follow-up. To our knowledge, the results of this study provide the first documented evidence that a oneness fantasy or schema may be related to positive adaptation, as hypothesized by Silverman et al. (1982) and Silverman and Weinberger (1985).

Discriminant Validity

McClelland et al. (1989) and Koestner, Weinberger, and McClelland (1991) have found that projective (implicit) and self-report (self-attributed) measures of motivation assess qualitatively different aspects of personality. They have been shown to be uncorrelated, to have different developmental antecedents, to relate to different types of behavior and to be sensitive to different aspects of the environment (see Weinberger & McClelland, 1990, for a detailed theoretical explication of this phenomenon).

On the basis of this work, Krass (1996) reasoned that both self-report and projective measures of oneness might relate to creativity but be unrelated to one another. He chose creativity because psy-

choanalytic writers have implicated the softening of reality boundaries in the creative process (Pao, 1983; Roth, 1975). Empirical work
also has shown that creativity is related to the capacity to become
engrossed in an activity to the exclusion of everything else (Csikszentmihalyi, 1990). Furthermore, it has been shown to be related
to a self-report measure assessing this quality, the Tellegen Absorption Scale (TAS; Tellegen, 1982). Tellegen (1982) defined *absorption* as "the readiness to undergo whatever experiential events,
sensory or imaginal, that may occur, with a tendency to dwell on
rather than go beyond them" (p. 269). OM also has this quality of
absorption, especially as reflected in its merger-flow and focus dimensions. Thus, OM also ought to be associated with creativity.
Krass hypothesized that, although oneness and absorption would
both be related to creativity, they would not be related to each
other.

Krass (1996) administered a battery of creativity measures to students in undergraduate fine arts classes. He also obtained their
professors' ratings of their creativity. Krass divided his participants
into those who scored relatively well on more than one of the creativity measures he used and those who did not (the measures
were largely uncorrelated). He thereby created a less creative group
(actually a basically uncreative) and a more creative group. He then
determined whether these two groups differed on OM and the
TAS.

As predicted, OM and absorption did not correlate. In addition
and more interestingly, both were higher in the creative than in the
noncreative group (Absorption: $t = 2.66$, $N = 30$, $p < .02$; OM: $t = 2.1$, $N = 30$, $p < .05$). Thus, absorption and oneness were related to
creativity but not to each other. These findings were replicated in
a second study using a larger sample. The results indicate that
although absorption and oneness both predict creativity, they capture qualitatively different aspects of it. This is consistent with the
reasoning of Weinberger and McClelland (1990) and further supports the notion that OM is an implicit motive and that the OMSS
measures it.

The present authors (Siegel & Weinberger, 1997) examined the
association between some other personality variables and OM to
provide additional convergent and discriminant validity for the
OM construct. They administered five well-validated self-report

measures: the Affect-Balance Scale (Bradbaum, 1969), a mood measure; the Coopersmith Self-Esteem Inventory (Coopersmith, 1967), a measure of self-esteem; the Inventory of Childhood Mental Imaginings (Wilson & Barber, 1981), a measure of fantasy proneness; and the NEO Five-Factor Inventory (NEO-FFI; Costa & McCrae, 1992). This last measure is based on the five-factor model of personality, which was developed from factor analyses of a massive set of self-report personality tests. It posits that there are five basic components of personality: Neurosis, Introversion/Extraversion, Openness to Experience, Conscientiousness, and Agreeableness. The TAS was administered once again, as were four TAT cards from the study described by Weinberger (1992), to assess OM.

Because the affect and self-esteem scales both are measures of explicit mood, we expected a minimal (probably nonsignificant) relationship between them and OM. This would be consistent with a previous finding (see the introduction) that demonstrated that MIO stimulation improved implicit, but not reported, mood. One might expect the degree of a person's oneness imagery to correlate positively with fantasy proneness (as measured by the Inventory of Childhood Mental Imaginings), and openness to experience (as measured by the Openness to Experience domain of the NEO-FFI). All of these constructs may imply a readiness to loosen one's ordinary sensory-perceptual focus on external reality in favor of experiencing whatever events, sensory or imaginal, that occur. However, consistent with the previous work of McClelland et al. (1989), Weinberger and McClelland (1990), and Koestner, Weinberger, and McClelland (1991), we predicted that they would be minimally related at best. We also thought that OM might correlate somewhat with measures of psychological health, as it did in the Weinberger et al. (1991) study. We therefore predicted correlations with the Affect-Balance subscale of the Affect-Balance Scale and with the Conscientiousness dimension of the NEO-FFI. The former is defined as a measure of psychological well-being and also has been shown to be related to it (Bradbaum, 1969). Similarly, previous research has shown the latter to be related to psychological well-being (Costa & McCrae, 1992). Again, consistent with the work on implicit and self-report variables, we predicted a weak relation at best.

We found that OM was marginally correlated with conscientiousness ($r = .23$, $p < .06$; $n = 75$). Similarly, affect balance (positive affect minus negative affect) also overlapped somewhat with OM ($r = .20$, $p < .10$; $n = 75$). Finally, there also was a marginal relationship with the Inventory of Childhood Mental Imaginings ($r = .21$, $p < .10$; $n = 75$).[2] This pattern of correlations could be interpreted to mean that OM is related to psychological health and fantasizing, but the variance it accounted for overlapped only slightly with that explained by these more traditional self-report measures.

Interpreting OM Findings: Are Researchers Measuring the Effects of a Schema or a Fantasy?

A series of studies has demonstrated that OM can be scored reliably (i.e., has interrater reliability) and is stable (i.e., has test–retest reliability). It also seems to be a valid measure of the OM we have hypothesized. It related to positive outcome in a behavioral medicine study; it correlated with other measures as expected; and it was higher in creative than in noncreative individuals. The question that originally inspired the creation of the OMSS still remains, however: What precisely mediates the effects measured by the system?

Recall that Silverman et al. (1982) believed that subliminal MIO stimulation achieves its dramatic effects by triggering a symbiotic-like, or "oneness," fantasy. Cognitivists might interpret Silverman's results and what the OMSS captures as the functioning of a schema. The idea of a schema is at the heart of cognitive psychology today, and it is conceptualized as a system or structure of cognitions (expectations and beliefs) about a given domain, orga-

---

[2]The oneness motive did not correlate with absorption, as measured by the Tellegen Absorption Scale ($r = .16$, $p < .20$; $n = 75$), even though the Inventory of Childhood Mental Imaginings and absorption correlated highly ($r = .81$, $p < .001$; $n = 78$). We do not know what to make of this and await further replication attempts.

nized in terms of the attributes of the domain and the relationships among those attributes (Demorest, 1995; Stillings et al., 1987). Such cognitive structures can be habitually learned under, and therefore linked to, mood states (Bower, 1981; Gilligan & Bower, 1984).

The modern conception of unconscious fantasy in psychoanalytic theory is compatible in some ways with the cognitive conception of a schema. Some psychoanalysts have already noticed this (Slap, 1986; Slap & Saykin, 1983). Fantasy representations are believed to become increasingly sophisticated, stable, and sensible as a person matures. As fantasies become increasingly influenced by reality and moral considerations, they can acquire significant conceptual organization and develop into narrative structures (Abend, 1979; Arlow, 1969, 1987; Inderbitzin & Levy, 1989). They can become organizing templates that provide the mental set through and in which experiences are perceived, understood, and integrated (Shapiro, 1983). They become the messages that guide the stories that patients tell. However, what still distinguishes the modern psychoanalytic conception of a fantasy from a cognitive schema is that fantasies are held to have affective cores, with cognitions assuming secondary importance. (This view is not without support in non-psychoanalytic areas of psychology, such as Posner & Rothbart, 1989.) For the most part, however, cognitive scientists believe that cognitions are central to schemas and that affect is secondary (Weinberger, Siegel, et al., in press).

We believe that there is enough evidence to establish that what is primed by MIO stimulation and captured by the OMSS does not fit the schema concept as it is usually used by cognitivists. Although schemas can and often do operate outside of awareness, they are conceived of as being accessible to consciousness (cf. Weinberger, Siegel, et al., in press; Westen, 1990). The OM construct has more unconscious character than this. MIO stimulation is subliminal and OM is implicit in the stories used to measure it. Participants cannot simply report on or talk about their OM. We know this to be the case because of the recurrent finding that our projective measure and the self-report measures with which one would expect it to be correlated are in fact uncorrelated. Moreover, OM is affective in nature. MIO stimulation and OM have been shown to be strongly related to mood (Weinberger, Siegel, et al., in press; Weinberger et al., 1991), and OM is an avowedly affective construct, as indicated by its scoring categories. Finally, schemas are not usually viewed as motivational constructs, but OM is implicated in motivated life experiences. It increases in the course of a behavioral medicine treatment and is positively related to a beneficial outcome in that treatment (Weinberger et al., 1991). It also is related to creativity (Krass, 1996).

If OM is a schema, it is of a different sort than what cognitivists usually mean when they use the term. Either the schema concept will have to be amended, different orders of schema identified, or the term *fantasy* continue to be used. On the weight of the evidence gathered thus far, we are apt to conceptualize OM as an affect-laden, motivational schema that has properties associated with the modern psychoanalytic view of a fantasy representation.[3]

Summary and Future Directions

We have attempted to demonstrate that an unconscious motive (i.e., the OM), described by psychoanalysts and experimentally investigated by Silverman (1976, 1983; Silverman & Silverman, 1964), can be assessed empirically. We used the motive measuring paradigm developed by McClelland and his associates for this purpose. That is, we compared an aroused with an unaroused group and developed a scoring system based on the differences and theoretical considerations. We described the basic characteristics and scoring categories of the system. We have shown that measure has respectable test–retest and interrater reliability. We also presented data attesting to its validity. It relates, as predicted, to treatment variables and to creativity as well as to measures related to psychological well-being, but not to self-report measures purporting to measure similar constructs.

Much work remains to be done. We need to replicate findings and expand the construct validity of OM. It would be valuable to

---

[3]Whether the particulars of the oneness motive fantasy can be more easily explained by any single school of psychoanalysis cannot be determined at this stage of the research. It can be seen as wishful, relational, or related to self-esteem. Of course, it can be related to all three. Perhaps future work can address this question.

determine whether OM increases over the course of, and relates to the outcome of, other behavioral medicine treatments. It would be particularly interesting to see how it relates to various kinds of psychotherapy. We plan to conduct another behavioral medicine study, with a larger sample, which would use medical reports as well as patient-reported symptomatology. We have not yet begun working seriously with the OM− score of the OMSS. It is possible that it would relate to the individuals with schizophrenia, described as not being well differentiated from their mother, who do not respond positively to the subliminal MIO message. We also want to examine its possible connections to other kinds of psychopathology and maladaptive behavior. We need to continue to clarify the nature of the affect-laden schema or fantasy that we believe we are measuring. Finally, we want to disseminate the OMSS to others for their purposes.

We are only at the beginning of our investigations of the OM construct. As more of this work emerges, we expect that we will be able to present a more complete and thorough picture of the place of OM in human psychological life.

References

Abend, S. M. (1979). Unconscious fantasy and theories of cure. *Journal of the American Psychoanalytic Association, 27*, 579–596.

Antonovsky, A. (1984). The sense of coherence as a determinant of health. In J. D. Matarazzo, S. M. Weiss, J. A. Herd, N. E. Miller, & S. M. Weiss (Eds.), *Behavioral health.* New York: Wiley.

Ariam, S., & Siller, J. (1982). Effects of subliminal oneness stimuli in Hebrew on academic performance of Israeli high school students: Further evidence on the adaptation-enhancing effects of symbiotic fantasies in another culture using another language. *Journal of Abnormal Psychology, 91*, 343–349.

Arlow, J. A. (1969). Unconscious fantasy and disturbances of conscious experience. *Psychoanalytic Quarterly, 38*, 1–27.

Arlow, J. A. (1987). The dynamics of interpretation. *Psychoanalytic Quarterly, 56*, 68–87.

Atkinson, J. W., & Birch, D. (1970). *The dynamics of action.* New York: Wiley.

Balay, J., & Shevrin, H. (1988). The subliminal psychodynamic method: A critical review. *American Psychologist*, *43*, 161–174.

Bergmann, M. S. (1971). On the capacity to love. In J. B. McDevitt & C. S. Settiage (Eds.), *Separation-individuation: Essays in honor of Margaret S. Mahler* (pp. 15–40). New York: International Universities Press.

Bornstein, R. F., & Masling, J. M. (1984). Subliminal psychodynamic activation: Implications for psychoanalytic theory and therapy. *International Forum for Psychoanalysis*, *1*, 187–204.

Bower, G. H. (1981). Mood and memory. *American Psychologist*, *36*, 129–148.

Bradbaum, N. M. (1969). *The structure of psychological well-being*. Chicago: Aldine.

Cohen, J. (1977). *Statistical power analysis for the behavioral sciences* (2nd ed.). New York: Academic Press.

Coopersmith, S. (1967). *The antecedents of self-esteem*. New York: Freeman.

Costa, P. J., & McCrae, P. R. (1992). *Revised NEO Personality Inventory (NEO-PI-R) and NEO Five-Factor Inventory (NEO-FFI) professional manual*. Odessa, FL: Psychological Assessment Resources.

Csikszentimahalyi, M. (1990). *Flow: The psychology of optimal experience*. New York: Harper & Row.

Demorest, A. P. (1995). The personal script as a unit of analysis for the study of personality. *Journal of Personality*, *63*, 569–592.

Derogatis, L. R. (1983). *SCL-90: Administration, scoring and procedures manual for the revised version*. Baltimore: Clinical Psychometric Research.

Entwisle, D. R. (1972). To dispel fantasies about fantasy-based measures of achievement motivation. *Psychological Bulletin*, *77*, 377–391.

Freud, S. (1963). The dynamics of transference. In P. Rieff (Ed.), *Freud: Therapy and technique* (pp. 112–123). New York: Macmillan. (Original work published 1912)

Gilligan, S. C., & Bower, G. H. (1984). Cognitive consequences of emotional arousal. In C. Izard, J. Kagan, & R. Zajonc (Eds.), *Emotions, cognitions and behavior* (pp. 547–588). New York: Cambridge University Press.

Hardaway, R. (1990). Subliminally activated symbiotic fantasies: Facts and artifacts. *Psychological Bulletin*, *107*, 177–195.

Inderbitzin, L. B., & Levy, S. J. (1989). Unconscious fantasy: A reconsideration of the concept. *Journal of the American Psychoanalytic Association*, *37*, 113–130.

James, W. (1902). *The varieties of religious experience*. New York: Modern Library.

Jung, C. G. (1969). The archetypes and the collective unconscious. In *The collected works of C. G. Jung* (Vol. 9). Princeton, NJ: Princeton University Press. (Original work published 1936)

Kabat-Zinn, J. (1990). *Full-catastrophe living*. New York: Delacorte Press.

Kobassa, S. C. (1977). Stressful life events, personality and health: An inquiry into hardiness. *Journal of Personality and Social Psychology, 37,* 1–11.

Koestner, R., Weinberger, J., & McClelland, D. C. (1991). Task-intrinsic and social-extrinsic sources of arousal for motives assessed in fantasy and self-report. *Journal of Personality, 59,* 57–82.

Krass, M. (1996). *Oneness and creativity.* Unpublished doctoral dissertation, Adelphi University, Garden City, NY.

Limentani, D. (1956). Symbiotic identification in schizophrenia. *Psychiatry, 19,* 231–236.

Linehan, E., & O'Toole, J. (1982). The effects of subliminal stimulation of symbiotic fantasy on college students' self-disclosures in group counseling. *Journal of Counseling Psychology, 29,* 151–157.

McAdams, D. P. (1988). *Power, intimacy, and the life story.* New York: Guilford Press.

McClelland, D. C. (1951). *Personality.* New York: Holt, Rinehart & Winston.

McClelland, D. C. (1985). *Human motivation.* Glenview, IL: Scott, Foresman.

McClelland, D. C., Koestner, R., & Weinberger, J. (1989). How do self-attributed and implicit motives differ? *Psychological Review, 96,* 690–702.

McClelland, D. C., & Meterko, M. (1983). *Manual for the Competency Mood Profile.* Boston: Boston University, Center for Applied Social Science.

McClelland, D. C., & Winter, D. G. (1969). *Motivating economic achievement.* New York: Free Press.

McNair, D. M., Lorr, M., & Droppleman, L. F. (1981). *Manual for the Profile of Mood States.* San Francisco: EDITS. (Original work published 1971)

Mendelsohn, E. M., & Silverman, L. H. (1982). Effects of stimulating psychodynamically relevant unconscious fantasies on schizophrenic psychopathology. *Schizophrenia Bulletin, 8,* 532–547.

Morgan, C. D., & Murray, H. A. (1935). A method for investigating fantasies: The Thematic Apperception Test. *Archives of Neurology and Psychiatry, 34,* 289–306.

Murray, H. A. (1962). *Explorations in personality.* New York: Science Editions. (Original work published 1938)

Murray, H. A. (1943). *The Thematic Apperception Test: Manual.* Cambridge, MA: Harvard University Press.

Palmatier, J. R., & Bornstein, P. H. (1980). The effects of subliminal stimulation of symbiotic merging fantasies of behavioral treatment of smokers. *Journal of Nervous and Mental Disease, 168,* 715–720.

Pao, P. (1983). Suspension of the reality principle in adaptation and creativity. *Psychoanalytic Inquiry, 3,* 431–440.

Parker, K. A. (1982). The effects of subliminal merging stimuli on the academic performance of college students. *Journal of Counseling Psychology, 29,* 19–28.

Posner, M. I., & Rothbart, M. K. (1989). Intentional chapters on unintended thoughts. In J. S. Uleman & J. A. Bargh (Eds.), *Unintended thought* (pp. 450–469). New York: Guilford Press.

Rosenthal, R. (1979). The file-drawer problem and tolerance for null results. *Psychological Bulletin, 86*, 638–641.

Roth, N. (1975). Free association and creativity. *Journal of the American Academy of Psychoanalysis, 3*, 373–381.

Salovey, P., & Birnbaum, D. (1989). Influence of mood on health-relevant cognitions. *Journal of Personality and Social Psychology, 57*, 539–551.

Salovey, P., & Rosenhan, D. L. (1989). Mood and prosocial behavior. In H. L. Wagner & A. S. R. Manstead (Eds.), *Handbook of social psychophysiology* (pp. 371–391). New York: Wiley.

Searles, H. F. (1979). Concerning the development of an identity. In H. F. Searles (Ed.), *Countertransference and related subjects* (pp. 45–70). Madison, CT: International Universities Press.

Shapiro, T. (1983). The unconscious still occupies us. *Psychoanalytic Study of the Child, 38*, 547–567.

Siegel, P., & Weinberger, J. (1997, August). *Reliability and validity of the oneness motive*. Poster session presented at the annual convention of the American Psychological Association, Chicago, IL.

Silverman, L. H. (1976). Psychoanalytic theory: The reports of my death are greatly exaggerated. *American Psychologist, 31*, 621–637.

Silverman, L. H. (1983). The subliminal psychodynamic method: Overview and comprehensive listing of studies. In J. Masling (Ed.), *Empirical studies of psychoanalytic theory* (Vol. 1, pp. 69–103). Hillsdale, NJ: Erlbaum.

Silverman, L. H., Lachmann, F. M., & Milich, R. H. (1982). *The search for oneness*. Madison, CT: International Universities Press.

Silverman, L. H., & Silverman, D. K. (1964). A clinical-experimental approach to the study of subliminal stimulation: The effects of a drive-related stimulus upon Rorschach responses. *Journal of Abnormal and Social Psychology, 67*, 158–172.

Silverman, L. H., & Weinberger, J. (1985). Mommy and I are one: Implications for psychotherapy. *American Psychologist, 40*, 1296–1308.

Slap, J. W. (1986). Some problems with the structural model and a remedy. *Psychoanalytic Psychology, 3*, 47–58.

Slap, J. W., & Saykin, A. J. (1983). The schema: Basic concept in a nonmetapsychological model of the mind. *Psychoanalysis and Contemporary Thought, 6*, 305–325.

Smith, C. P. (Ed.). (1992). *Motivation and personality: Handbook of thematic content analysis*. New York: Cambridge University Press.

Stillings, N. A., Feinstein, M. H., Garfield, J. L., Rissland, E. L., Rosenbaum, D. A., Weisler, S. E., & Baker-Ward, L. (1987). *Cognitive science: An introduction*. Cambridge, MA: MIT Press.

Tellegen, A. (1982). *Brief manual for the Differential Personality Questionnaire*. Unpublished manuscript, University of Minnesota, Minneapolis.

Weinberger, J. (1989). Response to Balay and Shevrin: Constructive critique or misguided attack? *American Psychologist, 44*, 1417–1419.

Weinberger, J. (1992). Validating and demystifying subliminal psychodynamic activation. In R. Bornstein & T. Pittman (Eds.), *Perception without awareness: Cognitive, clinical, and social perspectives* (pp. 170–188). New York: Guilford Press.

Weinberger, J., & Hardaway, R. (1990). Separating science from myth in subliminal psychodynamic activation. *Clinical Psychology Review, 10,* 727–756.

Weinberger, J., Kelner, S., & McClelland, D. C. (in press). The effects of subliminal symbiotic stimulation on free-response and self-report mood. *Journal of Nervous and Mental Disease.*

Weinberger, J., & McClelland, D. C. (1990). Cognitive versus traditional motivational models: Irreconcilable or complementary? In E. T. Higgins & R. M. Sorrentino (Eds.), *Handbook of motivation and cognition* (Vol. 2, pp. 562–597). New York: Guilford Press.

Weinberger, J., & McLeod, C. (1989, August). *The need to belong: A psychoanalytically-based affiliative motive in the McClelland-Atkinson tradition.* Paper presented at the 97th Annual Convention of the American Psychological Association, New Orleans, LA.

Weinberger, J., Scroppo, J., McLeod, C., Santorelli, S., & Kabat-Zinn, J. (1991, June). *Motivational change following a meditation-based stress reduction program for medically ill patients.* Paper presented at the meeting of the International Society for Behavioral Medicine, Uppsala, Sweden.

Weinberger, J., Siegel, P., & DeCamello, A. (in press). What kind of integration do we want? In H. Kurtzman (Ed.), *Cognition and psychodynamics.* London: Oxford University Press.

Weinberger, J., & Silverman, L. H. (1987). Subliminal psychodynamic activation: A method for studying psychoanalytic dynamic propositions. In R. Hogan & H. Jones (Eds.), *Perspective in personality* (Vol. 2, pp. 251–287). Greenwich, CT: JAI Press.

Weinberger, J., Stefanou, S., Scroppo, J., & Siegel, P. (1996). *The Oneness Motive Scoring System.* Unpublished manuscript, Adelphi University, Garden City, NY.

Westen, D. (1990). Psychoanalytic approaches to personality. In L. Pervin (Ed.), *Handbook of personality: Theory and research* (pp. 21–65). New York: Guilford Press.

Wilson, S., & Barber, T. (1981). Vivid fantasy and hallucinatory abilities in the life histories of excellent hypnotic subjects (somnambules): Preliminary report with female subjects. In E. Klinger (Ed.), *Imagery: Vol. 2. Concepts, results, application* (pp. 133–149). New York: Plenum.

Winter, D. G. (1973). *The power motive.* New York: Free Press.

4

Cognitive–Experiential Self-Theory:
A Dual-Process Personality Theory With Implications for Diagnosis and Psychotherapy

Seymour Epstein

Cognitive–experiential self-theory (CEST) is a global theory of personality that integrates the psychodynamic unconscious of psychoanalysis with the cognitive unconscious of modern psychology. It accomplishes this by modifying each of these two approaches. The modification of the psychoanalytic unconscious consists of the substitution of an adaptive unconscious for the Freudian maladaptive unconscious, which has the advantage of making it more defensible from an evolutionary perspective. The modification of the cognitive unconscious consists of assuming it is emotionally driven, which transforms a kinder, gentler cognitive system into one that has the capacity for emotionally intense, psychodynamic reactions. I will show that nothing is lost in either psychoanalytic or cognitive theory by this modification and that much is gained.

A critical flaw in the Freudian conceptualization of the unconscious is that it makes little sense from an evolutionary perspective.

Preparation of this chapter and the research reported in it were supported by National Institute of Mental Health Research Grant MH01293 and NIMH Research Scientist Award 5K05 MH00363 to Seymour Epstein.

The constructive critique by Alice H. Epstein of an earlier version is gratefully acknowledged.

It was through the study of dreams that Freud (1900/1953) inferred the principles of operation of the unconscious mind, which he referred to as the *primary process*. The major principle underlying the primary process is wish fulfillment, according to which people, when a need is activated, hallucinate the objects that have gratified the need in the past. Other principles of the primary process are displacement, condensation, association, and symbolic representation. Such principles are useful for interpreting dreams and psychotic delusions and hallucinations but are not very useful for explaining adaptive behavior in the real world. If people or nonhuman animals operated solely in terms of the primary process, they would starve to death amidst blissful hallucinations of unlimited gratification. Does it follow from such reasoning that Freud's conceptualization of the primary process is simply invalid and should be discarded? Not necessarily. It implies that there is an important void in Freud's theory of the unconscious that needs to be filled by positing another kind of unconscious, one that, rather than being the stuff that dreams are made of, is reality oriented and primarily adaptive. Primary process, in this approach, can retain a useful place in psychoanalytic practice and theory through its contribution to dream interpretation and the elucidation of esoteric phenomena, such as delusions and hallucinations.

Freud (1900/1953) accounted for realistic and adaptive functioning in everyday life by a conscious mind that operates according to the principles of the *secondary process*. The secondary process functions in the medium of language and makes inferences on the basis of a person's understanding of conventional principles of logical reasoning. This leaves the question unanswered of how nonhuman animals, who presumably have a primary process, but not a secondary process, can adapt to reality. CEST remedies this situation by adding a reality-oriented adaptive unconscious that learns from experience to Freud's dream-inferred maladaptive unconscious. This "experiential" unconscious has been a source of adaptation through learning from experience for millions of years in nonhuman animals and is assumed to operate in a similar manner in humans.

As I noted previously, nothing in cognitive theory nor in psychoanalytic theory or practice is lost with the inclusion of an adaptive, emotionally driven cognitive unconscious. If anything, the realm of unconscious influence is expanded, including its biasing influence on conscious thinking. The concept of psychodynamics is retained and expanded, and the importance of transference is retained (albeit subsumed under stimulus generalization) and therefore expanded to include all distortions of current relationships as a result of their resemblance to previous emotionally significant earlier relationships, including those with siblings no less than with parents. The psychosexual stages are replaced by information from developmental research. Questionable, esoteric constructs such as *cathexis, libido, energy transformations*, and *death instincts* are replaced by simpler, more comprehensible, and operationally definable terms from learning and cognitive theory. Relatedly, an esoteric theory beyond the comprehension of untrained laypeople is replaced by one that is consistent with personal experience and can be communicated readily to nonprofessionals. The primary process is not lost but is retained either as an additional state, or, alternatively, as a degraded form of processing of the experiential system in an altered state of consciousness, such as sleep.

It will be seen that the proposed modification of psychoanalytic theory is consistent with later developments in Freud's own thinking and with more recent developments by others with diverse psychoanalytic approaches, including ego psychologists, object relations theorists, and self-theorists. Moreover, it is more consistent with the actual practice of psychoanalytic therapy than is Freud's early theory of the unconscious, with its emphasis on primary process—which, although useful for dream interpretation, is not very useful for other clinical phenomena, including transference and superego reactions.

With respect to modifying the unconscious of modern cognitive psychology, nothing is lost and much is gained by the assumption that the cognitions are emotionally driven. Given a conceptual tool for adapting to the environment, it is inconceivable that it would not be used in the service of maximizing positive affect and minimizing negative affect (the Freudian *pleasure principle*, and the source of *reinforcement* in learning theory). What is gained is making the cognitive unconscious relevant to an understanding of how people behave in the real world, including their passions, conflicts, and self-destructive as well as adaptive behavior.

In the remainder of this chapter, I present a summary of CEST, followed by a brief description of a research program undertaken to test its assumptions. I then consider the implications of the theory for diagnosis and psychotherapy.

Cognitive–Experiential Self-Theory

CEST was introduced more than two decades ago (S. Epstein, 1973). It has undergone considerable development since then and has been supported by an extensive research program. A brief summary of the basic principles in CEST follows; more complete information is available elsewhere (for reviews of the overall theory, see S. Epstein, 1973, 1980, 1991c, 1993c; for in-depth discussions of particular aspects of the theory, see S. Epstein, 1976, 1983b, 1984, 1985, 1987, 1990, 1991a, 1991b, 1993a, 1993b; Epstein & Erskine, 1983; Epstein & Katz, 1992; Epstein, Lipson, Holstein, & Huh, 1992; Epstein & Meier, 1989).

In reading the summary of CEST that follows, it may appear that the theory suddenly appeared to the author full blown, without precursors. It should be recognized that the most important distinguishing feature of the theory is that it is highly integrative and, accordingly, shares views with several other theories. The assumption of an adaptive unconscious in CEST is foreshadowed by developments within classical psychoanalytic theory itself. In his later writings, Freud introduced the view that there are adaptive, reality-oriented aspects of the unconscious that are concerned with the consequences of the expression of id impulses and safety issues and not simply wish fulfillment (see review in Weiss and Sampson, 1986). This position is further developed by ego psychologists, such as Hartman (1964), Gill (1959), Rapaport (1959), and G. S. Klein (1970), among others. Object relations theorists, including Fairbairn (1954), Melanie Klein (1952/1975), Mahler (1952), Kernberg (1976), and, in particular, Bowlby (1988), also have overlapping views with those of CEST, such as in their departure from the Freudian instinct model and their recognition of the importance of relatedness as a fundamental human need. Bowlby's belief that people's everyday behavior is guided by internalized models of relationships with significant others is very similar to the assumption in CEST that people's behavior is determined by the schemas in their personal theories of reality that are derived primarily from emotionally significant experiences.

There is also a convergence of ideas between CEST and several nonanalytical theories of personality, most notably those of constructionist psychologists, such as Rogers (1951, 1959), Adler (1954), and Kelly (1955), who emphasize the importance of people's models of reality.

Despite shared views with other personality theories, CEST differs from all other theories in important ways. For example, although CEST agrees with traditional psychoanalytic theory on the importance of psychodynamic formulations and, relatedly, on the ubiquitous influence of unconscious information processing on conscious thought and behavior, it has a very different view of the principles by which the unconscious operates. Also, despite its agreement with modern psychoanalytic views on an adaptive unconscious, CEST has a far more articulated view of the operating principles of the adaptive unconscious, and it completely rejects the concept of the primary process as a viable system in its own right, which the other theories accept alongside their views of an adaptive unconscious. As previously noted, primary process is retained either in its own right or as a degraded form of experiential processing that is useful for understanding dreams and other esoteric reactions, such as delusions and hallucinations, but it is not regarded as a fundamental adaptive system.

Although CEST has much in common with constructionist theories that emphasize the importance of maintaining the stability and coherence of personal conceptual systems, it considers other needs equally important, including the need to maintain a favorable pleasure–pain balance (the pleasure principle), the need for relatedness, and the need to maintain self-esteem. Moreover, CEST is concerned with the interactive influence of these basic needs on conscious and unconscious thought and behavior as well with the more general interaction of conscious and unconscious processing. Thus, unlike the constructionist theories, CEST is predominantly a psychodynamic theory and has more in common with the psychoanalytic tradition than with other approaches in this respect.

Basic Principles

It is assumed in CEST that people automatically construct an implicit model of the world, or *theory of reality*, that has two major divisions, a *world-theory* and a *self-theory*, and connecting propositions. (It is assumed that nonhuman, higher order animals also construct a model of the world, but it does not include a self-theory.) A theory of reality is not developed for its own sake, but in order to make life as livable (meaning as emotionally satisfying) as possible. Thus, a fundamental assumption in CEST is that the experiential system is emotionally driven and that behavior is reinforced by positive and negative affect.

People have constructs about the self and the world in two systems, experiential and rational. Those in the rational system are referred to as *beliefs* and those in the experiential system as *schemas* or, alternatively, as *implicit beliefs*. The schemas consist primarily of generalizations derived from emotionally significant experiences. It is important to recognize that the schemas are assumed to be organized into an overall adaptive system and that they are not just isolated constructs. Thus, they affect and are affected by other constructs in the system. Evidence attesting to an overall organization in the experiential system is provided by the coherent, complexly integrated behavior of animals lacking a rational system, and by the susceptibility of the experiential system, in both human and nonhuman animals, to total disorganization following unassimilable emotionally significant experiences. Such reactions are observed in the experimental neurosis in animals (Pavlov, 1941) and in acute schizophrenic disorganization in humans (Epstein, 1979; Perry, 1976). Disorganization of a system necessarily implies, of course, a prior state of organization.

There are two major kinds of schemas in the experiential system, descriptive and motivational. Descriptive schemas consist of implicit beliefs about what the self and the world are like. An example of a descriptive schema is, "Authority figures are uncaring." Motivational schemas are implicit beliefs about means–end relations. An example of a motivational schema is, "The way to get along with authority figures is to placate them."

Attributes of the Experiential System

Exhibit 1 provides a summary of the comparative features of the experiential and rational systems. The experiential system has a long evolutionary history and, as already noted, operates in a similar manner in nonhuman and human animals. At its lower levels of operation, it is a relatively crude system that automatically, rapidly, effortlessly, and efficiently processes information. At its higher reaches, and particularly in interaction with the rational system, it is a source of intuitive wisdom and creativity. Although it represents events primarily concretely and imagistically, it is capable of abstraction in the form of generalization gradients, prototypes, metaphors, and narratives.

The rational system, in contrast, is a deliberative, effortful, abstract system that operates primarily in the medium of language and that has a very brief evolutionary history. It is capable of high levels of abstraction and long-term delay of gratification. However, it is a relatively inefficient system for responding to everyday events, and its long-term adaptability remains to be demonstrated. (It may yet lead to the destruction of all life on this planet.)

Psychodynamics

All behavior is assumed, in CEST, to result from the combined operation of the two systems. Their relative contribution is determined by parameters such as (a) individual differences in thinking style and (b) situational variables (e.g., the degree to which situations are identified as requiring formal, logical reasoning, as in solving mathematics problems). Emotional arousal and relevant past experience tend to shift the balance of influence in the direction of the experiential system.

Most theories of personality posit a single fundamental need or motive. For Freud (1900/1953), it was the pleasure principle, that is, the need to maximize pleasure and minimize pain; for Rogers (1959), Lecky (1961), and other phenomenologists, it was the need to maintain a stable, coherent conceptual system; for Bowlby (1988), Fairbairn (1954), and other object relations theorists, it was the need for relatedness; and for Adler (1954), Allport (1961), and Kohut (1971), it was the need to overcome inferiority or enhance

Exhibit 1

Comparison of the Experiential and Rational Systems

Experiential System	Rational System
1. Holistic	1. Analytic
2. Automatic, effortless	2. Intentional, effortful
3. Affective: pleasure–pain oriented (what feels good)	3. Logical: reason oriented (what is sensible)
4. Associationistic connections	4. Logical connections
5. Behavior mediated by "vibes" from past events	5. Behavior mediated by conscious appraisal of events
6. Encodes reality in concrete images, metaphors, & narratives	6. Encodes reality in abstract symbols, words, & numbers
7. More rapid processing: oriented toward immediate action	7. Slower processing: oriented toward delayed action
8. Slower and more resistant to change: changes with repetitive or intense experience	8. Changes more rapidly and easily: changes with strength of argument and new evidence
9. More crudely differentiated: broad generalization gradient; stereotypical thinking	9. More highly differentiated
10. More crudely integrated: dissociative, emotional complexes; context-specific processing	10. More highly integrated: cross-context principles
11. Experienced passively and preconsciously: we are seized by our emotions	11. Experienced actively and consciously: we are in control of our thoughts
12. Self-evidently valid: "Experiencing is believing"	12. Requires justification via logic & evidence

From "Cognitive–Experiential Self-Theory: An Integrative Theory of Personality," by S. Epstein. In R. C. Curtis (Ed.), *The Relational Self: Theoretical Convergences in Psychoanalysis and Social Psychology* (p. 123), 1991, New York: Guilford Press. Copyright 1991 by Guilford Press. Adapted with permission.

self-esteem. According to CEST, these motives are equally important, and behavior is determined by their combined influence.

Like psychoanalysis, CEST is a psychodynamic theory that posits two levels of information processing, each functioning according to its own principles. Also, like psychoanalysis, CEST assumes that the unaware level continuously influences the conscious level. This has been well illustrated in studies in which priming the automatic level of information processing influences people's conscious thinking without their awareness (e.g., Bargh, 1989; Epstein et al., 1992; Higgins, 1989). Like psychoanalysis, CEST emphasizes the interaction of needs, both within and across levels of processing. However, unlike psychoanalysis, which emphasizes the pleasure principle, CEST, as already noted, considers three other needs equally important.

Several interesting consequences follow from assuming the interaction of four basic needs. One is that behavior represents a compromise among the basic needs. A second, not unrelated, consequence is that the needs serve as checks and balances against each other. When one need is fulfilled at the expense of the others, the motivation to fulfill the others increases, which normally moderates the influence of the first need, keeping it within normal limits. An important source of maladaptive behavior occurs when a particular need becomes so insistent that fulfillment of the other needs is sacrificed. A third, related principle is that good adjustment is fostered by fulfilling the basic needs harmoniously and poor adjustment by fulfilling the needs conflictually.

The interaction of the four basic needs provides a useful framework for understanding some otherwise anomalous findings. For example, it has recently been concluded by some that the widespread view that realistic thinking is an important criterion of adjustment is incorrect because research has demonstrated that well-adjusted people characteristically maintain positive illusions (see review in Taylor & Brown, 1988). According to CEST, this paradox is readily resolved once it is recognized that self-evaluation is influenced by both the need to maintain a realistic, coherent conceptual system *and* the need for self-enhancement. The interaction of these two needs fosters a modest degree of self-enhancement. Thus, the observation that well-adjusted people have moderate positive illusions does not indicate that reality awareness is not an important criterion of adjustment, but only that it is not the only one. That is, self-evaluation is influenced jointly by the need for accurately representing the data of reality and the need for self-esteem enhancement.

The experiential system is assumed to be intimately associated with the experience of affect, including "vibes," which refer to subtle feelings of which people may be unaware. When a person responds to an emotionally significant event, the sequence of reactions is assumed to be as follows: The experiential system automatically searches its memory for related events and their emotional accompaniments. The feelings, which may be activated with or without conscious recall of the associated events, influence the course of further processing and reactions, which, in nonhuman animals, are actions, and in humans, conscious and unconscious thoughts as well as actions. If the activated feelings are pleasant, they motivate actions and thoughts anticipated to reproduce the feelings. If the feelings are unpleasant, they motivate actions and thoughts anticipated to avoid the feelings.

As in psychoanalysis, CEST assumes a ubiquitous influence of automatic thinking outside of awareness on conscious thinking and behavior. Processing in the experiential system is normally dominant because it is automatic, less effortful, and therefore less demanding of cognitive resources than processing in the rational system. Moreover, since the influence of the experiential system is normally outside of awareness, the rational system fails to control it because the person does not know that there is anything to control. The advantage of insight in such situations is that it facilitates control. Thus, CEST does not diminish the importance of the unconscious in human behavior relative to psychoanalysis, but it emphasizes a different unconscious.

Two fundamental orientations toward responding to needs are a fulfillment orientation and a defensive orientation. For the need to maximize the favorability of the pleasure–pain balance, a fulfillment orientation consists of seeking pleasure, and a defensive orientation consists of avoiding pain. For the need to maintain a coherent conceptual system for assimilating the data of reality, a fulfillment orientation involves seeking stimulation and new experiences, and a defensive orientation involves avoiding stimulation and new experiences and thinking in familiar, stereotypical ways. For the need to enhance self-esteem, a fulfillment orientation consists of seeking new challenges that can increase feelings of efficacy, and a defensive orientation consists of avoiding challenges and using strategies to protect self-esteem and to avoid disappointment. For the need to maintain relatedness, a fulfillment orientation involves meeting new people or becoming more deeply involved in relationships, and a defensive orientation involves avoiding the establishment of new or deeper relationships.

People adopt a defensive or a fulfillment orientation as a function of their degree of security. Just as children in the absence of a secure base cling to whatever support is available, whereas those with a secure base eagerly explore their environments, insecure adults tend to adopt a defensive orientation, and secure adults, a fulfillment orientation. Both styles are adaptive within limits; there is a time for defending the stability of a conceptual system and a time for expanding it, a time for defending self-esteem and a time for enhancing it, a time for seeking pleasure and a time for avoiding pain, a time for establishing new or deeper relationships and a time for avoiding them. Maladaptive behavior consists of maintaining a defensive orientation when there is no longer a threat beyond a person's adaptive capacity. Adaptive behavior consists of pacing exposure to threat, so that the person remains neither locked into a rigid defensive position nor exposes himself or herself to challenges beyond coping capacity (Epstein, 1983a).

Basic Beliefs

Associated with the four basic needs are four basic-belief dimensions that form the nuclei of important cognitive–affective networks. Because people automatically attend to events associated with fulfillment and frustration of their basic needs, they develop a network of descriptive and motivational schemas related to those needs. For example, given the need to enhance self-esteem, people attend to events related to success and failure. The result is that they develop implicit beliefs about their abilities and the opportunities the world affords for fulfilling and frustrating their need for self-esteem enhancement.

The basic-belief dimension associated with the need to maximize favorability of the pleasure–pain balance is the degree to which the world is viewed as benevolent versus malevolent. The basic-belief dimension associated with the need to maintain a coherent conceptual system for assimilating the data of reality is the degree to which the world is viewed as meaningful (including predictable, controllable, and just) versus unpredictable, unjust, and chaotic. The basic-belief dimension associated with the need to maintain relatedness is the degree to which people are viewed as trustworthy and supportive versus untrustworthy and dangerous. The basic-belief dimension associated with the need to enhance self-esteem is the degree to which the self is regarded as worthy (including competent, lovable, and good) versus unworthy (including incompetent, unlovable, and bad).

Positions on the four basic-belief dimensions are among the most important schemas in people's implicit theories of reality. Therefore, serious threats to the validity of any of these beliefs can produce overwhelming anxiety and, relatedly, a tendency of the conceptual system to disorganize. Should the beliefs actually be invalidated through emotionally highly significant experiences, disorganization of the entire personality structure, that is, the person's implicit theory of reality, may follow. This explains why people are desperately driven to defend their basic beliefs, even their unfavorable ones. It also suggests that understanding a person's basic beliefs is one of the most important steps in understanding a person's personality structure. An instrument for measuring the four basic beliefs, the Basic Beliefs Inventory, was constructed for this purpose (Catlin & Epstein, 1992).

Repression and Dissociation

According to psychoanalysis, repression occurs when a person has thoughts or impulses that are too guilt-arousing or otherwise threatening to be consciously accepted (Freud, 1933/1965). The result is that the material is kept in a state of inaccessibility by the expenditure of psychic energy. The repressed material strives for expression, generating conflict with the forces of repression, resulting in tension and displacement, manifested in the form of symptoms, dreams, and slips of the tongue. The task of psychoanalysis is to eliminate the more troublesome repressions. By making the unconscious conscious, people are able to bring their intelligence to bear on solving important problems in living. Thus, psychoanalysis places great store in rational thinking.

CEST presents an alternative view. According to CEST, material is dissociated when it cannot be ignored, denied, or assimilated. The dissociation helps maintain the coherence and organization of the remainder of the conceptual system. There are two kinds of dissociation, that between the experiential and rational systems (which corresponds to repression), and that within the experiential system itself. If dissociated material within the experiential system is activated to the extent that the dissociation cannot be maintained, the unassimilable material can threaten the stability of the entire experiential system. An example of this is an acute state of schizophrenic disorganization following arousal of unacceptable homosexual impulses.

The striving for expression of dissociated material is not because it has an energy of its own that seeks expression, as proposed by Freud, but because there is a fundamental need to assimilate emotionally significant experiences into a unified, coherent conceptual system. Material that cannot be assimilated keeps reemerging into consciousness in a belated attempt at assimilation. This process continues until assimilation, if ever, is accomplished. The process is essentially adaptive, as it promotes assimilation and, therefore, the construction of a coherent model of the world that is consistent with experience.

Basic Sources of Maladjustment

CEST assumes there are three major sources of maladjustment: discordance (including dissociation and incoherence within and between the two systems), failure in need fulfillment, and sensitivities and compulsions.

Discordance. Although dissociation *between* the two systems is widely recognized as a source of maladjustment, the importance of dissociation within the experiential system has been unappreciated because psychoanalytic theory does not view the unconscious as an adaptive, organized system, but rather considers it to be a loose system with rampant inconsistencies. This is in marked contrast to the view in CEST, which considers the experiential system as an adaptive, organized system (although less tightly organized than the rational system) and one that, because it is the major source of information processing in everyday life, must maintain a reasonable degree of organization in order for people to function. The result, as previously noted, is that threats to the organization of the experiential system can produce overwhelming levels of anxiety and disorganization.

Failure in basic-need fulfillment. One important reason that basic needs are frustrated is that the environment is not conducive to their fulfillment. For example, someone may be in a situation in which it is impossible to avoid continuous ridicule, as in the case of a Marine recruit who is intellectual but physically poorly coordinated. Such a situation obviously would be highly frustrating with respect to the need to maintain self-esteem.

A second important reason for a failure to fulfill a basic need is that its fulfillment conflicts with other basic needs. An example is the case of someone with a delusion of grandeur who fulfills the need for self-enhancement at the expense of fulfilling the needs to maintain a realistic model of the world, to maintain rewarding relationships with others, and to maintain a favorable pleasure–pain balance (being in a mental institution is not very pleasant). It follows that good adjustment requires harmonious need-fulfillment, whereas poor adjustment is associated with conflictual need-fulfillment.

A third important reason for a failure to fulfill a basic need is that its fulfillment in the experiential system is unacceptable to the rational system. Awareness of the need does not have to be repressed for this to occur. A person may reject fulfillment of a need of which he or she is consciously aware. Sometimes such suppression can be successfully accomplished, as in some cases of voluntary celibacy. In other cases, control fails, and the person experiences overwhelming guilt as a result. In yet others, the struggle to inhibit the fulfillment of strong needs produces intense conflict and stress.

According to CEST, an inability to fulfill basic needs, no less than an inability to maintain basic beliefs, is associated with increased anxiety and a tendency toward disorganization. As fulfilling basic needs is a major function of a personal theory of reality, people have so evolved that when their implicit theories of reality seriously fail in this purpose, the conceptual system tends to self-destruct. It is therefore understandable why severe frustration of self-esteem or relatedness needs frequently precedes acute schizophrenic disorganization. Such reactions are sometimes adaptive, because dismantling the personality structure provides an opportunity for a new, more effective organization to be constructed (Epstein, 1979; Perry, 1976).

Sensitivities and compulsions. Sensitivities, in CEST, refer to experientially derived schemas with low thresholds of arousal and broad generalization gradients associated with the view that certain kinds of events are dangerous. Compulsions refer to experientially derived schemas that certain ways of behaving are effective for reducing the anxiety associated with sensitivities. Thus, sensitivities are descriptive implicit beliefs, and compulsions are motivational implicit beliefs, the former being a major source of anxiety, and the latter a driven way of reducing anxiety. Sensitivities and compulsions are learned under conditions of high arousal.

It will be recalled that the schemas in the experiential system are mainly generalizations from emotionally significant experiences. Most such schemas are learned at relatively low levels of arousal and can be applied flexibly in different situations. For example, a person with a broad schema that people are trustworthy can be trusting in most circumstances, yet can identify and appropriately cope with untrustworthy behavior when it occurs. In contrast, another with a sensitivity to untrustworthy behavior (derived, e.g., from having encountered highly distressing, untrustworthy behavior during childhood) will have a very low threshold for interpreting behavior as untrustworthy, will experience strong emotions at the slightest indication of untrustworthy behavior, and will tend not to give people the benefit of the doubt. Such a person will exhibit a driven, inflexible behavioral pattern, such as always attacking people perceived as untrustworthy.

Not only are sensitivities and compulsions maladaptive because of the biased perception and inappropriate behavior that they induce, but, relatedly, because they are also a source of self-fulfilling prophecies. Those with a sensitivity to untrustworthy behavior are apt to act antagonistically to anyone whose behavior is perceived as untrustworthy, which will tend to instigate antagonistic or rejecting behavior on the part of the target person. This only serves to confirm the initial interpretation of the untrustworthy person, and it now provides him or her with an objective basis for the perceived lack of trustworthiness.

Transference reactions, considered in psychoanalysis to be the most important source of maladaptive interpersonal relationships and to provide the key to successful therapy, are regarded in CEST as a particularly important kind of sensitivity and compulsion. Like other sensitivities and compulsions, they bias people's perceptions of reality; are associated with inappropriate, rigid behavior; and serve as self-fulfilling prophecies. However, CEST, in common with some modern psychoanalytic views (e.g., Greenson, 1967), does not restrict transference reactions to generalizations derived from early childhood relationships with parental figures, but includes inappropriate generalizations from all emotionally significant relations, such as those with siblings.

A Research Program on the Construct Validity of CEST

Research from a wide variety of dual processing theories other than CEST has produced many findings consistent with assumptions in CEST (see review in Epstein, 1994). Because a review of this extensive literature is beyond the scope of this chapter, I will confine the discussion to studies that my associates and I specifically designed to test assumptions in CEST. Three kinds of research are reported: verification of the operating principles of the experiential system, examination of the interactions within and between the two systems, and the construction of measures of individual differences with respect to the qualitative and quantitative use of the two systems.

Operating Principles of the Experiential System

My associates and I have used studies of *heuristic processing*— which refers to the use of cognitive shortcuts for reaching decisions under conditions of uncertainty—for studying the principles of operation of the experiential system. Because such processing occurs in a rapid, preconscious, automatic manner that is characteristic of the operation of the experiential system, I became highly interested some years ago in a series of studies by Tversky and Kahneman (e.g., 1974, 1983; Kahneman, Slovic, & Tversky, 1982) and their associates that demonstrated that people are much more irrational than had previously been suspected. I was particularly impressed by the observation that the principles of heuristic processing inductively derived by Tversky and Kahneman and others were consistent with the operating principles of the experiential system as proposed in CEST (Epstein, 1994; Epstein et al., 1992). As a result, my associates and I embarked on a research program to test the operating principles of the experiential system by employing modifications of the procedures used by Tversky and Kahneman. We used specially constructed vignettes to probe people's heuristic thought processes.

Reactions to Arbitrary Aversive Outcomes

People in everyday life often irrationally judge others by the arbitrary outcomes that follow their actions. We tend to view more favorably the bearer of good news than of evil tidings, despite knowing that the messenger is not responsible for the message. Such behavior is an example of the operation of the experiential system, which relates events associationistically rather than through an understanding of cause and effect relations.

We used vignettes with arbitrary outcomes to examine several basic operating principles of the experiential system. As an example, in one vignette, two people were said to have arrived at an airport 30 minutes after the scheduled departure of their flights. One learned that her flight had left on time; the other learned that, due to a delay, her flight had just left. Who was more upset? Tversky and Kahneman (1983) found that people typically reported that the one who barely missed her flight was more upset, although from a rational perspective it should make no difference, because both were equally inconvenienced and they were equally responsible for the outcome. We modified Tversky and Kahneman's experimental paradigm by having the participants respond from three perspectives: how they believed most people would react; how they themselves would react, based on how they have reacted to similar situations in the past; and how a completely logical person would react (Epstein et al., 1992). The first two perspectives were considered to be mainly under the jurisdiction of the experiential system, and the third under the jurisdiction of the rational system. In order to test the influence of each mode of processing on the subsequent ones, we counterbalanced the order of the perspectives.

The findings in our studies of arbitrary outcomes supported the following hypotheses: There are two different modes of information processing, experiential and rational, which most lay people can identify; the experiential system is an associationistic system that connects events by similarity and contiguity rather than by an understanding of causal relations; and the systems are interactive, as indicated by the influence of processing in one system on subsequent processing in the other. Support for the last hypothesis is particularly interesting, because it supports the assumption in CEST that automatic processing in the experiential system biases information processing in the rational system. Other unpublished research with arbitrary outcomes that varied the affective content of the vignettes supported the assumption in CEST that experiential processing is directly associated with affect.

The Ratio-Bias Phenomenon

Imagine that you are told that on every trial in which you blindly pick a red jelly bean from a bowl containing red and white jelly beans, you will receive $2. To make matters interesting, you can draw from either of two bowls, one containing 10 jelly beans, 1 of which is red, and the other containing 100 jelly beans, 10 of which are red. Which bowl would you choose to draw from, and how much would you pay for the privilege of drawing from the bowl of your choice, rather than having the decision made for you by the flip of a coin?

This situation is particularly interesting with respect to CEST because it pits the experiential system against the rational system. The conflict between the systems arises because the experiential system is a concretive system that is highly responsive to numerosity, an extremely fundamental heuristic that is within the capacity of 3-year-old children and nonhuman animals (Gallistel & Gelman, 1992). An understanding of ratios, on the other hand, is facilitated by formal instruction and therefore is largely in the domain of the rational system.

In support of hypothesis, we found that most adults were willing to pay small sums of money for the privilege of drawing from the bowl "that has more winners," while acknowledging that they know this is foolish because the probabilities are equal (Kirkpatrick & Epstein, 1992). We obtained even more impressive results of irrational behavior when we presented uneven odds in the two bowls (e.g., 1 in 10 red beans in the small bowl and 8 in 100 in the large bowl; Denes-Raj & Epstein, 1994). Under such circumstances, many adults made nonoptimal responses against the better judgment of their rational system.

Studies that examined the ratio-bias effect in children who did and did not understand ratios and in adults under various experimental conditions (e.g., Denes-Raj & Epstein, 1994; Kirkpatrick & Epstein, 1992; Pacini, Epstein, & Barrows, 1996) supported the following hypotheses derived from CEST: There are two independent information-processing systems that operate in parallel by different rules and sometimes conflict with each other; the experiential system is a concretive, associationistic, imagistic system; compromises often occur between processing in the two modes; there is an increasing appreciation, with maturation, that rational processing should be given precedence over experiential processing, but only when the discrepancy between the two choices is considerable.

A study with the ratio-bias paradigm (Pacini, Muir, & Epstein, in press) helped clarify the depressive realism phenomenon (Alloy & Abramson, 1988), which refers to the surprising finding that subclinically depressed students are more rather than less accurate in judging contingencies between events. We demonstrated that subclinically depressed students made fewer nonoptimal responses than their nondepressed counterparts only when stakes were minimal. We therefore argued that the depressive realism phenomenon can be attributed to an overcompensatory reaction among subclinically depressed people in trivial situations for a more general tendency to behave unrealistically in personally significant situations. Relatedly, we found that subclinical depressive participants reported more maladaptive experiential processing and a lower degree of rational processing than did normal controls.

In another study, we uncovered a new principle of experiential processing, the "affirmative representation principle." According to this principle, the experiential system encodes information affirmatively and is unable to represent directly the negation of an idea or event. Although the affirmative representation principle can be derived from the concretive principle, it is sufficiently important to warrant a designation in its own right.

The Good-Person–Bad-Person Heuristic

The good-person–bad-person heuristic refers to the widespread tendency of people to evaluate others as completely good or bad and to assume that good people do no wrong and bad people do nothing right. It is a particularly important heuristic because of its prevalence and the mischief it causes, such as exonerating people with presumably good character and an attractive appearance of crimes they committed, and convicting people with presumably poor character and an unattractive or otherwise unacceptable appearance, despite their innocence.

We formally studied the good-person–bad-person heuristic by having participants respond to a vignette adapted from a study by Miller and Gunasegaram (1990). According to the vignette, a rich benefactor informs three friends that if each throws a coin that comes up heads, each will receive $100. The first two throw heads, and the third, Smith, throws tails. When asked how each of the protagonists feels, the participants said that Smith feels guilty and the others feel angry. In an alternative version with reduced stakes, the ratings of guilt and anger were reduced. When asked if the other two would be willing, as they previously had intended, to invite Smith to join them on a gambling vacation in Las Vegas, where they would share their wins and losses, most participants said they definitely would not, "because he is a loser." These responses were made from the perspective of how the participants believed both they and others would behave in real life. When responding from the perspective of how a logical person would behave, the participants said a logical person would recognize that the outcome was completely arbitrary and would not hold it against Smith, nor would they refuse to invite him to join them on a gambling venture.

This study supports the hypotheses that people recognize that there are two systems of information processing that are consistent with the operating principles of the experiential and rational systems; that experiential relative to rational processing is increased when emotional consequences are increased; and that people tend to overgeneralize broadly in judging others, based on how the person's behavior arbitrarily affects them.

Conjunction Problems

The Linda vignette is without doubt the most researched vignette in the history of psychology. Linda is described as a 31-year-old woman who is single, outspoken, and very bright. In college, she was a philosophy major who participated in antinuclear demonstrations and was concerned with issues of social justice. The vignette then poses the question, How would you rank these three possibilities: Linda is a feminist, Linda is a bank teller, and Linda is both? Most people (Tversky & Kahneman, 1983) rank Linda as being a feminist *and* a bank teller ahead of being just a bank teller. In doing so, they have made a conjunction error (CE; referred to by Tversky & Kahneman as a *conjunction fallacy*) because, according to the conjunction rule, the occurrence of two events cannot be more likely than the occurrence of one.

The Linda vignette has evoked a great deal of interest because the conjunction rule is one of the simplest and most fundamental principles in probability theory, so it is surprising that about 85% of people make CEs when responding to it (Tversky & Kahneman, 1983). The usual explanation of the high rate of CEs is that people either do not know the conjunction rule, or, knowing it, do not think of it in the context in which it is presented. They respond instead by the representativeness heuristic, according to which being both is more representative of Linda's personality than being just a bank teller.

In a series of studies on conjunction problems, including the Linda problem, we demonstrated that a major reason for the difficulty of the Linda problem cannot be an absence of knowledge of the conjunction rule, as everyone has intuitive knowledge of it and readily uses it in contexts in which it is recognized as appropriate. For example, we found that nearly everyone, whether or not they have formal knowledge of the conjunction rule, correctly applies it when judging whether it is more likely that a person will win one or two lotteries (Epstein, Denes-Raj, & Pacini, 1995). This is particularly interesting from the perspective of CEST because it indicates that the experiential system (that knows the conjunction rule intuitively) is sometimes smarter than the rational system (that may not know it at all).

We conducted a series of studies with the Linda problem (Donovan & Epstein, 1997; Epstein et al., 1995; Epstein, Donovan, & Denes-Raj, in press), including some studies in which we provided participants with principles from which they had to choose the correct one; other studies in which we advised the participants to consider the vignettes as presenting probability, and not personality, problems; and still other studies in which we had participants respond from rational and experiential perspectives. We found the following:

1. The difficulty of the Linda problem cannot be fully accounted for by the misleading manner in which it is presented, because even with full disclosure that the problem should be regarded as a probability problem and not a personality problem, a substantial number of participants made CEs.

2. The difficulty of the Linda problem can be explained by the rules of operation of the experiential system, which is the mode used by most people when responding to it.

3. The outcome of processing in the experiential mode is extremely compelling, often overriding contrary knowledge in the rational mode. Thus, many people, despite knowing and thinking of the conjunction rule, nevertheless prefer a representativeness solution.

4. Priming intuitive knowledge in the experiential system facilitates solutions to problems that people are unable to solve in the rational mode.

The Interaction of Experiential and Rational Processing

A fundamental assumption in CEST is that there is a continuous interaction between the experiential and rational systems. They are assumed to influence each other not only sequentially but also simultaneously, as manifested in compromises between the systems. Some research on compromises was presented in the discussion of the ratio-bias phenomenon. It will be recalled that adults and children with a knowledge of ratios exhibited compromises between numerosity (in the domain of the experiential system) and their formal understanding of ratios (in the rational system).

With respect to sequential interactions, there is ample evidence that priming the experiential system by presenting stimuli at subthreshold levels influences subsequent responding in the rational system (see review in Bargh, 1989). Other evidence indicates that the mode (independent of the content) of processing can be influenced by priming the experiential system. When processing in the experiential system is followed by attempts to respond rationally, the rational mode itself may be compromised by intrusions of experiential reasoning principles (Chaiken & Maheswaren, 1994; Denes-Raj, Epstein, & Cole, 1995; Edwards, 1990; Epstein et al., 1992; Epstein, Donovan, & Denes-Raj, in press; Pacini, Epstein, & Barrows, 1996). The result is that presumed rational processing may be little more than a rationalization of outcomes derived from previous experiential processing.

The influence is not only of processing in the experiential mode on processing in the rational mode. In everyday life, the influence often proceeds in the opposite direction, as when people react to their spontaneous, maladaptive initial thoughts with more carefully reasoned rational thoughts. In a study in which my associates and I formally examined this process, we instructed participants to list the first three thoughts that came to mind when they imagined themselves in various situations described in vignettes (reported in Epstein, 1994). The first thought was usually an impulsive one, consistent with the operation of the associationistic principle of the experiential system, whereas the third thought was more often a more carefully reasoned response in the mode of the rational system. For example, in response to a situation in which a protagonist failed to win a lottery because she took the advice of a friend instead of following her own inclination to buy a ticket that had her "lucky" number on it, a common first thought was that the friend was to blame and the participant would never take her advice again. By the third thought, the participant was likely to acknowledge that the outcome was due to chance and that no one was to blame.

The Interaction Among Basic Needs

A basic assumption in CEST is that behavior often represents a compromise among multiply activated basic needs. This process is important because, as previously noted, it is a means by which the needs serve as checks and balances against each other. When one need is fulfilled at the expense of the others, the others increase in intensity until they moderate the fulfillment of the first need. To test the assumption that behavior represents a compromise among needs acting simultaneously, we examined the interaction of the needs for self-enhancement and self-verification.

Swann and his associates have demonstrated that verification and enhancement occur sequentially, with the latter tending to precede the former (e.g., Hixon & Swann, 1993; Swann, 1990). To demonstrate that they also operate simultaneously and generate compromises in the process, we constructed a stimulus dimension that contained five levels of evaluative feedback from different romantic partners (Epstein & Morling, 1995; Morling & Epstein, in press). Participants rated the degree to which they were attracted to each of the partners. In support of hypothesis, compromises were demonstrated between verification and enhancement motives.

Research on Individual Differences in Experiential and Rational Processing

A self-report measure of the intelligence of the experiential system. If there are two different cognitive systems for adapting to the environment, then it is reasonable to consider that there may be reliable individual differences in the efficacy with which people use each of the systems. It is assumed in CEST that each system has its own form of intelligence. The intelligence of the rational system can be measured by intelligence tests, but because there was no available measure of the intelligence of the experiential-system, we constructed the Constructive Thinking Inventory (CTI). People respond to this inventory by indicating the degree to which they tend automatically to think in certain adaptive and maladaptive ways. Examples of items are, "When I have a difficult task to do, I think about things that will help me do my best," and "I spend a lot of time thinking about my mistakes, even if there is nothing I can do about them" (reverse scored). The CTI provides a Global Constructive Thinking scale and six more specific scales, all but one of which have several subscales. The main scales are Emotional Coping, Behavioral Coping, Categorical Thinking, Esoteric Thinking, Naive Optimism, and Personal Superstitious Thinking. The scales have respectable levels of internal-consistency reliability and impressive evidence of construct validity (Epstein, 1990, 1992a, 1992b; Epstein & Katz, 1992; Epstein & Meier, 1989; Katz & Epstein, 1991).

The Global scale, composed entirely of a subset of items from the other scales, is strongly inversely correlated with measures of neuroticism and might therefore be considered the cognitive component of "nonneuroticism." It is important to know, in this respect, that many of the items indicate that a person does not respond in certain neurotic ways. Thus, low scores on the Global scale have implications for the diagnosis and remediation of neurotic disorders, a topic that I will discuss later.

Apart from the Global scale, the two most important scales are the Emotional Coping and Behavioral Coping scales. Between them, they provide information on adjustment to the inner and outer world of experience. The Emotional Coping scale provides a measure of thinking in ways that facilitate the achievement of peace of mind and the modulation of negative affect. It is directly associated with mental and physical well-being (Epstein, 1992a, 1993a; Epstein & Meier, 1989; Nadeau, 1994) and is inversely associated with absenteeism in the workplace (Nadeau, 1994).

The Behavioral Coping scale measures adaptive and maladaptive ways of thinking with respect to behavioral accomplishment and is associated with success in the workplace (Epstein & Meier, 1989; Geschwandtner, 1990; Nadeau, 1994). It includes subscales of Positive Thinking (a realistic form of optimism that is adaptive, unlike the optimism measured by the scale of Naive Optimism),

Action Orientation, and Conscientiousness. The Behavioral Coping scale is more strongly associated than the Emotional Coping scale with experiencing positive affect, and it is less strongly associated than the Emotional Coping scale with the absence of negative affect.

In a series of studies (e.g., Epstein, 1990, 1992a, 1992b, 1993a; Epstein & Brodsky, 1993; Epstein & Katz, 1992; Epstein & Meier, 1989; Katz & Epstein, 1991), it was demonstrated that scores on the Global CTI scale are independent of scores on intelligence tests and, unlike IQ, are positively associated with social facility and mental and physical well-being.

The measurement of individual differences in degree of rational and experiential information processing. If people process information by two independent systems, an important aspect of personality must surely be the degree to which they rely on each of the systems. To measure this, we constructed the Rational and Experiential Inventory (REI), which has independent scales of rational and experiential processing. For the scale of degree of processing in the rational mode, we modified Cacioppo and Petty's (1982) Need for Cognition (NFC) scale by simplifying the wording in some of the items and shortening the scale. The new scale contains items such as, "I would prefer complex to simple problems" and "I would prefer a task that is intellectual, difficult, and important to one that is somewhat important but does not require much thought." For measuring processing in the experiential mode, we constructed the Faith in Intuition (FI) scale, which contains items such as, "I believe in trusting my hunches" and "My initial impressions of people are almost always right." The internal-consistency reliability coefficient of the NFC is .87, and that of the FI is .77. The correlation between them is −.07, which is not significantly different from zero. They contribute in a supplementary way to the prediction of heuristic responding to vignettes, and they are differentially related to a variety of measures of personality and adjustment (Epstein, Pacini, Denes-Raj, & Heier, 1996), which I will discuss in the section on diagnosis. Because the scales are independent, groups can be compared that are high on both, low on both, and high on one and low on the other, thereby providing information on the independent and interactive influence of the two coping modes. Such studies are currently being conducted.

The measurement of individual differences in basic beliefs.
We constructed the Basic Beliefs Inventory (BBI) to measure the four basic beliefs proposed in CEST (Catlin & Epstein, 1992). The BBI is a self-report questionnaire that provides a global scale of overall favorability of basic beliefs and more specific scales that measure the favorability of the following beliefs: good versus bad world, good versus bad self, meaningful versus meaningless world, and good versus bad people. The internal-consistency reliabilities of the scales are between .77 and .91. The scales are moderately intercorrelated, with a median correlation of .42.

In a study of the construct validity of the inventory (Catlin & Epstein, 1992), we correlated scores on the BBI with reports of extreme life events, such as loss of a loved one, and with reports about relationships with parents during early childhood. It will be recalled that, according to CEST, beliefs in the experiential system are derived from emotionally significant experiences. It was therefore anticipated that basic beliefs would be related to extreme life events and to relationships with parents in childhood. In support of these hypotheses, regression analysis revealed that major life events and relationships with parents made supplementary contributions to basic beliefs. In addition, the quality of childhood relationships with parents moderated the relation between life events and basic beliefs.

Summary and Conclusions

In summary, the program of research on CEST has provided considerable support for its construct validity. The following basic assumptions of CEST have been verified: There are two information-processing systems that operate in parallel by different rules. The systems are interactive, with each influencing the other, and the interaction occurs simultaneously (as indicated by compromises between the processing modes) as well as sequentially. The influence of the experiential on the rational system is of particular importance because it identifies the mechanism by which people's rational thinking is routinely compromised by their automatic experiential processing. The experiential system is a concretive, associationistic, rapid, primarily imagistic system that is intrinsically highly compelling to the extent that it can override the rational system, leading people to "behave against their better judgment." When people are aware of the maladaptive thoughts generated by their automatic experiential processing, they often correct them through more deliberative reasoning in their rational system. There are reliable individual differences in the efficacy, or "intelligence" of the experiential system. The intelligence of the experiential system is independent of intellectual intelligence (the intelligence of the rational system) and more strongly associated with a variety of indexes of success in living, including social success and mental and physical well-being, than intellectual intelligence as measured by intelligence tests. There are reliable individual differences in *degree* of experiential and rational processing that are independent. Experiential processing is more strongly directly associated with esoteric thinking and establishing secure relationships with others, and rational processing is more strongly directly associated with measures of adjustment. There are reliable individual differences in the four basic beliefs postulated by CEST, as measured by the BBI. The basic beliefs influence behavior simultaneously through compromises and serve as checks and balances against each other, thereby helping to keep behavior within normal limits.

Implications of CEST for Diagnosis

It is beyond the scope of this chapter to consider in detail all the implications of CEST for diagnosis. A number of implications from the general discussion of the theory are already apparent, such as the importance of determining (a) the degree of fulfillment of each of the four basic needs, (b) whether people operate primarily from a defensive or a fulfillment orientation in general and in satisfying particular basic needs, (c) whether the attempt to fulfill basic needs occurs in a conflictual or a harmonious manner, and (d) a person's position on the four basic belief dimensions. Within present space limitations, the discussion must be confined to a brief consideration of a few specially devised diagnostic procedures.

The Diagnostic Use of the Three Self-Report Measures

The three self-report inventories—the CTI, REI, and BBI, which are individual-difference measures of particular significance to CEST —have obvious implications for diagnosis. It will be recalled that the CTI provides three levels of information about adaptive and maladaptive automatic thinking. The Global scale provides diagnostic information at the most general level, comparable to an overall IQ score in an intelligence test. At the next level are six scales that provide more specific information on the basic ways that people automatically think adaptively and maladaptively. At the most specific level, subscales provide more precise information on how people automatically think. Thus, it is possible to determine with the CTI, for example, not only that a person is poor at emotional coping, but that the reasons for the person's poor emotional coping are primarily negative overgeneralization and dwelling on past aversive events. Such diagnostic information has implications for remediation, for it suggests the kinds of steps that can be taken to correct maladaptive thought processes.

The REI provides diagnostic information on the *degree* to which people value and engage in experiential and rational information processing. Such information suggests the kinds of information to which people are most likely to be receptive, and it also reveals imbalances in reliance on the two modes that can benefit from correction. As previously noted, rational processing is more strongly associated with adjustment than is experiential processing. With respect to overall adjustment, one can afford to be or not be intuitive over a wide range, but one cannot afford to be irrational. We also found that experiential processing is more strongly associated with esoteric thinking and with establishing satisfactory interpersonal relationships than is rational processing (Epstein et al., 1996; Pacini & Epstein, 1996). Thus, those who are best adjusted obtain high scores on both rational and experiential processing. These are people who are well adjusted interpersonally as well as intrapersonally.

It would seem that people who are high on experiential thinking but low on rational thinking would profit from cognitive forms of therapy in which they would learn to be more rational and to identify and dispute their maladaptive ways of automatically construing events and otherwise processing information. Unfortunately, they can be expected to be resistant to such therapy, because it would threaten their most fundamental way of experiencing the world, which is to be guided by their emotions and intuitive impressions. On the other hand, people who are high on rational and low on experiential processing tend to be alienated from what Horney (1950) has referred to as the true self and may be lacking in authenticity and the ability to relate warmly to others and to experience joy from their accomplishments.

The BBI provides information on the four basic beliefs postulated in CEST. The overall level of favorability across the beliefs indicates a person's general level of positive relative to negative beliefs about the self and the world. The favorability pattern among the specific beliefs indicates particular areas of security and threat. It might be observed, for example, that a person tends to regard others as threatening rather than supporting. This knowledge can be useful to a therapist in managing his or her relationship with a client and, in particular, in providing corrective emotional experiences as well as in correcting particular kinds of maladaptive automatic thoughts. Specific negative beliefs can also provide important clues about the nature of a client's disorder. For example, the belief that the world is disorganized and unpredictable suggests the possibility of a psychotic disorder, whereas the belief that one is deeply unworthy suggests vulnerability to depression. Of course, the same belief may occur for different reasons, and the BBI should therefore be used in conjunction with other procedures.

Beyond Self-Report Procedures

An obvious limitation of self-report procedures is that their validity depends on a person's insight and willingness to respond accurately, and research has demonstrated that self-report measures are often inaccurate and inflated by self-presentation strategies (Shedler, Mayman, & Manis, 1993). It is therefore important to supplement self-report procedures with other approaches.

An important method for determining implicit beliefs in the experiential system is to infer them from behavior and emotions. The reader will recall that two basic assumptions in CEST are that behavior in everyday life is directed primarily by the experiential system and that emotions are intimately associated with the experiential system. It follows that what people feel and do provides more important information than what they say as a basis for determining the important implicit beliefs in their experiential systems.

Particularly important, according to CEST, is the detection of sensitivities and compulsions. These can be inferred from observations of real-life behavior, from distressing incidents that clients report in therapy, and from reactions of clients to their therapists. Another useful procedure is to have clients record their behavior in specific situations of interest.

A useful diagnostic procedure is to infer from emotions the schemas in personal theories of reality. It will be recalled that the experiential system is intimately associated with the experience of affect. An emotional reaction to an event suggests that a significant belief in a person's experiential system has been implicated. Thus, by attending to the events that a person reacts to emotionally, it is possible to infer the important beliefs in a person's implicit theory of reality.

Another important diagnostic tool is the use of fantasy to access beliefs in the experiential system. This follows from the assumption that the experiential system is primarily an imagistic system that represents lessons in living in the form of images and narratives. The narratives may be symbolic representations with means–end implications. The use of such representations for diagnostic purposes will be illustrated in the section that follows on psychotherapy.

Implications of CEST for Psychotherapy

According to CEST, the objective of therapy is to produce changes in the experiential system. There are three basic ways to accomplish this: (a) using the rational system to correct the experiential system, as in providing interpretations in psychodynamic approaches and in disputing irrational thoughts in cognitive–behavioral approaches; (b) learning directly from emotionally significant experiences in real life or through a constructive relationship with a therapist; and (c) communicating with the experiential system in its own medium, namely imagery and narratives. The latter approach is particularly interesting because not only can the rational system use directed fantasy to influence the experiential system, as in systematic desensitization, but it can learn from the experiential system about underlying maladaptive schemas in the experiential system. Moreover, as I will demonstrate shortly, it is possible to respond to the learning in the rational system from the experiential system therapeutically in the medium of fantasy. These three fundamental approaches provide a unifying framework for integrating a wide variety of approaches in psychotherapy, including insight approaches, cognitive–behavioral approaches, and experiential approaches, such as Gestalt therapy and psychosynthesis (Epstein, 1994; Epstein & Brodsky, 1993).

Because CEST is readily comprehended by nonprofessionals and makes sense to them in terms of their own experience, it can be shared with clients in a constructive manner. People are well aware that they have conflicts between the heart and the head and that they have unbidden maladaptive thoughts that they cannot control with their logical thinking. These are not deep, dark, inaccessible reactions, but are quite conscious. It is therefore easy to translate such observations into the language of CEST. A major advantage in instructing clients about CEST is that it allows them to separate the operation of their logical and experiential ways of thinking. When they comprehend that their problems lie in the domain of the experiential and not the rational system, their defensiveness is reduced because they do not feel compelled to defend their reasonableness but rather are more willing to discuss their problems at the experiential level. Thus, if a client engages in excessive rational discourse, the therapist can remind the client that this is not the way the experiential system operates and direct him or her to describe feelings, images, and behavior with the aim of elucidating the processing of events in the experiential system.

As already noted, fantasy and imagery are particularly important in CEST because they communicate directly with the experiential system in its own medium. As our research has demonstrated (Pacini, Epstein, & Barrows, 1996), fantasy can be used as a vicarious form of experience. This principle has been effectively applied in techniques such as systematic desensitization and in the training of athletes. However, it can also be used in more complex ways that communicate with deeper levels of the personality, as the following example from a case of psychotherapy that produced remarkably rapid personality reorganization illustrates.

Alice Epstein wrote a book (A. H. Epstein, 1989) that presents in intimate detail the fantasies she experienced in the course of psychotherapy. She attributes deep-seated changes in the way she experienced the world and a dramatic recovery from a life-threatening illness predominantly to this process. She entered psychotherapy after receiving a diagnosis of terminal cancer and having been told that she would not likely live more than 3 months. The statistics on her form of cancer, a metastasized hypernephroma, reveal that no more than 4 in 1,000 cases experience remission let alone cure from the disease. Now, more than 10 years later, Alice has no detectable signs of cancer and is considered completely cured. Whether her belief that the psychotherapy saved her life is correct is not our concern here. What is our concern is the rapid resolution of deep-seated problems that usually require much longer periods of intensive psychotherapy. However, given increasing evidence of the relation of emotions to the immune system, it would be unwise to summarily reject her belief that her psychological recovery contributed to her physical recovery. The functioning of the experiential system may have a much stronger relation to physical well-being than orthodox medicine has recognized.

The following is one of the early fantasies described by Alice. In the sessions preceding the fantasy, she had expressed hostility to her mother for the mother's behavior in a period of turmoil in the household when Alice was a young child. During this period, the mother's mother died and the mother, having masked her pregnancy, gave birth to a daughter. The previous session was followed by a pervasive feeling of isolation and loneliness that endured until after the session in which the fantasy described below was discussed.

My therapist[1] and I decided to try the same technique to try to

---

[1]*My therapist* is substituted throughout this extract for the name of the therapist.

understand my intense discomfort at being alone. Visualizing isolation was much more difficult than visualizing pain. After many attempts that we both rejected as trivial, I finally caught the spirit of what I was experiencing. I saw some figures with shrouds—very unclear. Then as they took on a more distinct form, I saw that they were witches standing around a fire. My therapist told me to ask them to come over to talk to us. They were frightening to me in the light of the fire, but they were more horrible as they came closer. They laughed at me and started to poke at me with their sticks. The visualization was so real and their presence was so chilling to me that I burst into tears over the interaction with them.

My therapist told me to ask them what I could do to get rid of the awful fear of isolation. Finally they revealed their price. It was that I make a sacrifice so that they could become beautiful and mingle with other people. When I heard their price I began to tremble. In an almost inaudible voice I whispered, "They want my children so they can turn them into witches like them, but I'll never do it. I'll never give them my children!"

My therapist then told me to destroy them, but I told him that I couldn't possibly do it. He urged me to try to turn my fear to wrath, to try to imagine a creature that could help me. The image that came to me was a white winged horse. He told me to mount the horse and to supply myself with a weapon that would destroy them. I refused to kill them myself, but said that the wings of the horse would fan the flames of their fire, which would turn back on them and destroy them.

There was only one problem with this scenario—the horse and I were one now and I couldn't get airborne. The wings were so heavy that I couldn't flap them hard enough to catch the breeze. The harder I tried, the more I failed and the more the witches laughed at me. My therapist . . . told me that another horse who loved the first horse very much would join her and together they would destroy the witches. The other horse flew above me and made a vacuum into which I could take off. Once in the air, I flew effortlessly and fanned the fire into a huge blaze. The witches ran here and there trying to avoid the flames, but in the end they were consumed by the fire.

I practiced the scene over and over again until it became easy, but I never enjoyed it. I liked to fly, but I felt sorry for the witches, no matter how mean they were to me. My therapist felt that it was a mistake to feel sympathy for them because they would take advantage of any mercy that I displayed. He felt they would use any deception and illusion they could to control me. I was not so sure but I did agree with him that I must assume the right to soar into the world and be free of their influence. After the session, my therapist and I discussed the meaning of the images. Although I had begun with the concept of isolation in mind, I knew that the witches related to my mother, particularly the way she would poke at me and shame me. They probably represented my fear of isolation if I did not acquiesce to her demands. My therapist added that in destroying the witches I was only destroying the hostile part of our relationship, the witch part of it, and leaving the loving part intact. This was necessary for me to be free, autonomous, and no longer ensnared by fear of abandonment.

The concept that I had a great deal of conflict between the need for association and the need for autonomy was not new. I believed I had to buy affection and that no one would love me if I were myself, i.e., if I attended to my own wants. I knew also that I felt that I had to carry the burden of being responsible for my mother's well-being, that she would die at some level if I broke the bond with her.[2]

There are several aspects of the fantasy that warrant comment. First, it is noteworthy that the only aspect of the representation that initially reached awareness was an enduring mood of loneliness and isolation. The reason for the feeling remained unconscious, and the emotion endured until the reason became conscious and was dealt with at the fantasy (experiential) level as well as at the rational level. Whether one or the other would have been sufficient cannot be determined.

Second, the insight represented in the fantasy, namely that the client had a conflict between autonomy and relatedness, was not new to her. As she noted, she had been consciously aware of this conflict before. What, then, did the fantasy accomplish? One important contribution was its dealing with the insight at an experiential level, including combining intense emotions with appropriate cognitions. The previous intellectual insight in the absence of involvement of the experiential system had accomplished little. To make a therapeutic contribution, it had to be felt and processed experientially.

---

[2]From *Mind, Fantasy, and Healing: One Woman's Journey from Conflict and Illness to Wholeness and Health* (pp. 45–47), by A. H. Epstein, 1989, New York: Delacorte Press. Copyright 1991 by A. H. Epstein. Reprinted with permission of the author.

Third, the fantasy provided useful diagnostic clues for the psychotherapist. The client could not free herself from the hold of the witches until a loving figure helped her, after which she could soar freely. This suggested that what she needed to resolve her conflict was to be convinced at a deep experiential level that it is possible to be autonomous and loved at the same time. This was duly noted by her therapist, who made a point of seeing that it was implemented in the family and in the therapeutic relationship as much as possible.

Fourth, the fantasy illustrates the usefulness of vicarious symbolic practice as a therapeutic tool. The client spontaneously began to practice soaring freely on imaginary wings and enjoying her newfound freedom without feelings of guilt or fear of abandonment. Although she had understood the nature of her problem before, she was now, for the first time, able to use fantasy to reach the experiential system at a level at which it mattered. What she learned spontaneously suggests a therapeutic technique that may be more generally useful: the practice in symbolic form of remedial efforts for coping with deep-seated problems that can be identified by fantasy techniques. What remains unknown in this case is the degree to which her rapid recovery was facilitated by using the fantasy techniques in their own right, as distinguished from the support she received from an extremely favorable environment. Very likely, both contributed. However, it should be considered, in this respect, that the equally favorable environment before the therapy was insufficient for resolving her conflict and the despair associated with it. As the client reported, the love that was offered all around her by her husband, her children, her extended family, and deeply caring friends could not penetrate, so long as she felt that the price of that love was self-sacrifice and a lack of autonomy. Having developed a lifelong pattern of self-sacrifice in order to maintain relationships, she had no way of learning that it was unnecessary before undergoing therapy.

Conclusion

There is overwhelming evidence from observations of everyday behavior and from formal research, including the research summarized in this chapter (see also review in Epstein, 1994), that the prevalent mode in which humans process information is automatic, preconscious, influenced by schemas directly learned from experience, and corresponding in many other respects to what is referred to in CEST as the experiential system, which is distinguished from another major system, the rational system. It is noteworthy that psychoanalysis (except, perhaps, in the most general way of recognizing a preconscious system that serves as a gateway between unconscious and conscious systems) virtually ignores the experiential system, with its own principles of information processing that correspond to neither those of the primary nor secondary process. Thus, there is a very significant gap in psychoanalytic theory. This gap can be filled by recognizing the important role of the experiential system. Nothing is lost by such an addition, and much is gained, including an increase in the coherence of psychoanalytic theory, both within itself and with recognized principles of evolution and modern cognitive psychology. CEST also provides an integrative framework and suggests promising new directions for diagnosis and psychotherapy.

References

Adler, A. (1954). *Understanding human nature.* New York: Fawcett.

Alloy, L. B., & Abramson, L. Y. (1988). Depressive realism: Four theoretical perspectives. In L. B. Alloy (Ed.), *Cognitive processes in depression* (pp. 167–232). New York: Guilford Press.

Allport, G. W. (1961). *Pattern and growth in personality.* New York: Holt, Rinehart & Winston.

Bargh, J. A. (1989). Conditional automaticity: Varieties of automatic influence in social perception and cognition. In J. S. Uleman & J. A. Bargh (Eds.), *Unintended thought* (pp. 3–51). New York: Guilford Press.

Bowlby, J. (1988). *A secure base.* New York: Basic Books.

Cacioppo, J. T., & Petty, R. E. (1982). The need for cognition. *Journal of Personality and Social Psychology, 42,* 116–131.

Catlin, G., & Epstein, S. (1992). Unforgettable experiences: The relation of life-events to basic beliefs about self and world. *Social Cognition, 10,* 189–209.

Chaiken, S., & Maheswaren, D. (1994). Heuristic processing can bias systematic processing: Effects of source credibility, argument ambiguity, and task importance on attitude judgment. *Journal of Personality and Social Psychology, 66,* 460–473.

Denes-Raj, V., & Epstein, S. (1994). Conflict between experiential and rational processing: When people behave against their better judgment. *Journal of Personality and Social Psychology, 66,* 819–827.

Denes-Raj, V., Epstein, S., & Cole, J. (1995). The generality of the ratio-bias phenomenon. *Personality and Social Psychology Bulletin, 10,* 1083–1092.

Donovan, S., & Epstein, S. (1997). The difficulty of the Linda conjunction problem can be attributed to its simultaneous concrete and unnatural representation, and not to conversational implicature. *Journal of Experimental Social Psychology, 33,* 1–20.

Edwards, K. (1990). The interplay of affect and cognition in attitude formation and change. *Journal of Personality and Social Psychology, 59,* 202–216.

Epstein, A. H. (1989). *Mind, fantasy, and healing: One woman's journey from conflict and illness to wholeness and health.* New York: Delacorte Press. (Available from Balderwood Books, 37 Bay Road, Amherst, MA 01002 for $18.00 postpaid.)

Epstein, S. (1973). The self-concept revisited, or a theory of a theory. *American Psychologist, 28,* 404–416.

Epstein, S. (1976). Anxiety, arousal and the self-concept. In I. G. Sarason & C. D. Spielberger (Eds.), *Stress and anxiety* (pp. 183–224). Washington, DC: Hemisphere.

Epstein, S. (1979). Natural healing processes of the mind: I. Acute schizophrenic disorganization. *Schizophrenia Bulletin, 5,* 313–320.

Epstein, S. (1980). The self-concept: A review and the proposal of an integrated theory of personality. In E. Staub (Ed.), *Personality: Basic issues and current research* (pp. 82–132). Englewood Cliffs, NJ: Prentice Hall.

Epstein, S. (1983a). Natural healing processes of the mind: II. Graded stress inoculation as an inherent coping mechanism. In D. Meichenbaum & M. Jaremko (Eds.), *Stress prevention and management: A cognitive–behavioral approach.* New York: Plenum.

Epstein, S. (1983b). The unconscious, the preconscious and the self-concept. In J. Suls & A. Greenwald (Eds.), *Psychological perspectives on the self* (Vol. 2, pp. 219–247). Hillsdale, NJ: Erlbaum.

Epstein, S. (1984). Controversial issues in emotion theory. In P. Shaver (Ed.), *Annual review of research in personality and social psychology* (pp. 64–87). Beverly Hills, CA: Sage.

Epstein, S. (1985). The implications of cognitive–experiential self-theory for research in social psychology and personality. *Journal for the Theory of Social Behaviour, 15,* 283–310.

Epstein, S. (1987). Implications of cognitive self-theory for psychopathology and psychotherapy. In N. Cheshire & H. Thomae (Eds.), *Self, symptoms and psychotherapy* (pp. 43–58). New York: Wiley.

Epstein, S. (1990). Cognitive–experiential self-theory. In L. Pervin (Ed.),

Handbook of personality: Theory and research (pp. 165–192). New York: Guilford Press.

Epstein, S. (1991a). The self-concept, the traumatic neurosis, and the structure of personality. In D. Ozer, J. M. Healy, Jr., & A. J. Stewart (Eds.), *Perspectives in personality* (Vol. 3A, pp. 63–98). London: Jessica Kingsley.

Epstein, S. (1991b). Cognitive–experiential self-theory: Implications for developmental psychology. In M. Gunnar & L. A. Sroufe (Eds.), *Minnesota Symposia on Child Psychology: Self-processes and development* (Vol. 23, pp. 79–123). Hillsdale, NJ: Erlbaum.

Epstein, S. (1991c). Cognitive–experiential self-theory: An integrative theory of personality. In R. C. Curtis (Ed.), *The relational self: Convergences in psychoanalysis and social psychology* (pp. 111–137). New York: Guilford Press.

Epstein, S. (1992a). Constructive thinking and mental and physical well-being. In L. Montada, S. H. Filipp, & M. J. Lerner (Eds.), *Life crises and experiences of loss in adulthood* (pp. 385–409). Hillsdale, NJ: Erlbaum.

Epstein, S. (1992b). Coping ability, negative self-evaluation, and overgeneralization: Experiment and theory. *Journal of Personality and Social Psychology, 62,* 826–836.

Epstein, S. (1993a). Bereavement from the perspective of cognitive–experiential self-theory. In M. S. Stroebe, W. Stroebe, & R. O. Hansson (Eds.), *Handbook of bereavement: Theory, research, and intervention* (pp. 112–125). Cambridge, England: Cambridge University Press.

Epstein, S. (1993b). Emotion and self-theory. In M. Lewis & J. Haviland (Eds.), *Handbook of emotions* (pp. 313–326). New York: Guilford Press.

Epstein, S. (1993c). Implications of cognitive–experiential self-theory for personality and developmental psychology. In D. Funder, R. Parke, C. Tomlinson-Keasey, & K. Widaman (Eds.), *Studying lives through time: Personality and development* (pp. 399–438). Washington, DC: American Psychological Association.

Epstein, S. (1994). Integration of the cognitive and the psychodynamic unconscious. *American Psychologist, 49,* 709–724.

Epstein, S., & Brodsky, A. (1993). *You're smarter than you think.* New York: Simon & Schuster.

Epstein, S., Denes-Raj, V., & Pacini, R. (1995). The Linda problem revisited from the perspective of cognitive–experiential self-theory. *Personality and Social Psychology Bulletin, 11,* 1124–1138.

Epstein, S., Donovan, S., & Denes-Raj, V. (in press). The missing link in the paradox of the Linda conjunction problem: Beyond knowing and thinking of the conjunction rule, the intrinsic appeal of heuristic processing. *Personality and Social Psychology Bulletin.*

Epstein, S., & Erskine, N. (1983). The development of personal theories of reality. In D. Magnusson & V. Allen (Eds.), *Human development: An interactional perspective* (pp. 133–147). New York: Academic Press.

Epstein, S., & Katz, L. (1992). Coping ability, stress, productive load, and symptoms. *Journal of Personality and Social Psychology, 62,* 813–825.

Epstein, S., Lipson, A., Holstein, C., & Huh, E. (1992). Irrational reactions to negative outcomes: Evidence for two conceptual systems. *Journal of Personality and Social Psychology, 62,* 328–339.

Epstein, S., & Meier, P. (1989). Constructive thinking: A broad coping variable with specific components. *Journal of Personality and Social Psychology, 57,* 332–350.

Epstein, S., & Morling, B. (1995). Is the self motivated to do more than enhance and verify itself? In M. H. Kernis (Ed.), *Efficacy, agency, and self-esteem* (pp. 9–29). New York: Plenum Press.

Epstein, S., Pacini, R., Denes-Raj, V., & Heier, H. (1996). Individual differences in intuitive–experiential and analytical–rational thinking styles. *Journal of Personality and Social Psychology, 71,* 390–405.

Fairbairn, W. R. D. (1954). *An object relations theory of the personality.* New York: Basic Books.

Freud, S. (1953). The interpretation of dreams. In J. Strachey (Ed. & Trans.), *The standard edition of the complete psychological works of Sigmund Freud* (Vols. 4 and 5). London: Hogarth Press. (Original work published 1900)

Freud, S. (1965). *New introductory lectures on psychoanalysis* (J. Strachey, Trans.). New York: Norton. (Original work published 1933)

Gallistel, C. R., & Gelman, R. (1992). Preverbal and verbal counting and computation. *Cognition, 44,* 43–74.

Geschwandtner, G. (1990). How superachievers think to reach consistent success. *Personal Selling Power, 10,* 12–19.

Gill, M. M. (1959). The present state of psychoanalytic theory, *Journal of Abnormal and Social Psychology, 58,* 1–8.

Greenson, R. R. (1967). *The technique and practice of psychoanalysis.* London: Hogarth Press.

Hartman, H. (1964). *Essays on ego-psychology: Selected problems in psychoanalytic theory.* Madison, CT: International Universities Press.

Higgins, E. T. (1989). Knowledge accessibility and activation: Subjectivity and suffering from unconscious sources. In J. S. Uleman & J. A. Bargh (Eds.), *Unintended thought* (pp. 75–123). New York: Guilford Press.

Hixon, J. G., & Swann, W. B. (1993). When does introspection bear fruit? Self-reflection, self-insight, and interpersonal choices. *Journal of Personality and Social Psychology, 64,* 35–43.

Horney, K. (1950). *Neurosis and human growth.* New York: Norton.

Kahneman, D., Slovic, P., & Tversky, A. (1982). *Judgment under uncertainty: Heuristics and biases.* Cambridge, England: Cambridge University Press.

Katz, L., & Epstein, S. (1991). Constructive thinking and coping with laboratory-induced stress. *Journal of Personality and Social Psychology, 61,* 789–800.

Kelly, G. A. (1955). *The psychology of personal constructs* (2 vols.). New York: Norton.

Kernberg, O. (1976). *Object relations theory and clinical psychoanalysis*. New York: Jason Aronson.

Kirkpatrick, L. A., & Epstein, S. (1992). Cognitive–experiential self-theory and subjective probability: Further evidence for two conceptual systems. *Journal of Personality and Social Psychology, 63*, 534–544.

Klein, G. S. (1970). *Perception, motives, and personality*. New York: Knopf.

Klein, M. (1975). Some theoretical conclusions regarding the emotional life of the infant. In M. Klein (Ed.), *Envy and gratitude and other works* (pp. 1946–1963). New York: Delacorte Press. (Original work published 1952)

Kohut, H. (1971). *The analysis of the self*. Madison, CT: International Universities Press.

Lecky, P. (1961). *Self-consistency: A theory of personality*. Hamden, CT: Shoe String Press.

Mahler, M. (1952). On child psychosis and schizophrenia: Autistic and symbiotic infantile psychosis. *Psychoanalytic Study of the Child, 7*, 206–305.

Miller, D. T., & Gunasegaram, S. (1990). Temporal order and the perceived mutability of events: Implications for blame assignment. *Journal of Personality and Social Psychology, 59*, 1111–1118.

Morling, B., & Epstein, S. (in press). Compromises produced by the dialectic between self-verification and self-enhancement. *Journal of Personality and Social Psychology*.

Nadeau, M. (1994). *Relation of constructive thinking to stress, health, work performance, and overall success in living*. Honors thesis, University of Massachusetts at Amherst.

Pacini, R., & Epstein, S. (1996). *The relation of rational and experiential thinking styles to personality, basic beliefs, and heuristic processing*. Manuscript submitted for publication.

Pacini, R., Epstein, S., & Barrows, P. (1996). *Lessons in intuitive reasoning from the ratio-bias phenomenon: Principles of operation of the intuitive system and their interaction with rational reasoning*. Manuscript submitted for publication.

Pacini, R., Muir, F., & Epstein, S. (in press). Depressive realism from the perspective of cognitive–experiential self-theory. *Journal of Personality & Social Psychology*.

Pavlov, I. P. (1941). *Conditioned reflexes and psychiatry* (W. H. Gantt, Trans.). Madison, CT: International Universities Press.

Perry, J. W. (1976). *Roots of renewal in myth and madness*. San Francisco: Jossey-Bass.

Rapaport, D. (1959). The structure of psychoanalytic theory: A systematizing attempt. In S. Koch (Ed.), *Psychology: A study of a science* (Vol. 3, pp. 155–183). New York: McGraw-Hill.

Rogers, C. R. (1951). *Client-centered therapy: Its current practice, implications, and theory*. Boston: Houghton Mifflin.

Rogers, C. R. (1959). A theory of therapy, personality, and interpersonal relationships, as developed in the client-centered framework. In S. Koch (Ed.), *Psychology: A study of a science* (Vol. 3, pp. 184–256). New York: McGraw-Hill.

Shedler, J., Mayman, M., & Manis, M. (1993). The *illusion* of mental health. *American Psychologist, 48*, 1117–1131.

Swann, W. B. (1990). To be adored or to be known? The interplay of self-enhancement and self-verification. In E. T. Higgins & R. M. Sorrentino (Eds.), *Handbook of motivation and cognition: Foundations of social behavior* (Vol. 2, pp. 408–448). New York: Guilford Press.

Taylor, S. E., & Brown, J. D. (1988). Illusion and well-being: A social psychological perspective on mental health. *Psychological Bulletin, 103,* 193–210.

Tversky, A., & Kahneman, D. (1974). Judgment under uncertainty: Heuristics and biases. *Science, 185,* 1124–1131.

Tversky, A., & Kahneman, D. (1983). Extensional versus intuitive reasoning. The conjunction fallacy in probability judgment. *Psychological Review, 90,* 293–315.

Weiss, J., & Sampson, H. (1986). Testing alternative psychoanalytic explanation of the therapeutic process. In J. Masling (Ed.), *Empirical studies of psychoanalytic theories* (Vol. 3, pp. 1–26). Hillsdale, NJ: Analytic Press.

Daydreams, the Stream of Consciousness, and Self-Representations

Jerome L. Singer

If there were a contest for people to choose their favorite writing by Sigmund Freud, my selection would be easy. It would be "Creative Writers and Day-dreaming" (Freud, 1908/1960). In this 10-page paper first presented as a lecture in 1907, Freud called attention to the phenomenon of daydreaming as the basis for the production and appreciation of literature. He noted that in essence, writers believe that almost everyone is indeed a "poet at heart" and that the "last poet will not perish till the last man dies" (p. 143). Everyone engages relatively often in conscious fantasies that reflect frequently current or sometimes continuing wishes from earlier days, but people often dismiss these as "airy" nothings and fail even to see the degree to which the more spectacular night dreams are simply relatively continuous with the daydreaming process. Freud (1908/1960)—well before Piaget (1962), Luria (1932), or Vygotsky (1966)—pointed out that the spontaneous make-believe play of children was very likely a precursor of adolescent and adult daydreams. He then proceeded to examine the extent to which conscious daydreams and perhaps repressed efforts at wish fulfillment may combine in the storytelling of creative writers to generate what today might be called "the shock of recognition" that brings such delight to the readers of great writers.

The article is terse but meaty, free of the straitjacket of the libido theory and the later metapsychology that many now believe burdened the ensuing 50 years of psychoanalytic development. By its very definition, daydreaming is a conscious experience, albeit one often not well recollected. This paper, as I read it, however, also pointed to the significance of waking consciousness as a foundation for the psychoanalytic unconscious.

Why is this paper a favorite of mine? In its brief compass, it posed questions that have engaged my nearly half-century of research on the phenomenon of daydreaming and its links to psychoanalytic theory on the one hand and to William James' concept of the *stream of consciousness* or to modern cognitive psychology on the other. I had not read this article when I first began my research program, and I was more influenced by the teaching of Gardner Murphy (1947) and the writings of Luria (1932), Piaget (1962), and Rorschach (1921/1951). It was likely that all of these authors had indeed been subjected to some influence by Freud. Certainly, soon after I started active research, I did make the connection with Freud's paper.

Consciousness as a Psychological Problem

Why focus on conscious experience in a volume devoted to the "psychoanalytic unconscious"? The position I will be taking is that—as to some extent is suggested in Freud's paper—the foundation of unconscious mental processes lies to a great extent in the conscious intentions, imaginings, and mental explorations evident patently in the pretend play of children and, more privately, in the waking, ongoing thought of adults. In the first years of psychology's emergence as a formal scientific discipline, consciousness was at the center of the field. This is clearly evident from the fact that William James' great chapter on "The Stream of Thought" is close to the beginning of his two-volume *The Principles of Psychology* (James, 1890/1950). From about 1910 until the 1960s, with the dominance of behaviorism in psychology, conscious thought was largely ignored in the interests of the study of behavior. This denial of the "obvious" was further fostered by the psychoanalytic movement, which was emphasizing, during the same half-century or so, the importance of recognizing unconscious mental processes and their influence on social relationships, behavior, and psychopathology.

Even with the paradigm shift toward cognitive psychology that has characterized the last 40 years of the twentieth century, many researchers have still underplayed the significance of conscious experience (Leahey, 1992, 1994). Over the past decade, however, philosophers of science have turned their attention to the great problem of how to reconcile the subtleties and nuances, or what are technically called the *qualia*, of human conscious experience with the new findings emerging from neurophysiological studies of the living brain. In one way or another, perhaps still subtly under the influence of Skinner or of the powerful computer metaphors of intelligent functioning, some philosophers or cognitive scientists have sought to finesse the problem by animadversions such as Dennett's *virtual machine* (Dennett, 1991). Searle (1992, 1995) has argued vigorously for a more commonsense and clear acceptance of the reality of human conscious experience as an emergent property of brain function, one that ultimately must be addressed directly. Even within a computer metaphor, as Baars (1988, 1993) has proposed, it is possible to sustain a conception of consciousness as a global workspace. Can one conceive of a realm of unconscious processes if one does not to some degree accept the reality of individuals' beliefs in their own ongoing conscious thoughts (Leahey, 1994; Searle, 1992; J. L. Singer & Bonanno, 1990)?

During the 1980s and 1990s, unequivocal empirical evidence has documented the common belief that there are indeed unconscious cognitive processes as represented by implicit memories, forms of implicit perception, functional grammars or musical skills, and a range of automatic processes that are carried on without conscious awareness or often apparently without conscious preparation (Kihlstrom, 1987, 1990). This "cognitive unconscious," although overlapping somewhat with Freud's cognitive psychology, as Erdelyi (1985) has shown, is largely outside the scope of the so-called psychodynamic or psychoanalytic unconscious that is the subject of this volume. Can one conceive of unconsciousness without at least affording some significance to ongoing conscious processes?

The position that I will be taking is that consciousness may be more extensive than is proposed in the psychodynamic literature. In the following pages and quite possibly from some of the hints in the article by Freud (1908/1960) that I cited previously, it is possible to argue that the mind may indeed carry on a continuous stream of conscious thought that anticipates or imagines and fantasizes a very large range of possible situations or self-representations. One may try out in the "mind's eye" or "mind's ear" a considerable array of possible social situations in which one participates. Kihlstrom (1987, 1990, 1993) has argued along similar lines that self-relevant or self-representational material may often be at the core of conscious processes. In the research I will describe, it seems likely that (as great writers like Virginia Woolf, James Joyce, William Faulkner, Saul Bellow, and John Irving have shown in their novels) people carry on reasonably continuous interior monologues or range through a variety of imagined situations. Some of these thoughts, in the form of memories, plans, or more full-blown fantasies, may be preparing the way for changing cognitive schemas or social scripts (J. L. Singer & Salovey, 1991), but the *sources* of these cognitions may be forgotten (at least temporarily) because of the interference effects of processing external cues necessary for safety or social adaptation. Perhaps people often do not recall how many times they have consciously thought about the "possible selves" (Markus & Nurius, 1986) that they have tried out as they go about their business. Those neuroscientists and molecular biologists now becoming interested in consciousness in their efforts to formulate a theory of brain function will have to pay increasing attention to the relatively continuous nature of the stream of thought and its implications for memory and learning. Similarly psychodynamically oriented theorists and clinicians will need to attend carefully to the extent to which it may be useful to tap ongoing conscious thought processes before moving to make elaborate assumptions about "unconscious fantasy" or presumed unconscious childhood wishes or object relations imagings ascribed to infancy.

Research on Daydreaming and Ongoing Consciousness

Projective Technique Approaches

Freud had assumed in his daydreaming paper that most people would be reluctant to report many of their fantasies. It was this assumption, perhaps supported at one time by the experience of psychoanalysts and clinical interviewers, that led to the development of projective techniques. One of the most daring hypotheses proposed by the Swiss psychiatrist Hermann Rorschach (1921/1951) was that individuals who reported human figures engaged in some action in response to the question "What might this be?" when exposed to a set of ink blots were more likely to fantasize and to be aware of their ongoing thought. They were also likely to be more restrained and controlled or even inhibited in their overt movements. This Imagination–Motor Inhibition hypothesis Rorschach claimed was supported by his observations of normal individuals and of patients responding to his ink blots. Because of the possibility that fantasy processes might indeed be related to one's ability to restrain oneself from impulsive overt behaviors, as Freud had earlier suggested (Freud, 1911/1962), I was led in the late 1940s with various collaborators into a series of investigations to explore the implications of this suggestion. Would one's fantasies and daydreams serve as a form of motoric self-control on the one hand and as an index of "ego strength" on the other? This series of studies generally supported Rorschach's propositions and was summarized in the review of literally dozens of research studies (Blatt, 1990; Moise, Yinon, & Rabinowitz, 1988–1989; J. L. Singer & Brown, 1977). Early on, I outlined the implications of some of this research for the important concept of delay of gratification and its relation to one's imaginative capacity. We also conducted factor analytic studies linking Rorschach's scores with other measures of imagination and forms of self-restraint or inhibited motor behavior (J. L. Singer, 1955; J. L. Singer & Brown, 1977; J. L. Singer, Wilensky, & McCraven, 1956).

Questionnaire Studies of Daydreaming and Related Imaginal Processes

Despite the generally supportive results linking the Rorschach Human Movement response (M) to fantasy processes, there was still something inherently unsatisfying about such an indirect measure. Although it is true that self-reported tendencies for daydreaming were correlated with the M response on the Rorschach ink blots (J. L. Singer, 1966, 1975a), too many layers of inference are still necessary. It seemed reasonable therefore to move on to attempts to study daydreaming more directly by simply interviewing people about their daydreams and eventually accumulating much larger samples and more normative data through questionnaires. This has led to considerable data that document the apparent universality of daydreaming and the acknowledgment by large numbers of people from different walks of life that this is a general phenomenon in their daily lives. We developed fairly precise measures of individual variations in styles of daydreaming that characterize the genders, cultural groups, or age groups (Huba, J. L. Singer, Aneshensel, & Antrobus, 1982; Segal, Huba, & J. L. Singer, 1980; J. L. Singer, 1974, 1975a). A factor-analytically derived instrument called the Imaginal Processes Inventory (IPI) in longer and shorter questionnaire forms has been developed and widely used. A review of the extensive range of correlates of self-reported fantasies and fantasy styles emerging from this direct form of questioning about individuals' awareness of their daydreams is reported elsewhere (J. L. Singer & Bonanno, 1990). For the purposes of this chapter, it seems enough to state that daydreaming is a normal, widespread, human phenomenon that many people are aware of quite consciously and can present reliably on the kind of direct inquiry that is possible through questionnaires. It can also be shown that these self-reports have reasonable degrees of construct validity. Persons who score as showing more daydreaming tendencies are also more likely to show such patterns when they are examined systematically under laboratory conditions (Antrobus, Coleman, & J. L. Singer, 1967). Similarly, many people are also willing and able to attest to a considerable range of sexual fantasies of a kind ordinarily thought to be mentioned in clinical sessions (Campagna, 1985–1986; Hariton & J. L. Singer, 1974).

Recently, a psychoanalyst (Person, 1995) has written extensively on the availability, widespread nature, and significance of fantasies obtained through direct inquiry. Although Person's conclusions are drawn largely from anecdote or from specific clinical interactions, she is particularly effective in calling attention to "shared fantasies"—that is, fantasies and daydreams directly communicated between two individuals that may sometimes become parts of the general mythology of a culture. Thus, a parent with a particular fantasy might share it with a child, who might then begin to attribute perhaps even a greater reality to the fantasy than did the parent. In this way, fantasies can become guiding motives or lead to significant precursors of pathology or social dysfunction, as well as in some cases serve inspiring and uplifting purposes. Person suggested that fantasies that often are expressed in terms of the rhetoric associated with a particular charismatic individual's sharing his or her "dream" can lead large groups of people in particular religious, social, or political directions. The fantasy of a Jewish state that Herzl as a journalist shared with his readers inspired thousands to the eventual creation of the modern nation of Israel. The fantasies about the "equal rights of man" that were widely current during the French Revolution had similar far-ranging effects. Consider the shared personal fantasy of workers around the world uniting with "nothing to lose but [their] chains," as written by Marx and Engels. That image led undoubtedly to millions of people eventually participating in the communist revolutions that reshaped the world maps of the twentieth century. And, alas, the superman Aryan fantasy of Hitler was taken up by large numbers of Germans for at least a period of time and may still be found as a recurring image in the neo-Nazis, White supremacists, or skinheads of today. On a more constructive note, one may also consider the consequences of Martin Luther King, Jr.'s great "I have a dream" speech. As Person wrote, "I have analogized instances of a cultural change to mutations: a fantasy is to cultural revolution as mutation is to biological evolution, and cultural mutations, like biological mutations, may benefit us but they may also kill us" (Person, 1995, p. 117).

However sweeping one may find Person's speculations, they are prefigured by Freud's own references to religion as an "illusion" (from a fantasy about a powerful father). They do suggest an area of research hitherto neglected. In all of the questionnaire studies I conducted alone and with various collaborators, as well as by others working independently, little reference is made to the sharing of fantasy experiences, whether with intimate others or of cultural fantasies. Here is a potential area for extensive study by social psychologists or sociologists. Questionnaire approaches could prove fruitful.

Laboratory Studies of Ongoing Thought: Task-Unrelated Images and Thoughts

The questionnaire approach suffers to some extent from being based on retrospective reports by individuals who ordinarily do not keep track of the extensiveness and timing of their day-to-day fantasies or daydreams. Thus, even with reasonable evidence of reliability and construct validity for these inventory approaches, one cannot be sure that individuals are always in a position to report very accurately when presented with a questionnaire. Those who know this field have increasingly come to agree that it is not useful to cast daydreaming into an evaluative form or to limit it to the more improbable kinds of ongoing speculation or imagery. Rather, the evidence from these normative studies suggests that people often have rather mundane daydreams or fantasies about practical events that are upcoming in their lives, or else they spend time reshaping memories or fantasies into what become well-practiced schemas or scripts (J. L. Singer & Salovey, 1991). Such processes may well go on throughout the day and, quite possibly, at night as well. They reflect the fleeting thoughts so well portrayed in the stream-of-consciousness "fictional" literature of which James Joyce, Virginia Woolf, and Dorothy Richardson were among the earliest practitioners.

How can one capture these ongoing processes in a fashion that meets reasonable laboratory standards of reliability and replicability? In the late 1950s, John Antrobus and I began to use a carefully controlled procedure based on so-called vigilance and signal detection procedures (Antrobus, 1968; Antrobus, J. L. Singer, Goldstein, & Fortgang, 1970; Antrobus, J. L. Singer, & Greenberg, 1966; J. L. Singer, 1975a, 1975b). A participant is seated in a light-free and soundproof booth, wearing headphones through which pure tones of two different frequencies are broadcast at intervals (depending on the particular experiment) of between $1/2$ to $1^1/_2$ seconds. The individual is asked to press a button whenever a "high" tone is presented (or a "low tone" if that is the particular instruction). Correct signal detections are financially rewarded over a period of perhaps an hour in the booth. Most people can sustain a 90% accuracy level. Every 15 seconds, "white noise" interrupts the task, and the subjects report by a "Yes" or "No" button-press whether during the immediately preceding 15-second interval they experienced a "task-unrelated image or thought." Preexperimental training trials in which participants, when interrupted, reported the content of such thoughts along a criterion made it possible to assume a common definition. A "Yes" report indicated that even as participants were correctly identifying the signal tones, they were also producing a variety of extraneous, self-generated thoughts unrelated to their mental concentration on the tones and on the accuracy of their performance. Content reports of these task-unrelated images and thoughts have indicated that they range widely from fantasies about the experimenters to highly personal memories or daydreams. Researchers in this field have accepted the acronym proposed by Giambra (1995) referring to these reports as *TUITs* (task-unrelated images and thoughts), a suggestive term because of the link to "intuition."

Some selected findings from the numerous studies completed with this general laboratory methodology will be summarized briefly (see Giambra, 1995; J. L. Singer, 1975a; J. L. Singer & Bonanno, 1990; J. Singer & Kolligian, 1987 for further reviews). During a 1-hour "watch," individuals reported such TUITs during more than 50% of the 15-second signaling periods. Such TUITs generally do not impede accuracy of detections. They can be systematically related to the cognitive processing load borne by the participant. Special preexperimental circumstances such as overhearing a simulated radio broadcast announcing dramatic U.S. war involvement can sharply increase TUITs without, however, reducing accuracy; randomly timed rather than regular presentation of signals may reduce TUITs by forcing more task concentration; persons predisposed to greater daydreaming according to self-reports on our questionnaires showed more and more TUITs over time in the booth. In one study, simply systematically varying gender of the experimenter and participant led to increases in TUITs when the two were of the opposite sex. Results were significant for both male and female participants, but with women generally showing greater increases in TUITs than shown by men (Algom & J. L. Singer, 1984–1985). Giambra (1995) has shown that TUIT likelihood can be reliably measured across a considerable range of signal detection procedures and that TUITs show test–retest reliability in short-term and long-term assessments. Klinger (1990) has documented

the widespread nature of TUITs and Giambra (1995) and collaborators have used the procedure in studies of aging, depression, and
hyperactivity.

Even if one concedes the relative artificiality of the laboratory
procedure, one cannot avoid the recognition that ongoing conscious thoughts are persistent, intrusive, and ubiquitous and can
operate sequentially or in parallel with task performance (Antrobus, J. L. Singer, Goldstein, & Fortgang, 1970). Of importance is
that people who reported more frequent daydreaming on questionnaires actually showed such performance by producing more
TUITs than did low-daydream reporters in the signal detection
tasks. These frequent daydreamers sustained high accuracy in the
early half of an hour's watch, but as time passed, they shifted more
and more attention to their TUITs, and their accuracy dropped (Antrobus, Coleman, & J. L. Singer, 1967).

In summary, the laboratory methods using a signal detection
procedure indicate that human beings engage in a considerable
degree of what might be called task-unrelated thought, even as
they go about the business of dealing with specific demands of a
given piece of work. Klinger (1978, 1990) has summarized many
of the findings of these thought sampling approaches by proposing
the useful distinction between what he calls "operant" and "respondent" thought processes. Operant thought has a conscious in-
strumental characteristic. It attempts to solve a specific problem or
to engage in the examination of a particular issue presently con-
fronting the individual. Operant thought generally is acted on and
directed toward a specific immediate objective and can often be
considered a more operationalized form of what Freud called
"secondary-process" thought (Freud, 1911/1962). Particularly relevant in operant thought is its systematic checking against new
information in order to determine the effectiveness with which the
thought process is moving toward some solution or for the consequences that the new information may have for this solution.
Considerable effort is expended to sustain an operant line of
thought, lest it shift off target toward extraneous irrelevant cues.
Such operant thought probably resembles what neurologists such
as Henry Head (1926), Kurt Goldstein (1940), and Pribram and
McGuinness (1975) have called "vigilance," "the abstract attitude,"
or "effort." It is a fundamental human capacity to concentrate on

high-level syllogistic processes, which are especially prone to suffer from massive brain damage (J. L. Singer & Bonanno, 1990). As Klinger's (1978) own research has shown, one of the central characteristics of operant thought is that such a task-related focus is correlated highly with mental monitoring of progress toward a particular goal as well as conscious efforts to resist distraction (Klinger, 1978).

Contrasting with these operant processes are what Klinger has called respondent thoughts. These appear often to be nonvolitional, that is, "unbidden" or peremptory, they are mental distractions one becomes aware of when trying to focus on a task, as our participants do in the signal detection experiment. Most of what are now considered daydreams and fantasies and, naturally, nighttime dreams are examples of respondent processes.

Naturalistic Thought-Sampling Approaches

Although the laboratory approaches have considerable value in identifying the frequency of situational determinants and contingent features of respondent thought processes, they tell us little about the content of ongoing fantasies at the conscious level because, for quantitative purposes, we usually have to rely on simple "Yes–No" button presses rather than detailed reports. There are, however, increasing uses being made of naturalistic methods for investigating the individual's spontaneous thought in daily contexts (Quattrone, 1985; J. Singer & Kolligian, 1987). Such procedures often involve having individuals talk out loud over a period of time while sitting in a relatively controlled environment (e.g., a quiet room), tape recording their verbalizations. These comments are then scored for indications of particular patterns of thought or content categories. Another approach requires an individual to sit, recline, or stand quietly for a period but then be interrupted as in the signal detection studies to provide reports of thought or perceptual activity. Still another approach involves having the person carry a button-press device that can be used to indicate shifts in the chain of thought and then allowing the person to report verbally on these (Pope, 1978). Finally, most extensively used is the valuable method of Csikszentmihalyi and his collaborators (Csikszentmihalyi & Larson, 1987). This approach involves having ordinary individuals carry around a paging device that is now commonly used not only by physicians but also by teenagers. This "beeper" signals randomly during the day, at which point the participants in the study fill out a questionnaire they are carrying, reporting what thoughts they just had, what activities they were just engaged in, and their current emotional state. In a sense, these thought-sampling methods are especially intriguing because they seem to extend to daily life a version of the couch-based free association method that Freud introduced.

Psychoanalysts may be suspicious that thought-sampling procedures such as those just cited or the widespread use of self-report questionnaires may be susceptible to conscious falsification or simply may often reflect self-deception in the respondent. In the case of personality questionnaires, the greatly improved psychometric sophistication and demonstrated reliability and validity of such instruments for *group* comparisons far surpasses any current data available for projective methods or clinical interviews (John, 1990; Kiesler, 1996; Wiggins & Pincus, 1992, 1994). For thought-sampling reports, one cannot offer the same strong assertions of demonstrated "validity." Participants always have the option of marking their data cards as "Private" or "Choose not to respond." Such reports are rare. The immediacy of reactions to being beeped precludes elaborate or systematic fabrication or distortion, however. It seems to me that the burden of proof lies with skeptical clinicians who must provide empirical evidence that their own data are not susceptible to similar report biases or that experience-sampling reports are not as accurate as the material provided during a therapy session.

Because the results of these thought-sampling approaches have been reviewed elsewhere (J. L. Singer & Bonanno, 1990), one can identify the verbalizations and the contexts reported in such approaches as well as the specific emotions accompanying the individual's pattern of thought. To what extent is thought organized? Is it sequentially presented, or is it somehow degenerative or confused? Does the thought involve imagery of related episodes or event memory material, or is it rather organized along logical–semantic structures? To what extent does such thought reflect major current concerns, or is it perhaps more related to symbolic fantasies that are less easily identifiable? One can also determine whether the focus of ongoing thought involves largely reminiscences or whether it is oriented more toward the future. One can finally ask to what extent the content is realistic or improbable and further relate such thought to events that occurred just prior to the individual's actual physical positions or social situation.

Findings from this growing and intriguing body of studies demonstrate that one can actually conduct useful studies to determine the ways in which ongoing thoughts relate to a person's emotional state, physical health, and recent or long-standing unfulfilled intentions (J. L. Singer, 1988). Although Freud seemed to be more or less correct in the early paper on daydreaming, he may have overemphasized the belief that the fantasies of ongoing consciousness were determined largely by wishes. Klinger's (1990) useful distinction of the concept of "current concerns" has made it possible to measure such concerns psychometrically. In a way, these concerns incorporate the Freudian wish, at least in its form prior to libido theory, as Holt (1976) has explicated it. Such unfulfilled intentions may range all the way from the mundane examples used by Kurt Lewin (1935) in his studies of incompleted tasks (e.g., remembering to bring home some butter) to more long-standing unresolved desires (e.g., a recurrent thought about wanting to succeed in one's job in order to please one's father or mother or to prove to a sibling that one can accomplish things in life after all). By using a scoring method for current concerns, it is possible to estimate from thought sampling the relative importance of intentions and to establish a temporal hierarchy of such intentions and the individual's perception of the reality of actually achieving such intentions or the degree to which the intentions are relatively recently formed or related to earlier life experiences. The position of those who study thought sampling and ongoing consciousness is that they must explore the range and influence of current conscious concerns through sampling of a given person's thoughts, emotions, and behavioral responses before moving on to make elaborate inferences about the influence of presumed unconscious wishes or fantasies. This is a challenge that psychoanalytic theories of the unconscious will have to confront.

It is certainly possible to conduct a variety of controlled, hypothesis-testing investigations of individuals using thought-sampling methods. In a study Dennis Klos and I conducted (Klos &

J. L. Singer, 1981), for example, we developed a set of specific predictions about what prior factors might determine the ongoing conscious thoughts of an individual in a specific experimental situation (Klos & J. L. Singer, 1981). We recorded a group of late adolescents as each was seated quietly in a room and interrupted periodically to report on their thoughts. To what extent did these reports reflect uncompleted and completed activities engaged in shortly prior to the thought sampling as Lewin (1935) might have proposed? Did they also reflect recently developed concerns about imagined activities with a parent under different emotional or conflictual conditions? Perhaps the most central question was whether all their thoughts were moderated by a longer term history of unresolved conflict with parents. I will turn shortly in this chapter to descriptions of both research and clinical work of thought-sampling approaches.

Studying Imaginative Play in Children

At the outset of his daydreaming paper, Freud (1908/1960) described the links between the child's early play and the creative activities of the writer. Indeed, Freud outlined briefly the way the German language links play to fantasy in various ways in adults. He also attempted to show that adults, although they do not openly play, may engage in fantasies or daydreams. In my own research and in my collaborative efforts with my wife, Dorothy Singer, I have elaborated the implications of Freud's few pages in this area (J. L. Singer, 1973; D. G. Singer & J. L. Singer, 1990). We have examined the earliest forms of pretend play in childhood, the occurrence of imaginary playmates, various forms of make-believe play manifested in the day-care center or nursery school, and then, as the child moves on to the regular school situation, how such play—while persisting somewhat more privately at home—may become internalized increasingly into fantasies. We have not only reviewed the actual play behavior of children and the contingent characteristics that foster such imaginative play or impede it, but have also considered the implications of individual differences in imaginative play to determine whether it is largely a manifestation of early neurotic difficulties, as some have proposed (Segal, 1964) or can be viewed as a manifestation of a healthy adaptive development. Our evidence suggests that children who are more imaginative players early on are not only likely to appear happier in their day-to-day behavior but are also able to function more effectively in a variety of ways.

Using autobiographical data, we have also collected reports of many writers about the extent to which their early childhood make-believe play influenced their later writing (D. G. Singer & J. L. Singer, 1990). Freud's focus in his paper was primarily on wishes. Our data suggest that clearly, specific wishes are often involved in much of the early imaginative play of children. A great deal of such play, however, involves children's efforts toward mastery of the world through attempts to miniaturize the complexities of their milieu into a form that they can manipulate. In this way, they strive to experience some power over the grown-up environment in essentially a healthy sense.

Freud identified a gender difference in early fantasies, hypothesizing that male focus is on heroic activities, whereas those of females are more erotically oriented. More recently, Gottlieb (1973), working through direct observations of middle-school children, found that the boys were more inclined to engage in heroic fantasies and that the girls were more inclined to have social relationship daydreams as well as romantic fantasies. Despite the widespread psychoanalytic emphasis on middle childhood as the so-called latency period, again and again our observations have suggested that a gradual differentiation process characterizes children who move into school age. In preschool, they play most of their games out in the open and verbalize their thoughts. Under the constraints of regular school attendance, they are more likely to minimize overt play and to practice increasingly the use of private fantasy and thought. Such fantasy seems indeed to flower vigorously in middle childhood with rich and elaborate imaginings.

Play can of course reflect a tendency toward repression or suppression of certain kinds of wishes and family conflicts. Extremely repetitive, monotopical, or fragmented play can suggest pathology (D. G. Singer, 1993). From our observations, children appeared to show less avoidant tendencies and more active seeking to express desires in the course of their private play and then later in their conscious fantasies. We were also especially struck by the degree to which imaginative play was indeed about making sense of and exploring the world around them. In his paper, Freud (1908/1960) suggested that the child's motives were dominated by "a single wish—one that helps in his upbringing—the wish to be big and grown up" (p. 146). If we broaden this notion to a need for organizing the cognitive complexity of the world and for mastering it through miniaturization, we can only agree. Remember, however, that this daydreaming paper was written before Freud had moved so fully into his metapsychology and emphasis on psychosexuality and libido theory. He wrote, however, "a happy person never fantasizes, only an unsatisfied one. . . . Every single fantasy is a fulfillment of a wish, a correction of unsatisfying reality" (Freud, 1908/1960, p. 146). I find this statement overly general and missing the purely adaptive nature of daydreaming and play, in which the very act of fantasizing provides a method for orienting oneself in the world and is often characterized by a sense of excitement and happiness. If indeed a happy person never fantasizes, as Freud suggests, then either no one is ever happy or satisfied people are living in a kind of dull blur. To the contrary, our hundreds of observations as well as the formal research studies we and others have conducted attest to the fact that imaginative play in childhood not only is practically adaptive but also is associated with consistent evidence of smiling, laughing, and satisfaction in the children who engage in such behavior.

Daydreaming, Thought Sampling, and Night Dreaming

I have so far focused primarily on the indications that daydreaming and fantasy are part of a broader range of ongoing thought processes and that they are not necessarily limited only to wish-fulfillment scenarios. In the article that I have taken as the text for this chapter, Freud (1908/1960) also hypothesized that night dreams were simply the continuation of the daytime fantasy process, with his caveat that some of the obscurities of the night dreams reflected the attempted repression and disguise of unacceptable daydreams. It was critical for him in relation to his recently published dream theory to assert "repressed wishes of this sort and their derivatives are only allowed to come to expression in a very distorted form" (Freud, 1908/1960, p. 149). His thinking at this point was that many daydreams may well be conscious initially as part of the normal thought stream, but that somehow, the individual becomes ashamed or threatened by them. This leads to a repression effort that emerges in the distortions of the night dream. Without getting into an extended discussion of the process of night dreaming, it is important to recognize that there has been a whole body of research that has questioned Freud's emphasis on the primarily symbolic and disguising nature of the night dream (Domhoff, 1996; Fisher & Greenberg, 1996).

In a recent updating of their extensive reviews of the theories of Freud, Fisher and Greenberg (1996) concluded that Freud's emphasis on a distinction between the manifest content of a dream and its latent content and also his hypothesis that a significant feature of dreams is an attempt to release tensions and repress conscious wishes has not been empirically supported. A collection of hundreds of night dreams (with extensive quantitative analyses of these) carried out by Domhoff (1996) concluded with the statement that the findings of many different studies as well as Domhoff's own work provide "good evidence for our claim that the conceptions and concerns found in dream content appear to be the same ones operating in waking life. The waking mind and the dreaming mind seem to be basically one and the same, which is a strong argument for the idea that there is meaning in dreams" (Domhoff, 1996, p. 189). The review presented by Fisher and Greenberg (1996) and the specific research carried out by Domhoff suggest that our waking fantasies and conscious concerns are reflected relatively directly in our night dreams, even though they may appear in forms not immediately obvious, perhaps because of the greatly reduced external stimulation that characterizes the sleeping state. Freud, of course, early on introduced the concept of "day-residues" as a clear determinant of night dreams. He was obviously much more involved with demonstrating that the night dreams served the wish-fulfillment objective that was so central to his thinking and that they also were involved in defensive processes against unconscious fantasies and (in his later theory) libidinal strivings usually from early childhood.

It is not my purpose in this chapter to discuss the extensive

psychophysiological research in the sleep cycle as well as quantitative research of dream content by investigators such as Antrobus
(1986, 1991, 1993a, 1993b), Domhoff (1996), and Foulkes (1985,
1993). What I would like to suggest is that more indications of
relatively clear continuities might be found if more samples of the
waking fantasies of individuals could be obtained through fairly
direct inquiry. One such approach is through thought sampling.

I would like at this point to introduce a brief case study of an
individual who simply volunteered to engage in a thought-
sampling exercise for a week. He was not a clinical patient and did
not have any extensive exposure to psychoanalytic theories or to
psychological therapy in general. What I suggest is that it may be
possible by using an approach of this kind to identify indications
of the day-residues that come together in predicting a vivid dream
by examining thought samples randomly obtained over a period
of several days.

Case Example: Mr. V's Dream

After a period of 5 days of using a paging device and writing down
as well as scoring in various ways his own ongoing thoughts, Mr.
V, an engineer for a high-tech corporation, reported that he had
the following night dream with which he woke on the last morning
that he was scheduled to engage in thought sampling:

> I seem to be in Canada visiting Bill, a younger man who is a
> former associate of mine in the company for which I now work.
> We are on an extremely steep mountain with snow all around.
> There are dozens of skiers who are coming down this incline
> with great speed. Often they seem to be taking long leaps before
> coming back down to earth, probably jumping moguls. Bill
> points upwards and says, "Let's keep walking up there and we
> can get some skis and ski down." I find myself appalled as I
> see the steepness of the mountain. As we climb higher, I become
> more and more aware that I am not a good enough skier to
> come down at the rate of the other skiers.
>
> I put on some skis and I am trying in my slow fashion to cut
> slowly sideways across the mountains, traversing, rather than
> schussing straight downhill as others are. I notice my friend Bill
> whizzing by with great confidence. Suddenly, however, he takes
> a very bad fall and lies in the snow, obviously having hurt his

leg. The scene seems to shift at that point so that I find myself visiting Bill and a younger man who now shares an apartment with him. I realize that both Bill and his new roommate have recently had marital problems and are living bachelor lives. I say to them that while I appreciate some of the advantages of bachelorhood, I am really quite happy with my own wife after 20 years of marriage.

Since we had 28 samples of waking thoughts for the 4 days before Mr. V reported this dream, it is possible to identify a number of themes from these thoughts and fantasies he reported. Specific events in which he was engaging are also relevant, as the reader will see.

Mr. V was a middle-aged man who was an executive in a well-established engineering firm. In his thoughts, he recurrently questioned seriously his ability to master some of the new required technologies, especially more advanced computer procedures and some new mathematical features of the work (reflected in the dream by schussing downhill). The firm had been moving into new areas of engineering with which he was less familiar. Some of his thoughts also involved his mental questioning or his fantasies about his intensive work for the company. He seemed to be wondering whether he could keep up the pace, considering his apparently diminished physical strength and skill in relation to the daily demands of this firm.

Several events in the 2 or 3 days prior to the dream had triggered some of these self-questioning thoughts. In one of them, he and his wife had set out on a quiet walk on a marked trail in the woods. They took the wrong path and, as it happened, ended up climbing a mountain or, probably more likely, a very steep hill. Once they had reached the top, they found themselves then having to retrace their steps down a very steep incline (the link to the steep ski mountain). Despite what seemed at times an impossible descent, they emerged finally at the base in the state park, apparently none the worse for this severe exercise.

During the evenings, a number of thought samples emerged that indicated that Mr. V had been watching the Winter Olympics on TV with his wife. He and his wife engaged in various conversations, and he also reported a number of thoughts and fantasies about the intensity and determination required for athletes to reach the levels of skill that they exhibited in the competition. He found himself fantasizing about whether he would ever wish to train so hard and so single-mindedly in order to attain such an Olympic skill.

The man's dream may now be understood in the context of the prior series of mental thoughts and brief fantasies that he had reported in the thought sampling. These thoughts included intense emotions at various points, which he rated along with the fantasies, as well as areas of what might be called unfinished business and current concerns. There were fears and doubts associated with his difficulty in maintaining the standards of scientific work as his company moved into new areas. In thinking about these, he reported thoughts about his colleague, Bill. Bill had always seemed to him more technically competent but had in recent years suffered significant setbacks at work and in his personal life. Indeed, Bill had found it necessary to transfer to another company despite his great technical skill. A new, younger colleague had joined the firm to replace Bill. He also showed greater technical computer skills than did Mr. V. At the same time, he showed a social immaturity as well as a lack of experience in maneuvering within the company, which emerged in some of Mr. V's thought samples. The dream thus seems to fade at some point into something like a wish, but one already clearly represented in the previous thoughts and fantasies reported. In effect, Mr. V seemed to be thinking in the dream, "Well, I can still climb that mountain, and I can also say that I have a more fulfilled personal life, even though I may not be at first glance as good a technical engineer [skier] as these guys."

It would seem therefore that the dream does indeed have an element of symbolism but that such symbolism was already foreshadowed by the thoughts produced during the actual climb of the high hill by Mr. V and his wife. He already had been thinking in competitive terms, as he reported in his thought samples obtained during and after the climb. Also, the dream metaphor of skiing clearly represents his observations of the Winter Olympics.

I have included this brief case example of how regularly accumulated waking samples of an individual's spontaneous thought randomly obtained by a beeper during the day may yield considerable information that might actually predict the nature of some of the person's dreams. What I am suggesting is that it is quite possible that had Mr. V not been carrying the pager and reporting materials on the spot, he might have largely forgotten (through interference by his other activities) many of the passing thoughts that accumulated over the period just before the night dream. It is possible that, were he in psychoanalysis, he might be a little more sensitive to such thoughts and might have recalled some of the day residues as part of the treatment. What I propose, however, is that even the more symbolic imagery of the night dream is already forecast by the daytime fantasies and ongoing thoughts of the individual. In this sense, I am making a case for the considerable importance of consciousness and for the role of consciousness in formulating the kind of material that emerges in the more "glamorous" form of nocturnal dreaming.

There are two important implications that I especially want to stress. One is that if we are serious about studying night dreams as representations of unconscious phenomena or, in Freud's famous term, as the "royal road to the unconscious," then it behooves us to sample daytime thought more extensively before drawing conclusions about unconscious fantasy or "long-buried" wishes as relevant to understanding night dreaming. It is certainly possible that, given a particular dream, one can, as so often happens in psychoanalysis, free associate indefinitely and of course produce many memories and associations that link one's thoughts further and further back in time. This is essentially using the dream as a projective technique, however, that simply stimulates sequences of memories.

A second possibility that emerges from the use of waking thought samples and of paging devices may have practical importance for clinicians. We see patients only a few times a week, and much happens in between. Why ought we not expect them, for at least periods of time, to carry paging devices and to report their thoughts as they accumulate and the context of such thoughts? We rely too heavily on the retrospective ability of the patient to produce such material during a therapy session. Would not more data accumulated over the week be valuable? Patients use a variety of monitors for cardiac functioning and wear them over periods of time. "Behavioral paging," if anything, is a simpler procedure and could have considerable value for therapists.

In the case of Mr. V, the opportunity to keep track of his own thoughts and then to see them expressed in a more dramatic and vivid form in the night dream reported led him to serious reconsideration of his own work situation. He decided that he was becoming increasingly frustrated by his vocational limitations, which had been produced as a result of the younger man's surpassing him quickly in the sophisticated use of computers for information retrieving, imaging of various structures, and mathematical analysis. As a result, he moved into a facet of his company where his administrative skills and longer social experience had particular value.

Schemas and Self-Representations in Relation to Daydreaming and Ongoing Conscious Thought

Data from reports, interviews, and questionnaire research suggest that people daydream mostly about themselves in varying situations. Although it is true that most people do not actually "picture" themselves, since they "see" themselves ordinarily only in mirrors, they usually actively participate in the plots of their fantasies and dreams (Domhoff, 1996). Daydreams about oneself in various social settings may be some of the building blocks for the formation of those organized mental structures that cognitive psychology has labeled *schemas* and *scripts*. Even before these constructs had been formally developed, I directed research that examined whether ways that people thought of themselves in relation to parental figures might influence patterns of daydreaming and functions such as creativity or achievement motivation. In several studies (J. L. Singer & McCraven, 1961; J. Singer & Schonbar, 1961), my colleagues and I had middle-class adults from a variety of ethnic backgrounds respond to questionnaires as their actual selves, as their ideal selves, and then as they thought their fathers or their mothers might answer the same list of questions for themselves. By scoring the degree of difference between one's own set of responses and those perceived for the parent, we assessed the degree of identification with a particular parental figure. We found that where one was more closely identified with one's mother, there was a somewhat greater tendency for producing daydreaming in both men and women. This may have reflected the more traditional family style of that period (the 1940s and 1950s) when mothers were more likely to be at home and also more likely to be the family storytellers while fathers went to work and reflected a life of outside action rather than imagination. We also developed a measure in which the discrepancy between self and father in response to questionnaires was related to the discrepancy between the self and mother so that a simple formula ([S-F]−[S-M])—for example, the greater distance from father and greater closeness to mother—would predict, for example, a positive relationship to reports of daydreaming or creativity. Our findings in general supported the hypothesized relationships (J. L. Singer & McCraven, 1961; J. Singer & Schonbar, 1961).

More recently, Tory Higgins (1987) developed an elaborate and testable theory of self-schemas or, as he termed them, "self-guides." This work is important because by linking the views of the self with schemas, one can use the highly efficient retrieval capacity both of schemas and of self-relevant material as well as consider for clinical purposes the biasing effects of self-referential schemas and scripts (J. A. Singer & J. L. Singer, 1994; J. L. Singer, 1985; J. L. Singer & Salovey, 1991). The importance of self-focus is manifested in studies of thought sampling and ongoing conscientiousness (Klos & Singer, 1981; J. L. Singer & Bonanno, 1990). Experiments on memory also attest to the importance of self-relevant material in incidental recall and in autobiographical recollection (Klein & Kihlstrom, 1986; Kreitler & J. L. Singer, 1991; J. A. Singer & Salovey, 1993). The motivational role of the ways in which one conceives of "possible selves" is also shown in other studies of Ruvolo and Markus (1992).

The cognitive conservatism that characterizes schematic structures, that is, the tendency to try to stick to one's schemas, sometimes at all costs, may also account not only for the phenomenon of transference in therapy (J. A. Singer & J. L. Singer, 1994; J. L. Singer, 1985) but also for the persistence of self-schemas in the face of contrary evidence and even after much therapeutic effort has been expended. Such conservativism in self-schemas not only was identified by Freud in his wistful paper, "Analyses Terminable and Interminable" (Freud, 1937/1959), but also was reflected by Sullivan (1956) in his recognition that self-concepts proved especially resistant to change in psychotherapy.

Self-representation both is the key product of a schematic memory system and also may be a critical feature of a life narrative. Explicit memories of how one has been treated by other people, of what one wants in different situations, and of how one behaved in dozens of settings form often enough an extremely dense and complex network for the general memory associative structure. Self-relevance generally yields a powerful effect in studies of memory. The study by Kreitler and Singer (1991) demonstrated that young adults were more likely to recall self-relevant lists of words, compared with words presented either as relevant to another person or under various other controlled conditions. Especially interesting was a personality measure of self-complexity that also correlated with the frequency of word recall under the self-relevant conditions.

It seems likely, as William James (1890/1950) long ago suggested, that one is prone to an awareness more of multiple self-representations than of a single "core" self. James had already identified the actual self and ideal self difference, or the actual self and possible self representations in his chapter on self, which incidentally was closely associated in his two-volume work with the chapter on the stream of thought. The experimental research of Markus and Nurius (1986) on possible selves has shown how some of James' conceptions can be translated into operational forms suitable for experimental and clinical study within a social cognition framework. The actual self versus an ideal self, or the actual self versus the beliefs about one's mother's or father's likely self-ratings have also been shown to yield discriminating psychological predictions. The research program initiated by Higgins (1987) within a social cognition orientation perhaps operationalizes most effectively some key elements of what might be called Freud's superego into the so-called self-guides of *actual self, ideal self, ought self,* and their relationships. Thus, the actual-self–ideal-self discrepancy (measured by scoring respondents' descriptions of each self-representation) identifies the degree of gap between a currently perceived functioning self and an ideally desired personal representation. This work has been especially effective in demonstrating how discrepancies between the actual and the ideal self-representations are linked to depression and saddened moods, whereas discrepancies between the actual self and the ought or socially obligatory self are linked to agitation and social anxiety (Strauman, 1992, 1994; Strauman & Higgins, 1988). Even more remarkable are the dramatic findings of Strauman linking these discrepancies between actual and ideal or ought selves to the functioning of the "psychologically silent" immune system of the individual (Strauman, Lemieux, & Coe, 1993).

I will describe briefly two very recent studies in which a group of us have sought to examine the concept of discrepancies between various self-representations using the Higgins method and a great variety of measures of personality and emotion (Garfinkle, 1994; Hart, Field, J. L. Singer, & Garfinkle, 1997). We also sought in these studies to examine the self-representations as measured initially with the ongoing thought of the individual over a week's time as measured through thought samples.

We initially tested more than 100 young Yale students, although some of the data to be reported reflect smaller sample sizes because of missing data or failure to complete all questionnaires. Student participants in those studies were recruited from courses in introductory psychology and personality. They were paid for participation, but they generally showed considerable interest in the whole process of responding to questionnaires and filling out daily paging forms. Comparison with nonparticipants showed no evidence of biasing tendencies in these samples. The respondents listed the traits or characteristics that they saw as representing their actual selves, their ideal selves, their ought selves, and their undesired selves. By looking at the relationship between the lists of up to 10 traits under each of these categories, we determined how close actual self was to ideal self, to ought selves, and to undesired self, and we created a quantitative score. We also asked these individuals to answer a number of other questionnaires designed to measure the so-called Big Five Personality Traits (Neuroticism, Extroversion, Agreeableness, Conscientiousness, and Openness; Costa & McCrae, 1985, 1989). This measure is designed to determine the extent to which well-established personality traits are associated in a systematic way with the measures of proximities or discrepancies between the different self-representations. In addition, we included measures of anxiety, depression, self-esteem, and interpersonal problems that are well standardized and have been widely studied in the research literature.

A unique feature of the study was that in addition to these approaches, we required our participants to carry paging devices for a week's time. They were interrupted randomly during the day and had to complete forms at the point of interruption, describing their situation when interrupted, the specific thoughts they had been having, and their moods associated with the period just at the point of interruption. In this way, we hoped to determine whether the measure of proximities between actual self and other self representations such as ideal, ought, or undesired might predict the ongoing thoughts of individuals as sampled over a week's time.

Table 1, which is drawn in modified form from the study published in detail elsewhere by Hart et al. (1997), provides the actual correlations obtained. For the thought samples, we accumulated the content reports and rated these along a number of dimensions, which appear in the table. One variable was based on indications in the thoughts and fantasies of the individuals that they sustained a positive evaluation of self. Ratings of their moods or emotions at the same point in time yielded measures of positive affect, lethargic or depressed affect, and calm affect.

In keeping with Higgins and Strauman's work, we first sought to determine the extent to which a proximity or discrepancy between actual and ideal would be linked differentially to self-reported depression and anxious emotionality and symptomatology. As can be seen from Table 1, the proximity between one's actual self-representation and one's ideal self-representation correlates significantly and negatively with neuroticism and also with anxiety and depression. In other words, the closer respondents had rated their actual and ideal selves, the less they were likely to be reporting neurotic, fearful, or sad traits on the Big Five questionnaire. On a separately developed measure of self-esteem (the Rosenberg Scale), there are predicted significant positive correlations between the relationship of a reported high proximity between actual self-representation and ideal self-representation. Regarding the kinds of interpersonal problems reported by these participants, those who showed a high actual–ideal discrepancy also reported

Table 1

Correlations of Proximity Measures to the Personality Measures

	Proximity to actual self		
Personality measure	AI	AO	AU
NEO-PI FFI			
Neuroticism[a]	−.41**	−.42**	.41**
Extraversion[b]	.41**	.40**	−.30*
Agreeableness[c]	.40**	.37**	−.51**
Conscientiousness[a]	.13	.14	−.05
Openness[a]	−.15	−.17	.15
Spielberger Trait-Anxiety			
Anxiety[c]	−.52***	−.53***	.48***
Beck Depression Inventory			
Depression[b]	−.36**	−.41**	.35**
Rosenberg Self-Esteem			
Self-Esteem[a]	.44**	.44**	−.46***
Experience-Sampling			
Positive View of Self[d]	.42***	.39**	−.29*
Positive Affect[e]	.33**	.36**	−.33**
Lethargic Affect[e]	−.26*	−.29*	.27*
Calm Affect[e]	.28*	.30*	−.35*

Note. AI = Actual−ideal; AO = actual−ought; AU = actual−undesired. From "Representations of Self and Others: A Semantic Space Model," by D. Hart, N. Field, J. L. Singer, and J. Garfinkle, 1997, *Journal of Personality, 65*, pp. 93 −94. Copyright 1997 by Duke University Press. Adapted with permission. [a]n = 64. [b]n = 65. [c]n = 63. [d]n = 66. [e]n = 68. *$p < .05$ **$p < .01$ ***$p < .001$.

more overall difficulties in interpersonal relationships and particularly for responsibility, intimacy, and submissiveness.

To what degree do proximities between actual and ideal views of self recur in the ongoing thought of the individual? From the accumulation of daily thought samples for the participants, there was a clearly significant correlation between these daily reports (which included fantasies of a positive nature involving the self) and the similarity between the actual self and the ideal self as tested weeks before.

Self-ratings of moods during the thought sampling are also consistent with the closeness between actual self and ideal self. There are positive correlations with positive emotionality and calm emotionality, and a negative association with a lethargic or melancholic mood. It might be argued that associations between the self-representations and the personality trait variables, especially neuroticism and extroversion, could account for the findings that emerge in thought sampling (i.e., those persons already given to being outgoing or to being neurotic might simply carry over their style of reporting to thought sampling). We conducted various analyses to see if the self-representation measures still correlated with thought samples even when the scores that these participants had obtained on the personality traits were partialed out or dealt with through multiple regression analyses. When the correlations between the actual–ideal-self proximity scores and the personality trait variables were considered, the self-representations still contributed significantly to the prediction of ongoing thought patterns (e.g., to greater positive view of self, more daily positive mood states). The actual-self–ought-self proximity predicted positive emotionality, whereas the actual–undesired (AU) self predicted agitated rather than calm affect as reported in the participant's daily thoughts. These results were also sustained effectively when we examined the data for only those participants who were able to complete 40 or more of the 49 samples accumulated across the week.

This particular study involved numerous analyses more generally related to personality psychology. The concern here is to examine how one's thoughts and fantasies bear on a relatively conscious view of one's actual self and one's ideal self. Thus, one could argue, as I have suggested earlier in this chapter, that people are almost continuously engaging in thoughts or daydreams that involve judgments about their own actual traits and, quite possibly, how these relate to ideal or socially expected patterns. One might propose that the actual–ideal (AI) and actual–ought (AO) are both forms of the psychoanalytic notion of ego ideal and a punitive superego. Higgins and Strauman in their work have indeed related these representations to earlier childhood experiences in which the parent was perceived as either providing positive reinforcement or providing systematic punishment of one kind or another (Strauman, 1992). These findings can also be linked to the more general concepts of superego and ego ideal. However, there is only limited advantage in referring to such vaguely defined concepts as superego and ego when there are available relatively precisely defined operational terms such as Higgins' self-guides that can be applied directly both in experimental research and, as I shall shortly show, in clinical usage.

The data from a large-scale study such as that conducted by Hart et al. (1997) do not answer the issue of causality in determining ongoing conscious thought of such self-representations. Working with me, Garfinkle (1994) investigated whether intensifying "normal" individuals' awareness of the discrepancy between an actual and an ideal self-representation or an actual and an ought self-representation would influence their ongoing thought as sampled over a week's time.

Effects of Priming Awareness of Self-Discrepant Self-Representations on Ongoing Conscious Thought

Garfinkle (1994) and I tested the hypotheses concerning self-representation and ongoing thought processes. Building on the work of Strauman and Higgins (1993), we proposed that participants whose actual selves were considerably discrepant from either their ideal or their ought selves would be likely to notice negative emotions (dejection and agitation, respectively) more frequently in their day-to-day lives than would participants for whom the actual self is close to the ideal and ought selves. We were especially interested in the continuities across ongoing experiences and therefore sought conditions in which individuals with different discrepancies (compared with "yoked controls") would indicate a heightening of an already demonstrated discrepancy through an experimental intervention. Thus, we used groups identified as either *discrepant* or *nondiscrepant* from their self, ideal, and ought ratings. Several weeks after this rating and after completing the same questionnaires described earlier in the Hart et al. (1997) study, they were exposed to an experimental intervention. This was based in part on the method employed in the Klos and Singer (1981) study. Groups were formed of those individuals who showed a high AI discrepancy but a modest AO discrepancy; those who showed a high AO discrepancy and an average AI discrepancy; and finally, those who showed no significant discrepancies at all. These groups were then put into situations in which individuals were asked to imagine a discussion with their "better self" involving a kind of "coercive confrontation" (e.g., a parent trying to win an argument or expressing disapproval of the person while listening to his or her point of view). If the study involved the parent, the task should be activating the ought-self mismatch, especially when used in conjunction with an issue raised by a trait word that had been part of each specific participant's mismatch between actual and ought words. In the AO situation, participants should feel that they had not lived up to the state that a parent and the participant both believed was a personal obligation or duty to fulfill. A series of such simulations occurred.

AI mismatches had to involve the use of an "inner voice" or "part of yourself that is wisest and most insightful." In this way, the AI mismatch trait words used in this self-conversation created a powerful feeling that the individual was not living up to a highly desired state. To create the dialogues as effectively as possible, each trial began with questions such as that posed by a "parent" as read to the participant by an experimenter, beginning with, "Why aren't you more _____?"(for an AO mismatch). A self word was inserted here drawn from the participant's own listing so that this question would ring especially true.

For the AI mismatch trials, the inner voice began with a question such as, "Why is it so important for you to be _____?" where again, a trait chosen from the ideal-self listing of each individual was involved.

On the basis of earlier work by Strauman (1989), eight dialogues were drawn up. The critical dialogues were those in which respondents imagined an inner voice questioning them about two attributes drawn from their own earlier ideal-self listing that did not coincide with their own actual-self listed attributes. These self-referential AI mismatches presumably heightened the participants' awareness of an actual-self versus ideal-self discrepancy.

For those participants who had no AI mismatches, ideal-self attributes that neither matched nor mismatched any actual-self attribute ("none-match" attributes) were used. In all cases, only attributes unique to the ideal-self state (i.e., not also listed as part of another self-state) were selected. A similar procedure was used for the AO mismatches. For yoked AI mismatches, the participant was presented with attributes that were drawn from the list of a *different* participant. The attributes used had not been included in the target individual's own questionnaire responses. These words were used as primes for an inner-voice dialogue. A similar procedure was used for the yoked AO mismatches.

The priming trials, that is, the simulated or imagined confrontational dialogues, were presented in random order to control for sequence effects. The experimenter was also blind to each participant's order of presentations. The yoked trials were necessary because it was important to test an alternative hypothesis that priming effects might themselves be due to the specific content of the attributes rather than to the activation of a self-relevant mismatch (Strauman, 1989). After participants had signed an informed consent, they were asked to complete a mood checklist to estimate emotions just prior to the primings situation. After this, instructions were then repeated and the role-playing situation began. Immediately following priming, participants were also asked to answer the mood questionnaire. On the next day, they began their 7 days of carrying paging devices with questionnaires on which they filled out their mood states. Some also completed dream logs to examine continuity in dream mood as well as in mood of daytime thought.

As it turned out, 71% of the 49 experience-sampling record sheets were handed in, with an average of 4.0 of the 7 daily dream reports. Missing experience-sampling questionnaires occurred for several reasons. Some participants had initially been told that they could leave their pagers when they were taking showers or napping or especially in intimate moments such as going to the toilet. Other situations in the participant's lives, such as sleeping late, also produced missing records because they conflicted inherently with the procedures. In some instances, participants could not take part in the study for a day or so because they were involved in athletic events.

No gender differences were found for the 113 participants in this phase of the experiment. Results are reported with combined men and women. Specific statistical analyses are too complex to report in this chapter and may be found in Garfinkle (1994).

Despite the clarity in differentiation between the three groups in performance initially, once the priming experience was begun, the results showed general similarity between the AI and AO groups, compared with controls. From a detailed step-by-step analysis of these data, it was clear that those individuals who were exposed to a discrepancy between their representations of actual selves and either their ideal or their ought selves and who also underwent the priming experience demonstrated clear differences from yoked controls. These participants' daily logs *decreased* in positive affect reports and indicated *increases* in the more negative, lethargic (depressed) moods as well as *decreases* in the calm (less agitated) mood state. This was an especially strong effect for those individuals with large AI discrepancies. Over time, they showed rather consistent increases in negative mood and in more agitation or depressed affect. The AO group followed generally closely behind, both groups tending to be significantly more affected by the priming situation than were the control groups.

These data indicate that the schematic structure of relatively conscious differences experienced between one's actual self-representation and one's ideal self-representation, and between one's actual and one's ought representation significantly influence questionnaire ratings of depressed mood or of tendencies toward agitation. These schematic structures, especially when primed, are influential over a week's time period. The ongoing conscious thoughts of individuals, as tapped by the 7 daily interruptions over a week's time, do indeed reflect the "chronic" self-representations as measured in the fashion developed by Higgins.

Garfinkle was also interested in whether mood continuities reflected in the daytime thoughts of the individual would show a continuity with night dream reports as measured by daily logs of night dreams kept by the participants during the same period. The dreams were analyzed in much the same way as daytime reports for evidence of mood. As it turned out, there was no indication that the moods of the dreams reflected the daytime mood reports. Indeed, they showed no differences overall in mood ratings. This may suggest that dream material is indeed not continuous with daytime thoughts, at least for the emotionality expressed in the material. This might seem at first to contradict the proposal I made in the case of the engineer I described earlier. As it turns out, the critical issue in that case related to content resemblances. This is similar to the report of Domhoff (1996). Garfinkle's study did not score actual content and current concerns and their relation to the content of the night dreams. Nevertheless, there is indeed a puzzle. One would hope that more detailed studies both of content and affective reactions would be feasible. Questionnaire studies of day-dreaming styles have shown continuity with the affective patterns of night dream reports in studies by Starker (1974, 1977, 1982, 1984–1985) and Starker and J. L. Singer (1975).

In summary, although Garfinkle's strenuous experimental approach offered evidence that self-discrepant representational schemas when heightened by priming of their key elements will lead to a persistence of negative affective thoughts over a week's time, the more specific distinctions between the ideal self and the ought self which had been proposed by Higgins (1987) did not emerge for this sample of about 100 participants. The concern in this chapter is not so much with the specific tests of the Higgins–Strauman hypotheses but with indicating that relatively accessible, conscious self-ratings and ongoing waking thoughts are linked and have emotional consequences. In the next section, I will discuss how the current findings about conscious self-representations and their relationship to the stream of thought actually influenced my own psychotherapeutic efforts.

Self-Ratings as a Therapeutic Focus: Two Case Studies

During the period between about 1983 and 1995, I had been involved as a senior scientist in the development and in various phases of the execution of the MacArthur Foundation–sponsored Program on Conscious and Unconscious Mental Processes (directed by Mardi Horowitz at the University of California, San Francisco School of Medicine). The project included not only experimental and large-scale empirical studies such as that by Hart et al. (1997) but also involved following patients seen in therapy through the use of videotaping and psychophysiological measurement. These records of patient–therapist interaction were then subjected to extensive analyses using Horowitz's Role Relationship Model Configural Analysis. Descriptions of this work and the general approach have appeared elsewhere (Horowitz, 1991; Horowitz, Eells, J. L. Singer, & Salovey, 1995). In the analyses of the therapeutic sessions carried out by teams at Yale and San Francisco, we attempted to identify formal schemas produced by individuals in the course of their conscious presentations to the therapists. Thus, we would score statements such as, "I believe I am . . ." or "I think that my parents expected me . . ." or "That's the way people are, they . . .". These organized belief systems or schemas of self and others were identified and accumulated over five sessions of therapy. Frequency counts provided actual self-representations, forms of ideal self-representations, dreaded selves, or socially expected selves. This work, along with the more large-scale empirical work described earlier, led me to believe that one might increase the efficiency of therapeutic interactions by having patients complete trait lists of actual, ideal, and ought representations right at the start of the therapy.

As a clinical psychologist trained further in an interpersonal psychoanalytic institute, I have practiced psychodynamically informed psychotherapy for more than 40 years. At the same time, my own research and my continuing exposure to the psychological advances in experimentation and theory on cognition and emotion, as well as my awareness of psychoanalytic shifts from classical through ego psychology and now to relational theory, led me to reexamine my own concepts and practice. The emergence of cognitive–behavioral therapy, initially spurred by the great two-volume work of George Kelly (1955) with its demonstrated effectiveness, forced me to reexamine my own work with clients. Even psychoanalytically derived systematic studies such as those led by Horowitz (1991) and by Weiss, Sampson, and the Mount Zion Psychotherapy Research Group (1986) provided indications that cognitive structures, not unlike Kelly's personal constructs, that were fairly accessible to therapeutic inquiry provided the key to therapeutic intervention. My own research on daydreaming had also led me to the conclusion that more of one's self-defeating fantasies or beliefs were reasonably available to consciousness and were rehearsed in one's ongoing stream of thought. Long-standing psychoanalytic concepts such as unconscious fantasies or very early childhood repressed memories were hard if not impossible to demonstrate scientifically or even to prove as manifest in psychoanalytic therapy. It seemed worthwhile, therefore, to adopt a more direct effort to address neurotic or self-defeating belief systems. One could still stay in the framework of a psychodynamic, relational framework by paying careful attention to issues of transference and countertransference and by fostering free-associative responses whenever possible from the patient.

In a somewhat cognitively oriented therapeutic intervention with a cocaine-dependent patient (Mr. D), Kelly Avants, Arthur Margolin, and I had used not only an initial set of ratings on self-representations by the client but had then used daily logs that were completed during the 10 weeks of therapy and that incorporated the patients' various self-representations. These ranged from desired ideal self through the "addict" self (Avants, Margolin, & J. L. Singer, 1994).

Case Example: Mr. D

In one case, the patient, Mr. D, included attributes such as "being honest with myself and others," "being open and receptive," "feeling centered," "being warm toward others," "setting goals," "being stable and responsible," "communicating my feelings," and "letting people get close." During each therapy session, he worked at making these selected attributes concrete. He did this by identifying specific behaviors that would reflect each of these traits mentioned, and he attempted to role-play how he might manifest such behaviors in situations involving significant people in his environment. This patient kept daily logs and complied with the proposal to engage in specific behaviors that involved reconciling himself with a family member with whom he had quarreled; studying for his high school equivalency examination; arranging to obtain a driver's license; and taking specific steps to maintain his job, which had become endangered by his previous drug use. These behaviors were mentally reenacted by him during the day, even as he engaged in specific overt actions. His daily log documented the steps he took each day and his carrying out of his "homework" of role-playing in preparation for them. At the conclusion of the 10-week treatment, Mr. D was actually shown the lists of words he had generated early in treatment. He rerated them on a 5-point scale for his experience of each of the self-representations during the previous week. His sense of being addicted had disappeared as measured by the rating. It was also verified through toxicology screens and by his exposure to certain "drug triggers." He had returned to school to prepare himself further for his high school examination, had reconciled himself with the estranged family member, and was continuing his relationship with this individual. During the previous weeks, he had applied for and obtained a driver's license, and his job performance was being well received.

Considering that this young man had been a drug abuser for 16 years, the progress made in the approximately 3 months of treatment by Dr. Avants was extremely impressive. It strongly suggests that careful attention to the schemas that people carry with them about their various forms of self may be critical in establishing a therapeutic focus.

In my own part-time clinical practice, I began to propose to patients that they list the traits or characteristics that they themselves linked to their actual, ideal, ought, and dreaded selves at the very beginning of the treatment. My patients, admittedly individuals of high intelligence and achievement in business and professional activities, were quite willing to engage in this process. Once they listed these traits (only important ones were requested), one could calculate the proximities or discrepancies between the actual self and the other self-representations. Because of my long experience in encouraging the use of concrete images, memories, and fantasies as part of an ongoing treatment process, the patients were also encouraged to visualize specific scenes or settings in which these behaviors were reflected. The patients were also encouraged to keep daily logs of their awareness of various self-representations in the course of their activities and ongoing thoughts.

Case Example: Mr. L

One example that I offer in a disguised form is that of Mr. L, a successful lawyer who was a partner in a specialized but very busy law firm. Mr. L had come to see me because he was experiencing a mixture of both depressive and anxious symptoms, which he attributed chiefly to the stresses of his work and also to a conflictual relationship with the senior partner in the firm.

Mr. L was in his early thirties and had been relatively recently married. He and his wife had two very young children. His wife was supportive throughout treatment, and his personal relationship with her seemed excellent. Mr. L was clearly intelligent, well educated, and seemingly gifted in his profession. He had risen relatively quickly to the partnership; in the course of his attaining greater significance in the firm, however, he became more and more distressed by the continuing pressure for productivity, which he felt often led to some marginally ethical practices on the part of the leadership of the firm.

Mr. L agreed to complete the list of self-representations shown in Exhibit 1. He then began by producing a series of memories and also fantasies about these various personality traits and characteristics over the 20 sessions that followed. He was the son of a physician who had amassed a sizable fortune through a combination of a very "high-quantity" practice and his keen business skill in real estate investment. After he had filled out the ought-self listing, Mr. L quickly noticed how much pressure he felt from his father to be extremely successful financially. This also was reflected in the dreaded self representations. In our twice weekly meetings, Mr. L also associated various memories and fantasies to the self-representations that he had initially provided, and he reported on events occurring daily through the logs he was keeping. Mr. L recognized more and more that the work stress he was experiencing seemed to reflect a transference response from his relationship with his father to the firm's senior partner, a man who shared at least some of the same financially driven qualities that Mr. L perceived in his own father. One can see how Mr. L's insight supports Higgins' views of the agitation associated with AO discrepancies in this circumstance. At the same time, a glance at the ideal-self listings indicates that there was a larger discrepancy between actual and ideal for this man. Especially striking were those aspirations for "respect," "leadership," "intellectual," and "scientist," among others. This discrepancy was reflected also in periodic episodes of sadness in addition to the anxiety and agitation. The daily logs presented by this young man called attention primarily to

Exhibit 1

List of Self Traits Provided by Mr. L at the Outset of Treatment

Actual self	Ideal self	Ought self	Dreaded self
Kind	Respected	Efficient	Failure
Humorous	Leader	Physical/athletic	Bankrupt
Chubby	Intellectual	Financial success	Unethical
Responsible	Scientist	Good business sense	Stupid
Nervous	Calm	Family leader	Loser
Fearful	Courageous	Devoted son	Weakling
Submissive	Assertive	Fast worker	Disbarred
Loving husband	Family man	Productive	Mediocre
Loving father	Self-assertive	Good team manager	Unable to hold family
Incompetent	Independent	Practical	Clown
Poor business sense	Specialist	Slim	

situations in which his own productivity in handling larger numbers of cases was being questioned by his boss and by another partner who was to some extent his rival. The quality of his work was not an issue, but there was pressure on him to handle and to locate more and more cases than he felt were appropriate to sustain a high quality of performance.

There was a critical turn in the treatment when as he sat working on his log one evening, he also found himself watching a TV movie. The story involved a young man who had been subjected to years of exploitation and public humiliation by an older sibling. The climax of the film came when the younger brother killed his older brother. As he was making a note of this experience, Mr. L suddenly began to weep and could not stop for some time.

In telling me about this on the following day, Mr. L once again began to weep. Actually, I had seen that same movie on TV the previous night, so I could appreciate the power of the story itself. What I did not know and what Mr. L revealed to me only later in the session was that this plot was surprisingly similar to a set of experiences he had had with an older sibling. We had to work through some resistance that he felt in telling me this story, a transference response to me as an authority figure and as a much older man. Once he was able to voice this resistance, he could then tell me about his own experience of teasing, physical abuse, and torment that he had received over many years from an older brother. This brother had often mocked him, sometimes actually supported by the patient's father, because he was at that time obese and also rather timid. What began to emerge as we reviewed these memories and their relation to his sense of self was that he had been systematically suppressing some of his own sense of independent thought and a considerable amount of intellectual curiosity that he had in his specialized law field in the interests of trying to meet the expectations of his father. This suppression was in part a carryover from his brother's bullying and the need to show that he could be "strong" by earning a good deal of money. In actuality, his brother was at this point a petty criminal and apparently a long-standing sociopath whose life was at a dead end in sharp contrast with Mr. L's. Mr. L after all had not only a successful career but a satisfying marriage and a very respectable family life.

As Mr. L reviewed his actual and ideal self-representations

through images of various possibilities and waking fantasies, he began to propose that these might be reconciled if he asserted himself more clearly to his boss at the firm. He tried this on a few occasions where he saw a clear-cut issue and found that these yielded good results. To his surprise, he was listened to and not mocked or humiliated. The success was reflected in his reexamining his own intellectual ambitions. He realized that his interests lay more in the theoretical and scholarly aspects of his specialized legal work. He then began to take steps to determine if he could move into academic law. When he tried this, he found within a very short time that his skills were quickly appreciated. It took some personal courage and considerable support from his wife for him to consider giving up his more lucrative practice. At the same time, as he moved along toward this new career, he experienced a great sense of autonomy and also a sense of relief from what he perceived as a more calm and reflective lifestyle.

What finally emerged was that our joint focusing in on his self-representations led this man to experience an increasing proximity between actual and ideal self. At the same time, he realized that his anxiety about the discrepancy between the actual and the ought self was illusory. It had been associated with early humiliation contrary to his own most cherished personal ideals. One might paraphrase in this case Freud's own dictum, "Where Id was, there shall Ego be," to say instead, "Where Superego was, there shall Ego and Ego-Ideal emerge."

A Final Word: Consciousness Counts

My goal in this chapter has been to call attention to the fact that ongoing conscious thought as reflected in reworking one's own memories, daydreaming about a range of daily life possibilities and current concerns, and various forms of self-representation are the stuff from which the preconscious, cognitive, and so-called dynamic unconscious features of mental processing draw their contents. The often fleeting daily fantasies, mental glosses on passing events, and even metaphors or symbols constructed by day may find their way into nocturnal dreams, slips of the tongue, or social behavior in a fashion that *seems* to come from an unconscious domain. I propose, however, that a great deal of the priming of seemingly out-of-awareness reactivity may be an outcome of the overlearning of various cognitive and affective schemas and scripts, first practiced consciously and then automatized to emerge as if without conscious effort (J. A. Singer & J. L. Singer, 1994; J. L. Singer & Salovey, 1991). The renewed interest of philosophers and neuroscientists in the human phenomenon of consciousness may be a welcome step in alerting psychoanalysts to the significance of what people think about all day long in the waking state.

References

Algom, D., & Singer, J. L. (1984–1985). Interpersonal influences on task-irrelevant thought and imagery in a signal detection experiment. *Imagination, Cognition, and Personality, 4*, 69–83.

Antrobus, S. (1968). Information theory and stimulus-independent thought. *British Journal of Psychology, 59*, 423–430.

Antrobus, J. S. (1986). Dreaming: Cortical activation and perceptual thresholds. *The Journal of Mind and Behavior, 7*, 193–212.

Antrobus, J. S. (1991). Dreaming: Cognitive processes during cortical activation and high afferent threshold. *Psychological Review, 98*, 96–121.

Antrobus, J. S. (1993a). Dreaming: Could we do without it? In A. Moffitt, M. Kramer, & R. Hoffman (Eds.), *The functions of dreaming* (pp. 200–222). Albany, NY: State University of New York Press.

Antrobus, J. S. (1993b). Thinking away and ahead. In H. Morowitz & J. L. Singer (Eds.), *The mind, the brain and complex adaptive systems* (pp. 155–174). New York: Addison-Wesley.

Antrobus, J. S., Coleman, R., & Singer, J. L. (1967). Signal detection performance by subjects differing in predisposition to daydreaming. *Journal of Consulting Psychology, 31*, 487–491.

Antrobus, J. S., Singer, J. L., Goldstein, S., & Fortgang, M. (1970). Mind-wandering and cognitive structure. *Transactions of the New York Academy of Science* (Series 11), *32*, 242–252.

Antrobus, J. S., Singer, J. L., & Greenberg, S. (1966). Studies in the stream of consciousness: Experimental enhancement and suppression of spontaneous cognitive process. *Perceptual and Motor Skills, 23*, 399–417.

Avants, S. K., Margolin, A., & Singer, J. L. (1994). Self-reevaluation therapy: A cognitive intervention for the chemically dependent patient. *Psychology of Addictive Behaviors, 8*(4), 214–222.

Baars, B. (1988). *A cognitive theory of consciousness.* Cambridge, England: Cambridge University Press.

Baars, B. (1993). How does a serial, integrated and very limited stream of consciousness emerge from a nervous system that is mostly unconscious, distributed, parallel and of enormous capacity? In Ciba Foundation Symposium 174, *Experimental and theoretical studies of consciousness* (pp. 291–302). New York: Wiley.

Blatt, S. (1990). Interpersonal relatedness and self definition: Two personality configurations and their implications for psychopathology and psychotherapy. In J. L. Singer (Ed.), *Repression and dissociation.* Chicago: University of Chicago Press.

Campagna, A. F. (1985–1986). Fantasy and sexual arousal in college men: Normative and functional aspects. *Imagination, Cognition, and Personality, 5,* 3–20.

Costa, P. T., & McCrae, R. R. (1985). *The NEO Personality Inventory manual.* Odessa, FL: Psychological Assessment Resources.

Costa, P., & McCrae, R. (1989). *NEO PI/FFI: Manual supplement.* Odessa, FL: Psychological Assessment Resources.

Csikszentmihalyi, M., & Larson, R. (1987). The experience sampling method: Toward a systematic phenomenology. *Journal of Nervous and Mental Disease, 175,* 526–536.

Dennett, D. (1991). *Consciousness explained.* Boston: Little, Brown.

Domhoff, G. (1996). *Finding meaning in dreams.* New York: Plenum.

Erdelyi, M. H. (1985). *Psychoanalysis: Freud's cognitive psychology.* New York: Freeman.

Fisher, S., & Greenberg, R. (1996). *Freud scientifically appraised.* New York: Wiley.

Foulkes, D. (1985). *Dreaming: A cognitive–psychological analysis.* Hillsdale, NJ: Erlbaum.

Foulkes, D. (1993). Data constraints on theorizing about dream function. In A. Moffitt, M. Kramer, & R. Hoffman (Eds.), *The Functions of Dreaming.* Albany, NY: State University of New York Press.

Freud, A. (1959). *The ego and the mechanisms of defense.* London: Hogarth Press. (Original work published 1937)

Freud, S. (1960). Creative writers and day-dreaming. In J. L. Strachey (Ed. and Trans.), *The standard edition of the complete psychological works of Sigmund Freud* (Vol. 9, pp. 141–154). London: Hogarth Press. (Original work published 1908)

Freud, S. (1962). Formulations regarding the two principles of mental functioning. In *The standard edition of the complete psychological works of Sigmund Freud* (Vol. 12, pp. 218–226). London: Hogarth Press. (Original work published 1911)

Garfinkle, J. R. (1994). *Discrepant representations of self: Relations to personality, emotion and continuous mood.* Unpublished doctoral dissertation, Yale University, New Haven, CT.

Giambra, L. M. (1995). A laboratory method for investigating influences on switching attention to task-unrelated imagery and thought. *Consciousness and Cognition, 4*, 1–21.

Goldstein, K. (1940). *Human nature in the light of psychopathology*. Cambridge, MA: Harvard University Press.

Gottlieb, S. (1973). Modeling effects upon fantasy. In J. L. Singer (Ed.), *The child's world of make-believe* (pp. 155–182). New York: Academic Press.

Hariton, E. B., & Singer, J. L. (1974). Women's fantasies during sexual intercourse: Normative and theoretical implications. *Journal of Consulting and Clinical Psychology, 42*, 313–322.

Hart, D., Field, N., Singer, J. L., & Garfinkle, J. (1997). Representations of self and others: A semantic space model. *Journal of Personality, 65*, 77–105.

Head, H. (1926). *Aphasia and kindred disorders of speech* (2 vols.). Cambridge, England: Cambridge University Press.

Higgins, E. T. (1987). Self-discrepancy: A theory of relating self and affect. *Psychological Review, 94*, 319–340.

Holt, R. R. (1976). Drive or wish? A reconsideration of the psychoanalytic theory of motivation. In M. M. Gill & P. S. Holzman (Eds.), Psychology versus metapsychology: Psychoanalytic essays in memory of George S. Klein. *Psychological Issues, 9*(4, Monograph No. 36).

Horowitz, M. (Ed.). (1991). *Person schemas and maladaptive interpersonal patterns*. Chicago: University of Chicago Press.

Horowitz, M. J., Eells, T., Singer, J. L., & Salovey, P. (1995). Role relationship models for case formulation. *Archives of General Psychiatry, 52*, 625–632.

Huba, G. J., Singer, J. L., Aneshensel, C. S., & Antrobus, J. S. (1982). *The short imaginal processes inventory*. Port Hurson, MI: Research Psychologists Press.

James, W. (1950). *The principles of psychology*. New York: Holt. (Original work published 1890)

John, O. P. (1990). The "Big Five" factor taxonomy: Dimensions of personality in natural language and in questionnaires. In L. Pervin (Ed.), *Handbook of personality: Theory and research* (pp. 66–100). New York: Guilford Press.

Kelly, G. (1955). *The psychology of personal constructs* (2 vols.). New York: Norton.

Kiesler, D. J. (1996). *Contemporary interpersonal theory and research*. New York: Wiley.

Kihlstrom, J. F. (1987). The cognitive unconscious. *Science, 237*, 1445–1452.

Kihlstrom, J. F. (1990). The psychological unconscious. In L. Pervin (Ed.), *Handbook on personality: Theory and research* (pp. 445–464). New York: Guilford Press.

Kihlstrom, J. F. (1993). The psychological unconscious and the self. In Ciba Foundation Symposium 174, *Experimental and Theoretical Studies of Consciousness* (pp. 147–167). New York: Wiley.

Klein, S., & Kihlstrom, J. F. (1986). Elaboration, organization and the self-reference effect in memory. *Journal of Experimental Psychology, 115,* 26–38.

Klinger, E. (1978). Dimensions of thought and imagery in normal waking states. *Journal of Altered States of Consciousness, 4,* 97–113.

Klinger, E. (1990). *Daydreaming.* Los Angeles, CA: Jeremy P. Tarcher, Inc.

Klos, D. S., & Singer, J. L. (1981). Determinants of the adolescent's ongoing thought following simulated parental confrontations. *Journal of Personality and Social Psychology, 41,* 975–987.

Kreitler, S., & Singer, J. L. (1991). The self-reliance effect in incidental memory: Elaboration, organization, rehearsal and self-complexity. *Imagination, Cognition, and Personality, 10,* 167–194.

Leahey, T. H. (1992). The mythical revolutions of American psychology. *American Psychologist, 47,* 308–318.

Leahey, T. H. (1994). Is this a dagger I see before me? Four theorists in search of consciousness. *Contemporary Psychology, 39*(5), 575–581.

Lewin, K. (1935). *A dynamic theory of personality.* New York: McGraw-Hill.

Luria, A. R. (1932). *The nature of human conflicts.* New York: Liveright.

Markus, H., & Nurius, P. (1986). Possible selves. *American Psychologist, 41,* 954–969.

Moise, F., Yinon, Y., & Rabinowitz, A. (1988–1989). Rorschach inkblot Movement Response as a function of motor activity or inhibition. *Imagination, Cognition, and Personality, 8,* 39–48.

Murphy, G. (1947). *Personality: A biosocial approach.* New York: Harper.

Person, E. S. (1995). *By force of fantasy.* New York: Basic Books.

Piaget, J. (1962). *Play, dreams and imitation in childhood.* New York: Norton.

Pope, K. S. (1978). How gender, solitude, and posture influence the stress of consciousness. In K. S. Pope & J. L. Singer (Eds.), *The stream of consciousness* (pp. 259–299). New York: Plenum.

Pribram, K., & McGuinness, D. (1975). Arousal, activation and effort in the control of attention. *Psychological Review, 82,* 116–149.

Quattrone, G. A. (1985). On the congruity between internal states and action. *Psychological Bulletin, 98,* 3–40.

Rorschach, H. (1921/1951). *Psychodiagnostics.* Berne, Switzerland: Hans Huber.

Ruvolo, A. P., & Markus, H. R. (1992). Possible selves and performance: The power of self-relevant imagery. *Social Cognition, 10,* 95–124.

Searle, J. (1992). *The rediscovery of the mind.* Cambridge, MA: MIT Press.

Searle, J. (1995). The mystery of consciousness. *The New York review of books, XLII*(17), 60–66.

Segal, B., Huba, G., & Singer, J. L. (1980). *Drugs, daydreaming and personality.* Hillsdale, NJ: Erlbaum.

Segal, H. (1964). *Introduction to the work of Melanie Klein.* New York: Basic Books.

Singer, D. G. (1993). *Playing for their lives.* New York: Free Press.

Singer, D. G., & Singer, J. L. (1990). *The house of make-believe: Children's play and the developing imagination.* Cambridge, MA: Harvard University Press.

Singer, J. A., & Salovey, P. (1993). *The remembered self: Emotion and memory in personality.* New York: Free Press.

Singer, J. A., & Singer, J. L. (1994). Social–cognitive and narrative perspectives on transference. In J. M. Masling & R. F. Bornstein (Eds.), *Empirical perspectives on object relations theory* (pp. 157–193). Washington, DC: American Psychological Association.

Singer, J. L. (1955). Delayed gratification and ego-development: Implications for clinical and experimental research. *Journal of Consulting Psychology, 19,* 259–266.

Singer, J. L. (1966). Daydreaming and planful thought: A note on Professor Stark's conceptual framework. *Perceptual and Motor Skills, 23,* 113–114.

Singer, J. L. (1973). *The child's world of make-believe.* New York: Academic Press.

Singer, J. L. (1974). Daydreaming and the stream of thought. *American Scientist, 62,* 417–425.

Singer, J. L. (1975a). Navigating the stream of consciousness: Research in daydreaming and related inner experience. *American Psychologist, 30,* 727–738.

Singer, J. L. (1975b). *The inner world of daydreaming.* New York: Harper & Row.

Singer, J. L. (1985). Transference and the human condition: A cognitive–affective perspective. *Psychoanalytic Psychology, 2*(3), 189–219.

Singer, J. L. (1988). Sampling ongoing consciousness and emotional experience: Implications for health. In M. J. Horowitz (Ed.), *Psychodynamics and cognition* (pp. 297–346). Chicago: University of Chicago Press.

Singer, J. L., & Bonanno, G. A. (1990). Personality and private experience: Individual variations in consciousness and in attention to subjective phenomena. In L. Pervin (Ed.), *Handbook of personality* (pp. 419–444). New York: Guilford Press.

Singer, J. L., & Brown, S. L. (1977). The experience-type: Some behavioral correlates and theoretical implications. In M. A. Rickers-Orsiankina (Ed.), *Rorschach psychology* (pp. 325–374). Huntington, NY: Krieger.

Singer, J., & Kolligian, J. (1987). Personality: Developments in the study of private experience. *Annual Review of Psychology, 38,* 533–574.

Singer, J. L., & McCraven, V. (1961). Some characteristics of adult daydreaming. *Journal of Psychology, 51,* 151–164.

Singer, J. L., & Salovey, P. (1991). Organized knowledge structures and personality: Person schemas, self-schemas, prototypes and scripts. In M. J. Horowitz (Ed.), *Person schemas and recurrent maladaptive interpersonal patterns* (pp. 33–79). Chicago: University of Chicago Press.

Singer, J., & Schonbar, R. (1961). Correlates of daydreaming: Dimensions of self-awareness. *Journal of Consulting Psychology, 25,* 1–17.

Singer, J. L., Wilensky, H., & McCraven, V. (1956). Delaying capacity, fantasy, and planning ability: A factorial study of some basic ego functions. *Journal of Consulting Psychology, 20,* 375–383.

Starker, S. (1974). Daydreaming styles and nocturnal dreaming. *Journal of Abnormal Psychology, 83,* 52–55.

Starker, S. (1977). Daydreaming styles and nocturnal dreaming: Further observations. *Perceptual and Motor Skills, 45,* 411–418.

Starker, S. (1982). *Fantastic thought: All about dreams, daydreams, hallucinations and hypnosis.* Englewood Cliffs, NJ: Prentice Hall.

Starker, S. (1984–1985). Daydreams, nightmares, and insomnia: The relation of waking fantasy to sleep disturbances. *Imagination, Cognition and Personality, 4,* 237–248.

Starker, S., & Singer, J. L. (1975). Daydreaming patterns and self-awareness in psychiatric patients. *Journal of Nervous and Mental Disease, 161,* 313–317.

Strauman, T. J. (1989). Self-discrepancies in clinical depression and social phobia: Cognitive structures that underlie emotional disorders? *Journal of Abnormal Psychology, 98,* 14–22.

Strauman, T. J. (1992). Self-guides, autobiographical memory, and anxiety and dysphoria: Toward a cognitive model of vulnerability to emotional distress. *Journal of Abnormal Psychology, 101,* 87–95.

Strauman, T. J. (1994). Introduction: Social cognition, psychodynamic psychology, and the representation and processing of emotionally significant information. *Journal of Personality, 62,* 451–458.

Strauman, T. J., & Higgins, E. T. (1988). Self-discrepancies as predictors of vulnerability to distinct syndromes of chronic emotional distress. *Journal of Personality, 56,* 685–707.

Strauman, T. J., & Higgins, E. T. (1993). The self-construct in social cognition: Past, present, and future. In Z. Siegel & S. Blatt (Eds.), *Self in emotional distress* (pp. 3–40). New York: Guilford Press.

Strauman, T. J., Lemieux, A., & Coe, C. (1993). Self-discrepancy and natural killer cell activity: Immunological consequences of negative self-evaluation. *Journal of Personality and Social Psychology, 64,* 1042–1052.

Sullivan, H. S. (1956). *Clinical studies in psychiatry.* New York: Norton.

Vygotsky, L. S. (1966). Play and its role in the mental development of the child. *Soviet Psychology, 12*(6), 62–76.

Weiss, J., Sampson, H., & Mount Zion Psychotherapy Research Group. (1986). *The psychoanalytic process: Theory, clinical observation, and empirical research.* New York: Guilford Press.

Wiggins, J. S., & Pincus, A. L. (1992). Personality structure and assessment. *Annual Review of Psychology, 43,* 473–504.

Wiggins, J. S., & Pincus, A. L. (1994). Personality structure and the structure of personality disorders. In P. T. Costa, Jr., & T. A. Widiger (Eds.), *Personality disorders and the five-factor model of personality* (pp. 73–93). Washington, DC: American Psychological Association.

Interpretation, the Unconscious, and Analytic Authority:
Toward an Evolutionary, Biological Integration of the Empirical–Scientific Method With the Field-Defining, Empathic Stance

Daniel Kriegman

Our destiny is to replace theology with psychology as the queen of the sciences.

—Friedrich Nietzsche

A sufficiently advanced technology is indistinguishable from magic.

—Arthur C. Clarke

[Scientist at a press conference:] *"I'm afraid I can't comment on the name Rain God at this present time . . . we are calling him an example of a Spontaneous Para-Causal Meteorological Phenomenon."*
"Can you tell us what that means?"
"I'm not altogether sure. Let's be straight here. If we find something we can't understand we like to call it something you can't understand, or indeed pronounce. I mean if we just let you go around calling him a Rain God, then that suggests that you know something we don't, and I'm afraid we couldn't have that. No, first we have to call it something which says it's ours, not yours, then we set about finding some way of proving it's not what you said it

For numbered notes to this chapter, please refer to the Notes section beginning on page 248.

is, but something we say it is. And if it turns out that you're right, you'll still be wrong, because we will simply call him . . . er, 'Supernormal'—not paranormal or supernatural because you think you know what those mean now, no, a 'Supernormal Incremental Precipitation Inducer.' We'll probably want to shove a 'Quasi' in there somewhere to protect ourselves. Rain God! Huh, never heard such nonsense in my life."

—Douglas Adams
So Long, and Thanks for All the Fish

Psychoanalysis was developed within the context of an objectivist, empiricist epistemology that was taken for granted as a given by its founder. This *scientific zeitgeist* was generally believed to be the crowning achievement of Western thought. When Freud's scientific education began, modern and postmodern challenges to this view were inconceivable: In the second half of the 19th century, only the most fanciful of foolish philosophers would have entertained wild notions suggesting that people ought to turn off the Enlightenment and reenter the darkness created by subjectivist[1] truth built on a foundation of received wisdom. Such dogmatic deduction had been the basis for all "knowledge" prior to the 17th century. It had taken (literally) death-defying courage for the first empiricists to challenge the received wisdom of the various churches and turn to what could be learned from actual observation of the world. Taking up Bacon's (1620) call for an inductive science, they progressed by leaps and bounds with astounding discoveries and theoretical breakthroughs rapidly following one after another. Operating, at first, outside of the universities that were controlled by the church and its melding of Aristotelian notions with Christian theology, the new scientists excited the world with a powerful new vision.[2]

Because of the success of this worldview, it may seem strange that there is now a call for psychoanalysis to abandon the scientific method (Orange, 1995; Stolorow & Atwood, 1994; Stolorow, Brandchaft, & Atwood, 1987; cf. Kriegman, 1996a). Analysts hear that psychoanalysis should not be considered to be—and should not strive to be—an empirical science (Atwood & Stolorow, 1984; Habermas, 1971), that it is more like an art form and should be classed with the humanities: Like a novelist creating a story, the analyst and patient co-construct a narrative, the value of which is determined by the aesthetics of the hermeneutic interpretations (meanings) they then find within their story (Geha, 1993; Ricoeur, 1970; Spence, 1982; cf. Holt, 1989). Because knowledge in general is a social construction, it can have no intrinsic truth value (Geha, 1993).[3] Objectivity is myth. Truth is contexual. In fact, we are told that only by abandoning notions of objectivity can we avoid the abuse of power relations that characterize most human interactions including psychoanalytic treatment (cf. Geha, 1993). Only by so doing can we provide an optimal analytic relationship and achieve the best therapeutic results. In such a view, it thus becomes a clinician's ethical duty to abandon notions of objectivity and truth: "The concepts of objectivity and distortion have no place in the theoretical lexicon of psychoanalysis" (Stolorow, 1995, p. xvi).

More than simply appearing strange, such notions appear to argue for abandoning the very foundations of the knowledge we now possess. This would inevitably lead to a return to superstitions and comforting beliefs as valid truths, regardless of how out of synchrony they may be with our experience of the world around us. It may be true that there are idiosyncratic, artistic (i.e., highly subjective and not objectively quantifiable) elements in psychoanalytic practice. However, architecture also is undoubtedly an art form. Despite this, we do not want the bridges we drive across and the buildings we enter to be designed and built by someone who eschews objectivity and the empirical accumulation of knowledge about the world. As Robert Stolorow (personal communication, 1995) noted, he would not want someone to drive a car using the epistemology he proposes for psychoanalysis. Yet, there is a reluctance to try to ground psychoanalysis in systematic observation that has made it vulnerable to sometimes scathing attacks by a wide variety of critics (Bornstein & Masling, 1994). Although the critics are often misinformed, they can (and do) aptly note that, when hermeneutic beauty is in the eye of the analyst, downright silly and even pernicious notions can be promulgated. Both of these trends—theoretical flights of fancy from within and vigorous attacks from the outside—have contributed to the loss of credibility of psychoanalysis among many serious scholars.

Psychoanalysis does indeed have important artistic elements in implementation and style. Yet, if artistic elements that are personal, idiosyncratic, and difficult to quantify or even describe in words are important to the process of psychoanalytic treatment, this does not prevent empirical research into the treatment process. Difficulties in measuring, accounting for, and controlling for such complex variables—difficulties that may be overcome only with arduous, extensive work that may necessitate expensive, complicated research designs that are unavailable today—should not be used to argue for a separation of psychoanalytic clinical theory and practice from science. For if such difficulties make psychoanalysis fundamentally unscientific, then the withdrawal of funding for the supercollider should lead particle physicists to declare that physics is no longer a science; it is now a hermeneutic art form.[4]

Why the postmodern cry? Although it is beyond the scope of this chapter to discuss the full range of antiscientific sentiments that abound today and the growing respectability among intellectuals of philosophical trends away from empiricist approaches to knowledge, I venture two thoughts, the second of which is at the heart of this chapter. The first is somewhat paradoxical in that, at first blush, it would seem to argue for a firm commitment to the scientific method. It is that, to a startling degree, empiricism has enabled us to gain enormous control of the inanimate and non-human biological world. And there is no end in sight. To a late 17th-century Enlightenment scientist, we now have powers that would surely seem magical. Even further: To an intelligent, well-educated person of the late 20th century, the world of technology is as mysteriously supernatural as the religions that, before modern science, were postulated as explanations of the origin of (and the order and disorder within) the world. How does a computer work? A TV? A CD player? A copy machine? A generator? A refrigerator?[5] We are presented with utterly unintelligible ideas—that we are told are now accepted as facts—about the physical world by famous scientists.[6] The distinction between a science grounded in observations and supernatural mysticism is becoming blurred. The virgin birth versus black holes. The resurrection versus time stopping at the speed of light. Transubstantiation versus an infinite universe (or, for that matter, a finite one in which space curves back on itself). For even the intelligent, educated person, science has progressed so far that, at its leading edge, knowledge and its foundation in empirical observation appear to be as far removed from human experience as any supernatural claim.

The second factor is the relative lack of progress in dealing with the human world. Our astounding success in dealing with the non-human world is matched by our dismal failure to cope with war, racism, political despots, religious fanaticism, martial discord, obscenely inequitable distributions of wealth, overpopulation, and the rapaciously destructive ways that technological prowess is used.[7] Those same Enlightenment thinkers who were thrilled by their advancing knowledge of the nonhuman world predicted similar success in dealing with human problems. If people only rejected dogma and opened their eyes and carefully observed the world, the power that would accrue to them would enable them to solve any problem. We know so much more about ourselves than about physics, for example, how rapidly we should progress when we apply scientific principles to ourselves. And yet, rather than progressing, the 20th century has been the most barbarous and destructive century of all time.[8] Although there is now a lull in the nuclear arms race and the collapse of communism provides some hope as the Cold War ends, genocidal racism is alive and well. Racial and religious intolerance are as widespread as ever. With both the massive misery of overpopulation and dramatic advances in technology that make inconceivable destructive power readily available on a wider scale than ever before, can we really hope to prevent the human-generated horrors that are likely to occur?

In this chapter I attempt to show how both psychoanalytic theory and evolutionary biology predict the differential success people have had in dealing with the nonhuman world on the one hand and the world of human meanings and actions on the other. Psychoanalytic theory, with its emphasis on the unconscious, suggests that, structured within the very design of the human psyche, there are tremendous obstacles to humans seeing themselves clearly without significant distortion. Evolutionary biology, in turn, predicts that the psyche would evolve in this direction and further the understanding of the adaptive value of such a design (Kriegman, 1996a; Slavin & Kriegman, 1992). I hope to show how this view is consistent with increasing concerns about the power differential in the analytic relationship and the need to acknowledge how analytic realities are co-constructed by two parties with their own individual distorting biases.

While operating under the guise of scientific objectivity, psychoanalysts have developed some fanciful metapsychological notions that are then reified (Holt, 1989). Claims that these notions are based on "objective" clinical "facts" that only analysts and their patients have access to have contributed to the ridicule that has been directed at psychoanalysis for being unfalsifiable (Popper, 1963) or for having no more of an objective base than religions or the Loch Ness monster (Eysenck, 1972; Masson, 1990; Torrey, 1992; cf. Bornstein & Masling, 1994). In essence, we are told by such critics that the psychoanalyst is wearing clothes that only the emperor and his court can see.

Yet the solution to dogmatic flights of fancy is not to reject objectivity and science and turn to hermeneutics. Rather, it is at the intersection of three theoretical systems—the juncture of scientific ways of accumulating knowledge of ourselves and our world (*empiricist epistemology*) with our depth knowledge of the human psyche (*psychoanalysis*) and both of these with our only "scientific theory of creation" (*evolutionary biology;* Trivers, 1985)—that I believe a new understanding of ourselves in our world can develop. I describe a convergence between psychoanalysis and evolutionary biology. This convergence is found as both of these theories struggle to understand deception and self-deception and the related psychoanalytic concept of the unconscious. I conclude that this convergent understanding of the way in which the human psyche is designed both to know accurately and to distort reality underscores the human need to ground knowledge—especially knowledge about ourselves—in an empiricist epistemology (Kriegman, 1996a).

Clinical Empiricism and Controlled, Statistical Empiricism

Wallace (1988) suggested that truth in analytic treatment is co-constructed by the patient and analyst (cf. Hoffman, 1991). However, he responded to the claim that clinical truth is therefore obscure by pointing out that, if both parties make a contribution and if the patient's contribution is somewhat stable (reliably similar from relationship to relationship), then the reality of the patient's contribution can be found, albeit with difficulty. In the self psychological perspective that I examine more closely, finding the "truth" is finding what is real in the analytic space that is brought to the analysis by the patient's experimental world (i.e., by the patient's sense of self, self-experience, and experience of others).

Masling and Cohen (1987) and Bornstein and Masling (1994), by contrast, suggested that the patient's experience as known by the analyst in the analytic setting cannot be a measure of "truth." They described a process of reinforcement in which the analyst shapes the patient's behavior. Therapists of different schools, by selectively reinforcing different aspects of their patients' verbal behavior, will generate patient data consistent with their theories. For example, through such a process, classical analysts will obtain evidence of oedipal issues and Kohutians will be able to provide evidence of narcissistic injuries, disappointments, and deficits. The empirical data—which, in their terms, means data from controlled, statistical studies—that Masling and Cohen were interpreting are the findings that different schools yield virtually identical results in systematic studies of therapeutic effectiveness. Also, the various schools of psychodynamic treatment yield equal benefit to other nonanalytic approaches such as cognitive–behavioral treatment. Talk therapy is almost equally effective regardless of the therapist's theory.

They are right in asserting that the empirical data call for the articulation of a theory that can account for them. However, I would suggest that the data do not necessarily call for the particular theoretical explanation they formulated: that clinical data are overwhelmingly biased by a process of selective reinforcement and therefore cannot be used to adjudicate truth claims. As an alternative explanation, I would argue that the findings of a general benefit from psychotherapy supports certain aspects of self psychology over other theories. That is, to varying degrees, all treatments provide what self psychology claims is essential. All treatments involve a therapist who takes the patient's feelings, suffering, or problems seriously. All treatments involve a therapist who pays careful attention to the patient's symptoms and considers the patient to be worth helping. Thus, all approaches essentially mirror the patient's worth as a human being whose suffering is worth attending to (providing an important component of a mirroring selfobject). All approaches present the patient with a trained "expert" therapist who believes he or she can help a suffering patient (providing an important component of an idealized selfobject). All approaches offer the patient, who may be extremely isolated, the unmistakable experience of being with another person (providing an important component of an alter ego selfobject). I would claim that the general beneficial effect of psychotherapy is attributable to the real impact of these powerful experiences. I also would suggest that the limited effect is attributable, in part, to the fact that the simple provision of such experiences is limited in its impact and that therapists (including those who consider themselves self psychologists) do not apply even these basic principles in a maximally effective manner. No specific analytic approach may be markedly more successful than others or than nonanalytic techniques because each approach uses specific interventions that may add to the general effect and be helpful to certain patients to varying degrees.

The point is not whether self psychology is *the* right theory. Rather, I am simply illustrating how the data Masling and Cohen (1987) examined might be better accounted for by one theory rather than another instead of concluding that clinical data are irretrievably contaminated and cannot be used to find out what is really going on. If there are other theories that can account for these data, they should be developed and then the different theories can be tested to see which works best. Masling and Cohen, by contrast, argued that the undifferentiated general effect of psychotherapy and the clear sources of bias in clinical data indicate that only controlled empirical (statistical) studies can provide objective conclusions. As Bornstein and Masling (1994) put it, "the validity and utility of . . . [psychoanalytic] ideas and hypotheses must be established through controlled empirical study" (p. xvi). I would differ on this and suggest that clinical observation and controlled, statistical studies are simply two forms of useful (potentially valid) empirical data. For example, consider the following test of theory, a test that occurred empirically in the clinical setting and that I present as part of an attempt to formulate a position between Bornstein and Masling's on the one hand and Freud's unwarranted assurances that psychoanalysis as he practiced it was objective and unbiased (Bornstein & Masling, 1994) on the other.

When first learning about self psychology, I responded to Kohut's call to try a self psychological approach myself—to test it empirically—and see how well the clinical data supported it. At the time, I was working as a therapist at the Treatment Center for Sexually Dangerous Offenders at the Massachusetts Correctional Institution at Bridgewater. A relatively new patient walked into the 7 × 10 ft (2.13 × 3.05 m) prison cell that was my office. I was a few minutes late and though I was prepared to make up the time at the end of the session, the patient—a "borderline" who in the past had been repeatedly diagnosed as "schizophrenic" and medicated with megadoses of Thorazine (measured in grams, not milligrams)—began screaming at me:

> You just wait. I'll be waiting for you and when you come around a corner, I'll break your goddam head in with a 2 by 4. This place is just a torture center run by Jews. Jews control the whole fuckin' thing. Hitler had the right idea. He should have killed all the fuckin' Jews.

Well, this was not the kind of experience that I was particularly able to empathize with as self psychology suggested I should. First of all, this was clearly a psychotic distortion because I was the only Jewish staff member and, at that time, I had no authority whatsoever. Also, try as I might, no amount of vicarious introspection was going to enable me to resonate empathically with the sense that we would all be better off if "Hitler had killed all the Jews." It was easy to fall back on ego-psychological notions and, as his rage continued, I thought about doing so. On the basis of the notion that his uncontrolled rage was insufficiently tempered aggression, I should insist that the session could not proceed and our psychotherapeutic work would have to wait until we could cooperatively try to understand what he was feeling. This would force him to accept that treatment was for the analysis of feelings rather than for acting out. Eventually, he would come to see the unreasonableness of his untamed aggression, and this insight would lead to progress in enabling him to mature into a more healthy individual.

Alternatively, I could see this as borderline splitting into good and bad objects. At that moment I was an all-bad annihilating other, and such a patient could not hold an ambivalent image of a whole object in his mind. Because of the degree of psychotic distortion frequently exhibited by this patient, I would have to accept that analysis was probably impossible and that I would have to settle for "supportive therapy" in which I would help the patient's ego learn techniques for functioning in a world that felt so alien.

Of course, there were many other possible responses. However, I had just read Kohut's (1972) article on narcissistic rage, in which he claimed that such rage responses were an attempt to ward off terrifying, psychotic fragmentation experiences in which patients feel themselves to be disappearing or literally disintegrating. Therefore, I decided to test Kohut's hypothesis that an empathic statement could reverse this process and—as I had no empathic understanding of my own of the patient—I actually asked myself, "What might Kohut say now?" The answer was immediate and clear. I waited a moment until I could feel just a small semblance of what I was about to say, a very small semblance, and then I looked him in the eye and said, "You must be in a lot of pain."

His reaction shocked me. I was just desperately, intellectually trying out something to cope with fairly painful confusion and bind my considerable anxiety. I did not really believe it would work. Instantly the "raging borderline" began to cry. Because I was now honestly able to tune in empathically to the pain that had been underlying the psychotic rage, my continued empathic responsiveness brought forth a torrent of painful sobbing. He did feel as if he was being annihilated. He felt as if he was going to be buried in prison forever and that my lateness was just another example of the profound indifference that would lead to his death in prison. Through many repetitions of this experience (over a period of 12 years), he was able to come to understand the terrifying depressive hopelessness that he covered with rage reactions. Eventually, his ability to feel the underlying despair without being overcome with terror made it less necessary to respond with such rage.

Literally hundreds of such experiences have verified this empirical finding: When my patients experienced an empathic response to them, they almost invariably felt better and functioned better. As we were able to analyze what stood in the way of finding empathic resonance in the world, they became better able to find empathic responses both within and outside of the therapeutic setting. Almost every premature and painful termination of treatment followed a clearly identifiable traumatic empathic failure. Failures of empathy in which we were able to reestablish an empathic connection—such as the example I just cited—were almost always accompanied by new insights into patients' intrapsychic dynamics and the vicissitudes of their relationships. Patients almost always found new strength through this understanding. In addition, new strength was derived from patients' experiences that they could sustain themselves through the disappointment and ensuing fragmentation that followed nontraumatic empathic failures, just as self psychology would have predicted.

Was this the systematic reinforcement of a pattern of responses? The evidence that this was not the case was that innumerable times during this treatment (and others) while learning this approach (and still continuing to the present day), I also tried (tested) numerous variants of the more ego-psychological and object-relational interventions described above. Invariably, the more traditional psychoanalytic interpretations and limit setting (e.g., attempts to forgo "gratifying" this particular patient and instead to interpret the drive demands or relational scenarios being played out) led to increased fragmentation. When I returned to the struggle to remain in the empathic stance, the patient would usually stop fragmenting, would reconstitute a nonpsychotic sense of self, and would start to function reasonably. I was not committed to this approach. I was often desperately fishing around through the theories I had heard of to find something, anything that would work with a patient who was often out of control. Repeatedly, I tested numerous theoretical approaches to interpretive interventions. Consistently, the struggle to understand the patient empathically worked better than other interventions.

Yet, could this perspective just be a self-deceptive, biased, self-fulfilling prophecy? Maybe. Again, however, in the example above, I had no belief system at the time to confirm. I was a young therapist in search of a belief system. Could this have been my finally finding a belief system to believe in that was compatible with my personality? Certainly it could have been. Yet, I continue to try other approaches and have found that certain extraempathic (non-self-psychological) responses also have been useful (this is discussed later in this chapter). However, the essential truths I experienced through this process of experimentation have remained valid. In addition, I would argue that this is how therapists learn clinically: They try various approaches and see what works best for them. To consider this anything but empiricism—even if uncontrolled and subject to considerable bias, individual interpretation, and distortion—seems unwarranted.[9]

This is a form of crude but generally somewhat effective empiricism that has been used by people since our socially sensitive brains began to grow larger (Kriegman, 1988, 1990, 1996a). To suggest that this is invalid clinical evidence and only controlled studies are empirical is, I believe, a mistake. Rather, they both are forms of empirical evidence each with enormous problems. The former is plagued by subjective, individual interpretation with enormous bias and self-deception while it retains the power of the ability to perceive complex mental states in the context of intimate relationships using our highly evolved empathic capacity (Kriegman, 1996a). The latter is plagued by the fact that much of the complexity and meaning of human experience is lost in the attempt to operationalize and atomize human experience[10] while it retains a much greater degree of control (but certainly not complete) over the human tendency to bias and distort experience. Both are *empirical* approaches, each with tremendous advantages and disadvantages.

For Masling and Cohen (1987), only controlled studies can disentangle the reinforcing influences of the analyst on the patient and the resultant "truths" that emerge in the clinical setting. Others, such as Spezzano (1993a, 1993b) and Mitchell (1993), have argued that the clinical setting is an adequate source of data for meaningful "conversations" (Spezzano, 1993a) with reasonable truth claims. Indeed, with regard to a concern that goes to the heart of Masling and Cohen's analysis (as well as being a main concern of this chapter), consider Spezzano's (1993b) counterproposal to Masling and Cohen's call for controlled studies: "Psychoanalysis is precisely that discipline that studies most closely the myriad ways in which the authority of one person in a conversation might be irrationally and uncritically internalized by the other" (p. 276). It is hard for me to imagine controlled studies (that could be conducted today or in the near future) that would provide the persuasive data needed to have a major impact on psychoanalytic conversations about a scientific understanding of the powerful bidirectional biases, resistances, and influences that characterize a long-term, intimate, analytic relationship. Yet, this crucial issue is being—must be—addressed by practicing psychoanalysts every day (cf. Kriegman, 1996c; Slavin & Kriegman, in press). Until less biased data are available, a responsible clinician must turn to clinical empiricism, to the clinical evidence (as opposed to the alternative that has been proposed of eschewing empiricism).

This book is part of a series that focuses on controlled, statistical studies as the primary source of data for empirical knowledge. For many years, beginning with Freud, such controlled empiricism has been discounted by clinicians who believe that their clinical experience is sufficient for establishing objective, unbiased theories and developing the most effective techniques (Bornstein & Masling, 1994). Masling and Cohen (1987) aptly pointed out the potential dangers of such a subjective, limiting approach to analytic knowledge and truth. Yet, I also agree with Spezzano (1993a) that clinicians need not seek a higher authority for psychoanalytic knowledge in either philosophy or controlled laboratory studies even though psychoanalytic theories must not be immune to knowledge produced by other disciplines; clinical theories will be most fruitful if they are consistent with the data available from as many sources as possible. Contrast this with Stolorow et al. (1987, pp. 5–6), who wanted to limit the data to be understood analytically to those that are obtained through empathy. In this chapter I examine both clinical and controlled statistical data that need theoretical explanation.

Yet, I am also aiming at a response to an even more pernicious tendency among modern analytic clinicians that should be of interest to readers of this series. Freud may have dismissed controlled studies as unnecessary. Now, however, there are a significant number of analysts who, in addition, dismiss objectivity, science, intersubjective verifiability, and empiricism of any kind as being irrelevant and inapplicable to human experience, especially the psychoanalytic interpretation of the unconscious. I think this is an absurd and dangerous trend when clinicians are also suggesting that suffering individuals pay them well to allow them to place themselves in the clinicians' hands for "treatment" (Kriegman & Solomon, 1985). To respond to such notions, I embrace both forms of empiricism: Clinicians need to turn to the empirical data from all sources to get their bearings, increase their effectiveness, and to safeguard their patients.

Problems With Objectivity and Authority in Psychoanalysis

A major motive for the rejection of empiricism in psychoanalysis seems to be a reaction to certain abuses of power that have been associated with psychoanalysis. Authoritarian abuse of power, in this view, is seen as stemming from an objective, scientific worldview that is the framework within which medical attempts at healing have traditionally operated. Supposed scientific objectivity provides a significant part of the context for the authority with which analytic patients have often been confronted as they are told the "truth" about their psychic life. This truth is known by the doctor-analyst who operates from a scientifically derived, objective, medical–clinical theory, not by the self-deceptive analytic patient who attempts to "resist" the truth.

I would suggest that the use of such a model has led—despite the benefit that many received from the new clinical method and understanding that Sigmund Freud created—to psychoanalytic history being replete with what must be acknowledged to be "abusive" interpretations and analytic relationships. Consider Freud's forceful confrontations with Dora, in which he insisted that her nervous fiddling with her pocketbook after she entered his consulting room indicated

> that Dora wanted to confess that she is a masturbator by opening and closing her reticule, and even putting her finger in it. (Did this last feature sexually arouse Freud?) "Dora's reticule was nothing but a representation of the genitals and her playing with it ... was an entirely unembarrassed, yet unmistakable pantomimic announcement of what she would like to do with them—namely, to masturbate" (Freud, 1905/1953, p. 79).
>
> Freud was only concerned that Dora accept his interpretation of her activity, which was masturbatory and fit his oedipal theory. ... He *refused* to explore the meaning of the activity to Dora, including the possibility that it had a totally contradictory meaning (Rachman, 1996b). What is more, Freud was unaware

of the subjective meaning of his so-called interpretive behavior, which could easily have been experienced as seductive and erotic, an issue that haunted him twenty-odd years later in his analysis of his daughter, Anna (Rachman, 1996a). (Arnold Rachman, personal communication, 1996)

Freud was convinced of the truth of his interpretation because (a) Dora suffered from the type of gastric pains that were "well known . . . [to occur] especially often in those who masturbate" (Freud, 1905/1953, p. 78), pains that Fliess, according to Freud, had "cured" in others by cauterization of the "gastric spot" in the nose. (b) Dora's cousin suffered from gastric pains and Dora "had good reasons for believing that her cousin was a masturbator. It is very common for patients to recognize in other people a connection . . . they cannot perceive in themselves" (Freud, 1905/1953, p. 79). And, possibly most important, (c) it fit Freud's nascent theory of the sexual origins of neuroses. Freud, the scientist, thus felt that he had plenty of objective evidence to forcefully confront Dora's resistance to his interpretations. Ultimately, Dora refused to acquiesce and left such "treatment."[11]

The point is not that the interpretation could not have been correct; most analysts have seen the unconscious express itself in such symbolic actions. Rather, it is unlikely to have been correct[12] because it appears to have been based more on *Freud's* theory bound ideas and other needs (e.g., his sexual desires or his possibly intense need to have his nascent oedipal theory confirmed) than *Dora's* (Rachman, 1996b). What we have here is just one example (of many) of "projective interpretation" backed by the type of objective, scientific, medical authority that postmodernists reject because of its biased, subjective, and potentially abusive nature. Indeed, what if Dora—either cowed by the authority of the "Doctor" or overwhelmed by the painful neurosis she suffered—had been unable to extricate herself from such treatment? What would happen after several years of such forceful interpretations? My own practice is actually composed, in significant part, of such wounded analytic patients. For me, there is abundant empirical evidence of analytic abuse that can result from long-term, authoritative, interpretive psychoanalytic treatment.

For example, consider the medical student who, hoping to one day become a psychiatrist and psychoanalyst himself, entered analysis to work on some relationship issues and to learn more about himself. Rather than learning to see himself more clearly, he experienced the analyst's interpretations as assaults. The analyst felt far away and as if he were criticizing him like his hypercritical, perfectionist, college president father. Although the transferential components of this patient's reaction may or may not have been open to productive analysis, in reality he was becoming less functional as the analysis proceeded. When he noted this fact, the analyst continued to hammer him with interpretations from the other side of the couch and—regardless of the accuracy or inaccuracy of the content of the interpretations—remained unresponsive to the patient's concerns (except for continuing to issue interpretations of them).

The patient continued to struggle with the interpretive assaults that he experienced when repeatedly confronted with his analyst's psychoanalytic "insights" until he was so riddled with self-doubt, shame, and confusion that he became almost totally dysfunctional. He dropped out of school, took relatively menial jobs such as temporary typing, began to engage in compulsive rituals that required most of his waking energy (e.g., washing and showering until his skin was raw and bleeding, walking 5 miles a day along the same route regardless of weather conditions, alternately wearing one of only two allowed shirts, etc.), and began an almost endless stream of journeys to therapists. Finally, after several years of treatment with another analytically oriented therapist who used a much different approach, the patient was able to reconstitute enough of his former level of functioning to return and finish medical school and engage in more satisfying relationships.

The horror of such treatments—and, as I noted, in my experience this is not uncommon—is that the analyst used his theory and his objective, scientific attitude and training to continue to engage in a relationship that was increasingly destructive to the patient. Even at the end of the 6-year analysis when the patient was nearly dysfunctional, the analyst was willing to proceed as before. Never did he ask for a consultation or question whether the analysis should continue.[13] The decision to terminate this destructive relationship was left to the patient, who had to pull his tattered remains of a self together and, from within a state of seriously diminished capacity, finally take a stand against the authority of the analyst who argued that the analysis—which, of course, continued to benefit the analyst—should proceed.

Schmideberg[14] (1970) reported knowing "of two patients treated by leading analysts for twelve and twenty years respectively, who eventually were sent by their analyst for lobotomy" (p. 199).[15] Regardless of what one thinks of Masson's (1984, 1988) vitriolic attacks on psychoanalysis, his story of his personal analysis and of the analytic community he subsequently inhabited (Masson, 1990) is to many an eye-opening horror story. However, given my clinical experience, I was not all that surprised and discussions with others have revealed that few analysts are unfamiliar with similar events. Some of those analysts who today use a postmodern rejection of science, objectivity, and empirical approaches to knowledge are reacting to such analytic horror stories as well as to the far more common, less horrifying but nevertheless destructive results of such clinical attitudes. Their call for a rejection of objectivity and empirical science is part of a move to replace analytic "objectivity" (authority) with humility (fallibility) and greater respect for their patients (e.g., Orange, 1995; cf. Teicholz, in press).

Interpretation and Confrontation

It's a rare person who wants to hear what he doesn't want to hear.

—Dick Cavett

Part of the problem I am trying to identify arises because interpretations are, by definition, confrontations. It is true that an analyst can make statements that clarify and help patients crystallize their feelings, ideas, and experiences and that such statements may not be confrontative. Yet, many if not most analysts would say such statements are just that: clarifications not interpretations; the unconscious is not being made conscious; conscious experience is simply being reorganized, more clearly perceived, and articulated. True analytic interpretations are confrontations.

In classic psychoanalytic theory, interpretation is resisted because the ego is threatened (signal anxiety) when unconscious material starts to become conscious; the danger is the reason for the repression in the first place. And though in modern, relational revisions of psychoanalysis, repression does not operate for the same reasons, there is still always some threat to the ego, to the maintenance of needed relational ties, to an old loyalty, to a way of organizing experience, to the cohesiveness of the self, and so forth that underlies the need to maintain the repression. Thus, any interpretation that attempts to undo repression must, by definition, pose some threat to a patient.

The notion of a well-timed, mutative interpretation (Strachey, 1934) is also consistent with this understanding. If delivered with great skill at precisely the right moment, virtually no sense of confrontation or threat may exist. Instead, the patient may have an "Aha!" experience that brings clarity, relief, and an increasing sense of insight and mastery. Yet, the fact that to bring about such a painless interpretive effect the analyst must wait, often for a considerable time, for the right moment and has to word such an interpretation with care makes the implicit confrontation clear. Just as the great artist provides the audience with the illusion that the performance is accomplished with little effort, it is the analyst's skill in deftly avoiding forceful confrontation that gives the appearance of a simple offering of helpful insight.

In addition, if one is listening carefully to the patient's associations, trying to enter the patient's experiential world, then any statement that is not an attempt to use empathy to clarify and deepen the analyst's understanding of the patient's experience must be perceived as an intrusion or confrontation. This must be particularly so when the analyst suggests, as by definition all true interpretations do, that, to some degree, the patient's conscious experience does not accurately reflect internal or external reality. At such moments, analysts bring their realities into *confrontations* —however well timed and gently done—with patients' conscious experiences. Also, because the interpretation is about the patient, in considering it the patient must undergo *self-confrontation*. Controlled studies show that self-confrontation has a general negative effect: increased arousal, negative self-evaluation, constriction of ideational themes, aversive reactions, and heightened anxiety (Sackeim & Gur, 1978). Merely by focusing attention on the patient, analytic interpretations can be aversive and threatening.

Stocking (1973) and Corwin (1973) attempted to distinguish between interpretation (hypothesis sharing) and confrontation (the more forceful, unilateral presentation of what the analyst considers to be reality). However, as Myerson (1973) noted, this is a polemicized way of viewing analytic interventions in which confrontation is a comparative rather than absolute way to characterize analytic interventions.[16] When troubled, confused people who are handsomely paying an expert for help are told that their inner or outer realities are not as they believe them to be, they must listen: "[A]ny confrontation . . . in spite of the fact that it was based solely on a genuine concern for the patient, also expresses the therapist's authority over him" (Arvidson, 1973, p. 166). Patients are forced by the inherent nature of the relationship to confront their own experiences with what their therapists offer.

Although it is true that the challenge and threat to the patient is affected by the state of the alliance and the therapist's concern, care, and gentleness—when people are destabilized by an upsetting experience, it surely matters if they have a caring ally nearby (even if the ally brought them the upsetting news)—it is still a mistake to suggest that a gentle presentation within a secure alliance means a confrontation has not occurred or that an interpretation offered as a "hypothesis" is not confrontative. Even caring interpretations within a secure alliance are delivered by an authority figure and contain information that for some reason was kept from awareness and that requires self-confrontation and reorganization of self-experience.

Indeed, traditional theorists such as Bibring (1954) went so far as to define interpretation (as opposed to clarification) by whether the intervention threatens the patient. According to Greenson (1967), if resistance is not obvious to the patient, and it often is not, it is essential to confront the patient with its existence. Every interpretation has an element of force according to Murray (1973). Traditional "therapeutic techniques, such as clarification, abreaction, and transference interpretation . . . *depend upon* confrontation" (Havens, 1973, p. 233) in which "in the long run it is the therapist alone against the resistances" (Havens, 1973, p. 238).

Furthermore, if, despite genuine care, love, concern, and mutuality, we live in a world that is also characterized by ubiquitous interpersonal conflict, then the human psyche must be adaptively designed to anticipate and cope with bias and pressure that inevitably emanate from the impingement of the self-interest of others on each individual (Slavin & Kriegman, 1992). Thus, every analytic interpretation that brings something into a patient's world from beyond its horizons must be evaluated: Is it true that what is being presented is a part of me emanating from (or operating within) my unconscious? Or is this something that emanates from the other and suggesting that it is me is really my therapist's biased view? Or is this something that is an outright attempt to manipulate me to promote my analyst's agenda? Or is this something that is a combination of more than one of these possibilities? If this view of the experiential dilemma facing the patient is correct, then an interpretation must not only be a confrontation, it must also, to some degree, be a problematic, confusing, and threatening confrontation. In this light, consider the previous discussion of analytic abuse and the problem of analytic authority.

Modern Analytic Responses

One can look at self psychology as just one example of the psychoanalytic response to such problems.[17] It was largely Kohut's concerns about the way in which patients' experiences become distorted to fit into the analyst's "objective" theories that led to his call for a return to an experience-near psychoanalytic theory that clearly acknowledged the field of defining nature of the empathic stance. His argument can be summarized as follows: Psychoanalysis is the study of complex mental states. Complex mental states can be known only through introspection and vicarious introspection (empathy). The observational tool that analysts use in knowing their own and others' mental states (introspection and empathy), in combination with the object of this knowledge—complex mental states—defines the field. Just as the field of astronomy is defined by the tools (telescopes) and the object of study (the heavens), psychoanalysis is defined by its tools and object of knowledge (Kohut, 1959, 1982). In Kohut's (1977) metaphor, although it may provide meaningful information to study the chemistry of pigments used by a greater painter, it is unlikely to provide much insight into the human experience one has when viewing a great painting. Just so, extrospective sources of knowledge such as neuroanatomy and biochemistry are unlikely to provide much insight into human experiences such as intense, ambivalent feelings in close relationships, loneliness, love, and the feeling of being understood (or misunderstood). Thus, empathy and introspection are the field-defining tools for the study of complex mental states (i.e., for psychoanalysis).

Although Kohut (1980) was unable and unwilling to follow others within self psychology who would eventually explicitly call for a separation of psychoanalytic self psychology and psychoanalysis from the *Weltanschauung* of the natural sciences (e.g., Orange, 1995; Stolorow & Atwood, 1994), he did use his definition of the limits of the psychoanalytic field to challenge the authority of the objective, analyzed doctor who could determine the truth and distortions in patients' communications. The notion that the analyst's role is not to be the arbiter of truth is an essential part of self psychology today. In this view, analytic confrontation is avoided. The constant call for an empathic stance and respect for the patient's experience has driven all but the most trivial and unanalytic confrontations from self psychological discussions. For example, consider Kohut's (1984) description of his use of confrontation, which consisted of yelling at a patient who was recklessly endangering his life. This was hardly the kind of interpretive confrontation that had historically formed the foundation of psychoanalysis. Over the years, I have gotten the impression that good therapists who are self psychologists continue to use interpretive confrontation judiciously, but they must now hide this fact from one another the way classical analysts once tried to hide their gratifying humanness.

Whether or not they use interpretive confrontations, self psychologists believe that analytic truth is truth about the complex mental state of the patient that can be known only through empathic observation. Thus, the ultimate authority about what is analytically true resides in the patient's experience, not in the analyst's experience or in psychoanalytic theory. Self psychologists view this as one of the fundamental differences between classical analysis and the new paradigm of psychoanalytic self psychology (Ornstein, 1995). Almost all analysts within—and despite the rejection of the patient's unequivocal authority regarding the truth of their experience by some (e.g., Mitchell, 1993), more and more, many outside of—self psychology would agree with Kohut's (1984) often-quoted observation:

> If there is one lesson that I have learned during my life as an analyst, it is the lesson that what my patients tell me is likely to be true—that many times when I believed I was right and my patients were wrong, it turned out, though often only after a prolonged search, that *my* rightness was superficial whereas *their* rightness was profound. (pp. 93–94)

The self psychologists today are split between those who now take such notions to mean that there is a fundamental problem with the empiricist epistemology of science and those who believe that psychoanalytic psychology is a branch of the scientific (i.e., empirical, objective) study of the human psyche. For the latter group, of which Kohut (1980) felt himself to be a member, Kohut reclarified the field defining relationship between the tools of observation for the science of psychoanalytic psychology and the object of knowledge. However, for the former group, Kohut issued a challenge to psychoanalysis that they continue to press using postmodern thought and other recent philosophical trends.

This conflict within self psychology reflects a larger conflict throughout psychoanalysis and, indeed, the Western intellectual tradition itself. The postmodern perspective has, in part, been based on a Marxist view of truth. Hegel had placed ideas in a historical context: Our beliefs cannot be seen as simple, correspondence reflections of a reality that exists independent of our observations. Rather, beliefs are shaped by the larger cultural context in which they take form. Marx then took Hegel's notion of how, as a culture changes, new ideas develop in an inevitable dialectic with older, culturally embedded ideas, and he systematically showed how the dominant ideas at any time support the interests of those currently in power. Following Marx, certain postmodernists have developed a trend toward deconstructing conceptual systems so that the underlying assumptions and values of a set of beliefs can be analyzed to reveal just whose interests are being served.[18]

Many of those now within psychoanalysis want to move psychoanalytic thinking into the "correct" postmodern view: It has been firmly established—postmodernists seem to declare, never fully dealing with the contradiction that in their view firmly establishing anything is an impossibility (including the impossibility of firmly establishing anything)—that truths are merely local, sociocultural, political constructions. Empiricism and science are only ways for those in power to argue that they know Truth in order to maintain the subjugation of others. They do not seem to see that antiempiricism, indeed pure subjectivism, can be and has been used for the same end. For example, Socrates attacked the sophists' use of extreme relativism to support a self-serving, "might makes right," view of morality: In the sophists' world, where truth was relative, there was nothing wrong with those in power determining truth to be whatever was consistent with their interests. Of course, this is in fact the way history proceeds. "Terrorist revolutionaries" become "founding fathers" if they win and are executed as "murderers" if they lose.

It is both ironic and simultaneously illustrative to note that epistemological stances are now reversed. The naked relativist assertion that might makes right would not win many elections in modern democratic societies. Those in power today must justify their privileged position differently. As societies changed from militaristic monarchies to pluralistic democracies, objectivist arguments were developed to support the claim that it is proper for those in power to rule and that the manner in which they wield power is both appropriate and necessary for the benefit of all. They are now opposed in this use of objectivism by those who, in their own attempt to gain greater power and influence, argue for a relativistic conception of truth that shows how supposed objective truths are really biases supporting the interests of the powerful. This reversal of epistemologies illustrates how flexible conceptions can be when placed in the service of the human tendency to use ideas to promote one's self-interest.

In a similar way, the evolutionary biological perspective that I turn to in a moment can be (and has been) used in a manner that supports the interests of those in power. It also can be used, however, to reveal the deceptive and self-deceptive ways in which those in power hide their pursuit of self-interest behind a whole range of notions (e.g., freedom, national interest, truth, caring concern, fairness, love of God, economic necessity). The evolutionary perspective itself predicts this flexible use of beliefs. The human tendency to create and hold to concepts, philosophies, and belief systems is derived from the benefit they provide to the self-interest of those holding them. This is the selective pressure (adaptive advantage) that shaped the tendency to develop and promulgate worldviews and perspectives on reality (Kriegman, 1996a). Also, note the irony: Bacon (1620) was attempting to undermine reasoning by appeal to authority when he formed the foundational arguments for empirical science. Now, we are told that only a rejection of natural science (i.e., a rejection of a method that was designed to systematically base claims of truth and meaning on empirical evidence instead of received wisdom from authority) can protect us from the abusive uses of authority (Orange, 1995).

An Evolutionary View of Truth, Authority, and the Unconscious

Man is, by nature, a political animal, while one who is unable to enter into political associations, or who, on account of his self-sufficiency, has no need of society,[19] is either an animal lower than a human, or else is a god.

—Aristotle
The Politics

As noted, the evolutionary biological perspective suggests that the entire human propensity to develop systems of belief has been brought about by selective pressures that shaped the human ability to use belief systems to further the individual's sociopolitical agenda (Kriegman, 1996a). Status is highly associated with access to resources and reproductive opportunities. The attainment of power and status within a social group appears to be a primary human activity; indeed, one could argue that it is *the* primary human activity. Also, the development, presentation, and promulgation of systems of belief appear to have been crucial in the power struggles that characterize human, political history (Kriegman & Kriegman, 1997).

Certain postmodernists are accurately noting how, throughout history, belief systems (e.g., religions, philosophies, scientific and pseudoscientific theories, aesthetics, and values) have been used in competitive struggles for dominance within the social setting. What the postmodernists have missed is that, like fire, a particular notion can be used for many purposes, some good and some bad. A belief can (and probably will) be used to support my agenda over someone else's, someone else's over mine, ours together, ours over others, and so on. All of this can occur regardless of the truth value of an idea. Truth is not a property of how people use ideas. Truth is a property of the way in which an idea relates to other ideas and the human experiences of being-in-the-world.[20] I now discuss how evolutionary forces shaped the human tendencies to perceive the world accurately as well as tendencies to distort and bias our perception of reality; in doing so, I adopt an adaptive, functional (evolutionary) perspective on the existence of a divided psyche with both conscious and unconscious mental processes.[21]

Distal, Ultimate Causes and Proximal Mechanisms

Central to an application to psychoanalysis of an evolutionary understanding of conscious and unconscious mental functioning is the distinction between *distal* and *proximal* causes. Distal causes—also known as "ultimate" causes—are those forces (selective pressures) that shaped a pattern of behavior, a motivation, or a mental process (conscious or unconscious) over evolutionary time. For example, people eat because if they did not they would die. Eating behavior is adaptive. However, this is the ultimate cause that is distal in the sense that those forces that shaped this behavior are distant in time from people as individuals. The selective pressure (i.e., only those who ate survived to reproduce and pass on their genes, which included the genetically influenced propensity to eat) operated on our ancestors and their compatriots over phylogenetic history. As a general rule, people are not consciously (or unconsciously) motivated to eat in order to live. As people experience it in ontogenetic, personal time, the proximal mechanism that was shaped by the ultimate cause that now causes eating behavior is hunger (or other forms of the desire or need to eat).

Proximal mechanisms include all of the affects people experience: rage, love, fear, anxiety, anger, jealousy, joy, sadness, lust, desire, grief, loneliness, shame, guilt, remorse, compassion, competitiveness, pride, envy, sympathy, and so on. These proximal mechanisms motivate human behavior and help determine responses by others. The ultimate cause that shaped our affects was the selective reinforcement by the environment of those proximal mechanisms (affects) that made certain behaviors more likely to occur. That is, the affectively motivated propensities to engage in the behaviors that were functional or adaptive (i.e., adaptive in that the individuals that engaged in them had a greater rate of reproductive success) were "chosen" by the differential outcome in reproductive success (i.e., "reinforced" by the environment) so that they had a higher frequency in each succeeding generation. The individuals motivated (by proximal mechanisms) to engage in more adaptive behaviors outreproduced those without such motivations, so that today those who have such proximal motives are the primary form.

As in the example of eating *in order to live* and *hunger*, it quickly becomes clear that the ultimate cause (functional, adaptive aspect of a behavior) may have little in common with the proximal cause (the mechanism actually motivating the behavior in the individual). Thus, an organism can be clearly pursuing an adaptive strategy *that may be obvious to observers* without any awareness or (conscious or unconscious) *intent* to do so. This can lead to major misunderstandings of motivation and may be the ground for some severe critiques of psychoanalysis. For example, consider the classical psychoanalytic understanding of the human preoccupation with sexuality. In men, this seems to be a reflection of reality: Anecdote, analytic experience, and empirical studies all conclude that men are in fact preoccupied with sexual thoughts and fantasies (Buss, 1995; Herman, 1993; Wright, 1994). Penis envy is alive and well. However, in my clinical experience, it is primarily found in men who are constantly comparing their size, potency, prowess, status, and so on. Feminists have rightly criticized psychoanalysis for the attempt to characterize female sexuality as a variant of male sexuality.

I now examine how confusion between ultimate and proximal causes can cause confusion in psychoanalytic theory and practice. If a female patient's associations do not demonstrate the type of preoccupation that men have with sex, then some analysts assume that such a preoccupation exists in her unconscious. If a female patient dresses in a manner that her male analyst finds sexually provocative, he may conclude that the motive to arouse him exists in her. In fact, the male analyst may be encouraged to explore his inner experience to see what feelings his patient is trying to arouse within him (or what she may be defensively avoiding through projective identification). If she denies any such conscious thought, she is either acting deceptively (lying) or she is telling what she believes to be the truth and the true motive is repressed, hidden away in her unconscious but exerting its influence as evidenced in her behavior.

Yet, males and females of all species may act in a manner that reliably brings about a particular effect without any conscious *or unconscious* motive containing any direct knowledge of the particular functional effect. This is assumed to be so in primitive species in whom the behavior looks mechanical (reflexive) and higher cortical awareness at either the conscious or unconscious level is assumed to be lacking. People have a harder time accepting their own highly effective mechanisms that govern their emotional life and behavior without necessitating the use of their higher, uniquely human mental processes. This resistance is a response to the blow to human narcissism that Freud (1917/1955) believed was central to both evolutionary biology and psychoanalysis.

To return to my example of the analytic interpretation of female sexuality. A woman may act enticingly without full awareness of how stimulating she may be to men. An example is the woman who does her best to be attractive, look young, wears makeup, wears stylish clothing designed to "advertise" her feminine figure by highlighting certain secondary sex characteristics (e.g., enhancing the apparent protrusion of her breasts, buttocks, and hips), and so forth, yet she is genuinely confused (and angry) when she is treated as a sex object. The classical analyst might insist that her behavior indicates an unconscious wish to be ravished or raped— or to be treated sexually in a manner consistent with male desires—and, in such a view, her anger is part of a reaction formation that helps to maintain the repression of her true motives. The evolutionary psychoanalytic view, however, suggests that such interpretations may be better understood as projections of male wishes mixed with confusions of proximal and ultimate causes. The woman's motive—both consciously *and unconsciously*—in the particular situation[22] may be to be found attractive (e.g., present-able, not ugly, likable, someone others would want to be seen with and want as a friend, as well as wanting to be attractive to the opposite sex) without wanting to stimulate fairly intense male lust and desire, as she may report. A repressed wish to drive men to distraction may not be operating, even in women whose appearance and behavior often does.

Am I saying that such female behavior is unrelated to the male response? Can it be that women spend enormous effort, time, and money to behave in a way that regularly and reliably produces a specific effect and yet the behavior and the effect are unrelated? It has been well documented in several societies that attractive women marry up the socioeconomic scale: The ability to arouse men has significant adaptive advantages for women (Buss, 1992; Elder, 1969; Fisher, 1992; Ridley, 1993). Women whom men find intensely arousing often have enormous power to select their mate from a large pool of possibilities. Compared with their responses to relatively unattractive women, men will take great risks and make extraordinary efforts to obtain reproductive rights with at-tractive women.[23] Certainly the vast preoccupation with beauty and the massive industries that arise from its existence and en-courage its development cannot be mere accidents. Whether one takes an overly simplistic biological view, a strictly cultural view, or the more reasonable view of a mixture of both biological and experiential factors as shaping human behavior, one cannot deny the ubiquitousness of women's attempts to enhance their beauty as well as men's preoccupation with it. When women go to such efforts to engage in this behavior and men are so aroused, how can I say that there may be no conscious or unconscious attempt on the part of women to arouse men sexually?

Although many women do experience the desire to be sexually exciting, there is no evidence that such a motive operates con-sciously or unconsciously on a minute-to-minute basis (e.g., in the school, on the bus, in the workplace, or in the analytic setting). Even if evidence suggests that most women have such desires at times, the notion that these desires are acting as nearly as ubiqui-tously, consciously or unconsciously, as the male sexual response suggests may be more accurately seen as a projection. Both the stimulating behaviors and the stimulation exist. Yet, it apparently does not require direct, intentional effort to stimulate fairly intense sexual desire in a sexually preoccupied creature. There may be motives (proximal mechanisms) that generate behavior that stimulates men without a conscious or unconscious *intent* to produce the male experience. With the distinction between proximal mechanisms (e.g., the motivation to maximize one's "attractiveness" through various means) and ultimate causes (e.g., the arousal of intense desire on the part of men that enhanced female choice and gave an adaptive [reproductive] advantage to the women in the past who were able to arouse such interest), evolutionary psychologists come to a different conclusion about what may exist in the female psyche today. In this view, the conclusion that stimulating raw, male lust, to the degree that men actually are stimulated to experience it, is the unconscious wish in women may largely be a projection of men's desire.

Yet, as noted, it is often obvious to men (and other women) that there is an enormous advantage to the attractive woman to be so perceived (i.e., women whose appearance and behavior arouse intense sexual excitement and desire in men are often able to use the male preoccupation with sex to gain numerous advantages, one of which is the extremely valuable ability to exercise a great deal of choice in selecting a mate). The ultimate cause (the enhancement of the self-interest of a woman through maximizing the stimulation of men) is thus obvious from observing the proximal mechanism in action today. However, this does not justify one to take the ultimate cause, meld it with the male experience, and then project it into the female psyche. The result of this confusion of proximal with ultimate causes and the male analyst's melding of this confusion with the human tendency to project leads to the presumption of a conscious or unconscious wish in women to produce the male sexual experience. The woman then becomes largely responsible for the man's sexual desire.

Although the crudest form of this projection is repugnant to us all—the rapist's claim that "she wanted it" because he may have experienced intense arousal in response to her appearance and behavior—I am, in fact, suggesting that this is only a more extreme version of the same interpersonal process that occurs in analysis.

I have heard numerous analysts and analytically trained psycho-therapists talk about their "hysterical" patients in just this manner. As an example, consider again Freud's (1905/1953) analysis of Dora. Dora recounted that she was alone with a handsome, married businessman, a friend of the family whom she knew well. Herr K "suddenly clasped the girl to him and pressed a kiss upon her lips. This was surely just the situation to call up a distinct feeling of sexual excitement in a girl of fourteen who had never before been approached" (Freud, 1905/1953, p. 28). Freud considered Dora's lack of such a response evidence of hysteria as if the normal feeling in an inexperienced girl of 14 who is suddenly sexually accosted by an adult male friend of the family should be sexual excitement.

From an evolutionary perspective in which sex can be a very costly act for the female and is relatively risk free (with a potential for terrific genetic payoff without much cost) for the male (Trivers, 1972), this is an interesting conclusion. No distinction is made between what is a normal response for a male and for a female; the normal female response ought to be like what one might expect from a 14-year-old boy who was suddenly kissed by an attractive adult woman whom he knew well and for whom he presumably had intense sexual desires. This type of assumption—that the analyst has objective knowledge of what is universal and normal (e.g., that the lack of a typical male response in a woman indicates hysterical repression of sexuality)—is a potentially iatrogenic projection that occurs in many forms, not only around sexuality, and I discuss this further shortly when I evaluate the notion of projective identification as it is commonly used. However, at this point, it is important to acknowledge the legitimacy of the feminist critique of psychoanalysis even though it may often be couched in extreme terms that reject much more than the real failings.

Another example of the confusion between proximal and distal causes is the simplistic interpretation of altruism as ultimately self-serving. This confusion is found in Freud's (1914/1957, 1915/1957a, 1915/1957b, 1921/1955, 1930/1961) writing as well as in the writing of evolutionists (e.g., Nesse, 1990; cf. Kriegman, 1990). In this view, the adaptive value to the individual of compassion and care for others is used to argue that such concerns are really selfish motivations. Yes, they ultimately are adaptive and thus "self-serving." However, this is the ultimate cause—those who cared for others were more reproductively successful than those who did not show concern for others—not the proximal mechanism, which in many cases is a genuine concern for the well-being of others (primary love and compassion). When compassion is considered nothing more than a reaction formation against sadism (Freud, 1915a/1957, 1915b/1957) and parental love is dismissed as born-again, childish narcissism (Freud, 1914/1957), psychoanalytic theory overlooks major points about the basic motivations found in social species, especially those in whom parental care is essential for the survival and well-being of the offspring (Kriegman, 1988, 1990).

Interpretations in which patients are told the "truth" about their feelings and intentions based on their analyst's subjective responses—responses that may be accurate clues to ultimate, functional aims that shaped the observed behaviors (for the response in others may be one of the effects constituting the selective pressure that shaped the behavior)—can be abusive to the patient. The interpretation can be iatrogenic even though it may be "correct," in a sense: The adaptive aims (ultimate causes) of the behavior of the individual may be correctly identified. For example, women may wear makeup because maximizing their ability to arouse men sexually is their ultimate (adaptive) aim, and a person may care for a friend because there are self-serving, adaptive benefits to being seen as a trustworthy ally[24] without these ends existing in their conscious or unconscious motivational system as the primary proximal mechanisms controlling the behavior in the here and now. Telling patients that their ultimate aims are their proximal motives, even if they are told that the motivating wishes and desires are unconscious, can be experienced as an assault. In such cases, the authority of the analyst who knows Truth and delivers it to a resistant patient is a dangerous arrangement.[25]

Those who reject empirical foundations for psychoanalytic knowledge because they feel a need to challenge the supposed scientific, clinical aura used to impute objectivity to such destructive interpretations may be trying to empty some truly dirty bathwater. As I proceed, I hope I can show that there is a way to save the baby.

Intentions, Projective Identifications, and the (Evolutionary) Psychoanalysis of Proximal Mechanisms

Although thus far I have critiqued classical misconceptions caused by a confusion of distal and proximal causes, the same misunderstandings can be found in relational approaches. Consider a Fairbairnian interpretation to a "borderline" patient such as, "You are enraged. You wish to destroy me because you fear that I am like your father who traumatically disappointed you in the past. You will not allow yourself to be 'tricked' and thus you need to destroy your treatment rather than risk being set up for another devastating disappointment." As the functional meaning of a particular patient's assault on a specific therapist, this interpretation may actually be correct. It may explain the ultimate, adaptive function of Fairbairn's "antilibidinal ego" (cf. Kriegman & Slavin, 1989). However, it may completely misrepresent and obscure the actual proximal mechanism operating in the patient both consciously and unconsciously. Rather than having any "wish to destroy" the therapist, which may be how the therapist experiences the situation, the patient may be validly sensing some degree of real danger in the limits of the therapist's ability to understand, to be helpful, and commitment not to harm the patient. The protective proximal mechanism serving the interpreted ultimate function (avoidance of retraumatization) may be to be hyperreactive to the sensed, real danger.

Consciously, then, the patient would certainly not be trying to destroy the treatment to protect against a new trauma. Rather, the patient might simply be trying to express what might be consciously experienced as a reasonable level of frustration or anger at the therapist's real limitations and errors. In addition, even on the unconscious level, the ultimate explanation may have little or no meaning to the patient. The unconscious proximal process may simply be a perceptual or cognitive tendency to exaggerate (distort) the degree of sensed danger with some self-deception about its fit with the actual injury or risk (i.e., to become adaptively hypersensitive after trauma).

Of course, the analyst can point to the maladaptive nature of the overreaction and the restriction of possibilities that hypersensitivity can cause. However, helping patients see the reasonable, adaptive aspects of a self-protective overreaction (even if it has debilitating effects) can lead to their feeling safe enough—patients understand that the danger is not being ignored—to put aside the self-protection. By contrast, pointing out the unreasonableness of the overreaction can lead patients to believe the danger is being minimized and the self-protective function must be clung to more tenaciously. This can lead to regressive spirals in which analysts keep trying to get patients to agree with their supposedly more "objective" perspective in which such reactions are overreactions. This, in turn, leads to increased anxiety as patients sense that a real danger to them is being minimized and thus can lead to a louder outcry that in turn is seen by the analyst as a more regressive, infantile, and even psychotically distorted overreaction, which, of course, leads to patients. . . . Such intractable interactions have been referred to as "repetition compulsions" (Freud, 1920/1961, 1933/1964), or "negative therapeutic reactions" (Freud, 1923/1961, 1924/1961, 1937/1964; Glover, 1955, 1956) and "id-resistance" (Glover, 1955, 1956). Using such conceptualizations, the responsibility for the impasse can be laid squarely on the patient (cf. Brandchaft, 1983; Kriegman & Slavin, 1989).

A Fairbairnian, relational interpretation may accurately identify the functional meaning of "what is going on" in the treatment without saying something with any meaning to the patient if the interpretation makes a claim about the patient's conscious or unconscious intention, as if the ultimate aim must be contained in some explicit form in some part of the patient's psyche that is available to direct or indirect observation.[26] The evolutionary perspective suggests that people may be designed to engage in functional actions (such as the interpreted one, in this case) without having any conscious or unconscious "awareness" of the function.

If an analysis of the proximal mechanism occurs instead (e.g., searching for the danger sensed by the patient and carefully elucidating how the felt danger leads to the rage reaction), after many occurrences its operation may become clear. After a clarifying analysis of the proximal, experience-near process—a process that is seen to have validity and an inherently adaptive function even if it causes enormous problems in its actual operation—most patients are willing to try to understand why they react so forcefully. At such a point, searching for an ultimate explanation (the functional "why") is often experienced as helpful because it emphasizes the adaptive goal (the healthy aim) of what the patient can then begin to see is an irrational response; understanding the adaptive (ultimate) function of a proximal mechanism can increase the patient's ability to see its distorting, dysfunctional aspects. In this view, the distortion is not seen as pathological with the inevitable shameful association connected to such an appellation. Rather, despite the problems it causes, the distortion is seen as an integral component of a valid, adaptive process. Frequently, therapists find that such patients long to disengage from—what they can see only after repeated analysis of the proximal mechanism—a process of distorting reality. This longing to be free from such overreactions may occur only after the analysis of the proximal mechanism (as it functions both within and out of treatment) has led to an increased awareness of its existence and nature as well as the difficulties it causes in relationships with others.

Patients then find themselves wishing to alter what has been identified as a formerly (or potentially) functional (but no longer necessary) process because of its troublesome (dysfunctional) effects. Rather than telling patients that they are trying to do something that they may actually be trying to do (in the ultimate sense)—for they are using proximal mechanisms that may include no conscious or unconscious awareness of their function and thus such interpretations can be experienced as missing the valid, vital meaning of the patient's here-and-now experience (i.e., the proximal mechanism in action)—this clear delineation of the difference between proximal mechanisms (including conscious and repressed aims or intentions) and functional meaning may result in a more facilitating mode of clinical communication.

The following clinical example helps illustrate some of the implications of this evolutionary perspective for the psychoanalytic concept of projective identification:

Case Example: S.

S. was a "psychotic" woman who, on several occasions, had gone into a coma after serious suicide attempts. During several of her descents into psychotic despair, she expressed her distress to me and I struggled to deal with the real danger that she would succeed in killing herself. The degree of distress I experienced and communicated had a great deal to do with whether she calmed down. If I was clearly upset and did not try to hide it, she usually calmed down. If I appeared calm and in control when I acknowledged the potentially fatal implications of my unwillingness to meet her needs more fully, she often became more agitated and despairing. My distress made the conflict in our interests palpable: She could directly feel the threat to my well-being (to my interests) that motivated the limits I placed on my investment in her. When my distress was hidden (i.e., unexpressed), or when I was able to repress the split-off affect and intellectualize, thus protecting myself from experiencing the anxiety that was caused by the conflict in our interests, she experienced me as rejecting and withholding. This is like Melanie Klein's (Segal, 1964) paranoid-schizoid position, in which the infant believes the mother's depleted breast is not dry; the angry infant believes the mother is withholding the fully available milk she is *unwilling* to give. S. often struggled until I more fully grasped her hopelessness and despair. Only when I sensed the massive hopelessness and pain and was moved out of my self-protective ensconcement in a theoretical (therapeutic) cocoon—which helped me to not experience her terror, helplessness, and despair—could S. finally feel truly understood and have the sense that her subjective experience had been grasped. Thus, she struggled until I suffered along with her.

Some analysts explain such phenomena with the notion of projective identification (Klein, 1946/1975). However, unlike projective identification, in this view I am not confusing intent with cause (cf. Stolorow et al., 1987). It was not S.'s intent to induce in me a sense of helplessness and thus sadistically (or defensively) project her helplessness into me in order to rid her of the experience. Rather, she fully experienced the helplessness and despair herself; she was not defensively avoiding it. She simply could not get the sense of being understood—and thus the isolating struggle with the despair continued and intensified the despair—until I appeared to grasp her horror fully. This "being with her" in the horrifying experience could not be sensed by her as long as I appeared to be comfortable in my role as analyzing therapist. To paraphrase S.'s complaint:

> How can you make sounds that supposedly indicate an understanding of my ugly, horrifying nonexistence as if you had just seen a poignant motion picture? I have just been exploded by a grenade; my guts are all over your office; my intestines are out and down around my knees; I'm screaming in pain and about to die; and you look at me with a sympathetic look and words that are supposed to indicate that you understand!?! You look as if in a few minutes you'll just say, "Next," and call in another sufferer to face with sympathetic looks. No, you don't just *look* that way. You really are going to dismiss me and say, "Next." You can't possibly understand!

Thus, until therapists seem to be in significant pain themselves, how could such patients believe that the understanding has any depth? The goal is not to rid the patient of pain by projecting it into the analyst. The goal is not to make the analyst feel as hopeless as the patient to act out some vengeful, sadistic fantasy or to change passive trauma into a sense of active mastery. The goal is to be understood. This cannot be experienced until therapists are visibly moved. Furthermore, if what is to be understood is truly horrifying, then the visible movement must be more than a look of concern. Only when therapists appear horrified themselves can such patients believe they are being seen.

Until therapists "get it," the struggle continues. To imply *intent* to make analysts suffer—which is, in fact, part of what this process was (ultimately) designed to produce—is the same logical error as the ironic saying, "You always find what you're looking for in the last place you look." As if there is something special about that last place. Or, as if the universe is designed with the intent to make people waste time looking until they have suffered enough and then they are allowed to find the lost item. As in the process misleadingly labeled *projective identification*, once the lost object is found (once the therapist is visibly and powerfully moved), the seeker (patient) can stop looking (stop struggling and claiming that the therapist does not "get it"). Only when the therapist is visibly moved can the patient have the selfobject experience of being understood. In this analysis, it is true—if the therapist does not get angry or find some way to blame the patient—that once the therapist is filled with despair, the patient may feel better. However, the subjective motive (proximal mechanism) on the patient's part was not to hurt the other. Patients do continue to hurt therapists (raising the ante) until they feel understood; their *behavior* is consistent with that which would be produced if the *intent* were to make therapists suffer. However, it is being understood—not to feel isolated, lost, and alone in despair—that is the patient's urgently experienced goal or intent. When this goal is achieved, the process stops spiraling into greater and greater fragmentation and despair on the patient's part. It can appear as if the patient's intent is to bring about the analyst's suffering when in fact the patient is struggling to bring about the analyst's palpable understanding, which (unfortunately) cannot be perceived unless the analyst shares some of the patient's discomfort.[27]

In the examples given thus far, the conscious and unconscious (proximal) motives may be very different in their intentional aim from the ultimate functions that they produce. Although the adaptive effect (ultimate function) is real, a direct intentional aim, desire, or wish for the attainment of the particular effect may not be operating (consciously or unconsciously), and it is often counterproductive—or even countertransference projection—to suggest that it is. However, evolutionists also have developed a functional understanding of a need to keep direct motives out of consciousness in order to hide one's true intentions from oneself. In this view, the evolutionary analysis strikes closer to home with the more classical psychoanalytic insight.

The Evolutionary Analytic View of Repression

In the actual act of deception . . . [great deceivers] are overcome by *belief in themselves*. . . . The founders of religions are distinguished from these great deceivers by the fact that they never emerge from this state of self-deception. . . . Self-

> deception has to exist if a grand *effect* is to be produced. For men believe in the truth of that which is plainly strongly believed.
>
> —Friedrich Nietzsche
> *Human, All Too Human*

Despite the complexity and unfamiliarity of the biological reasoning, analytic readers may agree with what I have said thus far. However, analytic experience shows that sometimes people are unaware of motives they appear to be acting on and that are nearly universal human motives other people can acknowledge consciously experiencing. Are analysts to believe that people do not have such unconscious motivations? What about empirical demonstrations of unconscious mental processing in which subliminal stimulation of certain affective themes changes behavior without the individual's awareness (Bornstein, 1990a; Patton, 1992)? What about individuals who are given posthypnotic suggestions and then confabulate logical (conscious) explanations for behavior that is actually motivated by the current influence of earlier instructions of which they are unaware? What about patients who deny the existence of motives and then later do not merely acknowledge their existence—in which case they may be reacting to suggestion—but embrace them as primary wishes that then clearly explain major aspects of their experience and behavior? Sometimes analysts do know things about their patients of which their patients are unaware. Sometimes such knowledge is actively resisted but ultimately is seen to be true. How does the evolutionary perspective explain this?

The human psyche appears, in large part, to be an organ for perceiving and organizing our perceptions of the world. Accurate knowledge of the structure of our environment, both the social and the physical world, and of ourselves and our place within the environment is clearly highly adaptive. However, there also are times when a lack of awareness is adaptive. Freud (1926/1959) suggested that repression was adaptive because it enables the ego to manage the competing and conflicting anxiety inducing forces impinging on it. Certain forces, mainly instinctual desires, would overwhelm the ego if allowed full access to consciousness. The whole idea of "defense mechanisms" is based on a notion of adaptive function:

The ego defends itself to maintain its integrity and ability to function. Without reviewing the classical analytic theory of repression, I simply suggest that Freud used adaptive explanations in his formulation of the divided nature of the human mind. Freud explicitly rooted these explanations in his attempt to develop psychoanalysis within a Darwinian (functional/adaptive) worldview. However, the Freudian notion of the adaptive nature of repression was biased in that, despite important caveats in which repression is clearly seen as normal, necessary, and adaptive, it tended to equate repression with pathology and treatment with making the unconscious conscious.

Evolutionary biology has developed an entirely new view of the adaptive function of repression, here called *self-deception*. This view deepens the psychoanalytic conception of how and why repression operates. The model is deceptively simple and can be readily demonstrated by looking at situations entailing intense conflict. It is a commonplace tenet of military science that a larger, better equipped army can surprisingly be beaten by a somewhat smaller, more poorly equipped force. Sometimes chance elements, brilliant tactics, or fatal blunders determine the outcome. But often it is the charismatic authority of a leader or the enthusiasm of the soldiers that carries the day. An important element of both phenomena is that the warriors are convinced of their eventual success, and the "enemy" becomes aware of their conviction. Whether true or not, it is far more adaptive, if one is in fact going to go into battle, to believe that one is going to win. In warfare, the belief can sometimes determine its own truth value.[28] Thus, there are clearly times when believing something to be true is more important than whether, independent of the belief, it is likely to be so.[29] Could such situations have been important enough to have shaped people over evolutionary history?

In answering this question, consider the ubiquitous experience of negotiations that characterize human social intercourse. For example, consider the frequency with which car salespeople say that the "final offer" has just been made; there is no way their managers could possibly consider going lower. Customers look at them trying to decide whether the salespeople are telling the truth. Now consider the two possibilities: (a) Although it is not so, the salespeople believe what they are saying to be the truth or (b) they know the dealership would in fact be willing to sell the car for less.[30] In which situation are the salespeople likely to be more convincing? Trivers (1976) noted that if

> deceit is fundamental to animal communication, then there must be strong selection to spot deception and this ought, in turn, to select for a degree of self-deception, rendering some facts and motives unconscious so as not to betray—by the subtle signs of self-knowledge—the deception being practiced. Thus the conventional view that natural selection favors nervous systems which produce ever more accurate images of the world must be a very naive view of mental evolution. (p. vi)

The question of the importance of such situations remains: Are there enough human interactions that require deception to render this a central feature of the human psyche? In fact, there appear to be more than enough.

In development, human children must adapt to the world that their parents provide. To maximize parental investment, children must be able to convince their parents that they are the kind of children in whom such investment is necessary and worthwhile. If children are to garner the full benefits of such parental investment, then they must convincingly demonstrate acquiescence to certain parental wishes, prohibitions, and values. But how to do this? Again, the most convincing display is one a child believes. Children repress significant aspects of themselves. Note that these repressed parts of the self are not deleted. They are still available, stored in the child's unconscious ready for resurfacing during adolescence when the child is leaving the parental environment and may be able to use those aspects of the self that had to be repressed for an optimal adaptation to the family (Slavin, 1985, 1990).

This is certainly a major universal developmental pattern that actually characterizes all of human social life: People pass through progressive adaptations to different environments. Some of these environments change rapidly (e.g., adolescence to adulthood, immigration to a new land, death of a spouse, war, etc.) and some change gradually (e.g., parental tasks change as children grow; aging; nonchaotic social, industrial, and economic change). Yet, in each of these environments, maximum social effectiveness is related to allowing only the acceptable parts of one's potential personality to be seen by others. The rest is best kept out of awareness where one's self-knowledge cannot betray its existence.

A similar link between self-deception and other-deception was suggested by Sackeim and Gur (1978), who also noted that in repression the contents are not eradicated (lost) but are stored and that self-awareness is related to conflicts with others (the environment). Laboratory studies of self-deception and repression have yielded data that are consistent with the conclusions suggested by the independent, evolutionary theorizing of Trivers (1976) that self-deception—rather than being a sign of psychopathology—may be related to the adaptive deception of others. For example, Sackeim and Gur (1978) presented evidence that shows that self-deception is negatively correlated with measures of psychopathology (e.g., the Manifest Symptom Questionnaire, the Eysenck Personality Inventory Neuroticism scale, and the Beck Depression Inventory) and positively correlated with other-deception (e.g., the Eysenck Personality Inventory Lie scale and Other-Deception Questionnaire).

Sackeim and Gur (1978) also reviewed experiments demonstrating greater autonomic arousal and inhibition of behavior after hearing one's voice (self-confrontation). The notion that self-awareness functions to monitor and then modulate and edit one's social presentation received support from the vocal masking experiments reviewed by Sackeim and Gur. If unable to hear their voice, participants' responses were more drive laden and less inhibited. This supports the notion that when less inhibited behavior is brought into play in pursuit of a goal (i.e., in conflict situations such as those frequently seen in the clinical "laboratory" of marital therapy), one should see maximal self-deception in which the individuals are minimally aware of aspects of their feelings as well as of their impact on others.

Indeed, this is consistent with my clinical experience: A great deal of what is communicated in marital therapy, and in the marital negotiations that have gone on for millions of years without the presence of a therapist, must be considered a bluff. I frequently hear statements of how "I will not live one more day with such and such behavior." When I began conducting marital therapy, I used to believe that my patients would divorce every other week. Although they do occasionally divorce, the frequency of divorce action is a tiny fraction of the threats to take immediate action. Such threats and the challenging accusations that accompany them are often extremely ugly. It is clear from working with couples that the individuals are often unaware of how they appear while they are ranting or attacking. This is to be expected: Decent people— and most of my patients are decent people who are trying hard to make their relationships and families work—could not possibly behave in such a manner if they were aware of how they appeared. Yet, they are often vicious (as their spouses are only too willing to point out to them). They are so caught up in their pain or anger that they cannot believe (much less see) that they are having such a destructive impact; suggesting that they are often intensifies their behavior.[31] As ugly as it is, this type of threatening often works. Although it also can be maladaptive, I would suggest that there are many circumstances in which such behavior may be a highly successful negotiating tool; self-deceptive bluffing—in which the bluffer believes the bluff—may be highly effective in forcing the other to acquiesce.

Such marital negotiations can be similar to the example of borderline rage discussed previously. In the evolutionary analysis of such rage, I suggested that repression was not operating along the typical psychoanalytic lines of interpretation (projective identification). Yet as in this example of marital conflict, repression may still be an important part of the clinical phenomenon. What is striking in this evolutionary analysis of either type of angry, conflictual interaction is the completely different content of what is repressed and may need to be brought into awareness. Rather than vicious, destructive wishes being repressed and projected onto the analyst or spouse by the raging patient or spouse—which is the more traditional interpretation based on the analyst's anger in response to the feeling of being assaulted or the marital therapist's horror at watching an assault—what is often repressed is the patient or spouse's dependency, need for love, and concern for the other.

If people are going to try to effectively intimidate someone into an accommodation to their agenda using either physical or abandonment threats, it is important that they believe their own threats and hate so that they do not betray the existence of softer, loving, or dependent feelings that might undermine their intimidation strategy. In such situations, it is adaptive to repress the positive or dependent feelings if they want the threat to be convincing. In traditional analytic theory, socially negative affects are repressed (hidden). In my experience conducting marital therapy, negative affects are flying all over the place in the attempt to get the spouse to change or acquiesce to the partner's agenda. It is love, caring concern, and dependent needs that are repressed to maximize the conviction with which the threats are made. The raging ("All you ever think about is yourself; you always distort the facts; you really are crazy; I hate you") or despairing ("I give up; I'm leaving") patients or spouses are essentially using self-deception to maximize the effectiveness of "bluffing": They usually do not hate the analyst or spouse so much—and are not actually in such unbearable despair—that they are willing to quit or divorce or kill someone at the moment. Note that the therapist's typical reaction (based on the belief that the rage is in fact the primary operative affect) may be an indication that "the bluff" (self-deception in the service of deception) worked. Whether the strategy worked to achieve the angry patient's or spouse's ends, the reaction of the therapist or spouse frequently indicates that the manifest behavior has effectively deceived all parties into believing the repressed feelings do not exist (or are not a significant factor at the moment).

Consistent with this evolutionary perspective, Sackeim and Gur (1978) noted that (a) there is a link between self- and other-deception; (b) in repression the contents are stored, not eradicated; (c) self-awareness is related to conflicts with others; and (d) there is a self-monitoring and modulating function of self-awareness in social situations. Yet, they failed to take the step the evolutionary biologist, Robert Trivers, took in realizing that self-deception and other-deception are *functionally* related, that a self-deceptive, divided psyche may have evolved as an adaptation to a social world in which conflicts of interest with others are ubiquitous.[32] That is, they looked for a proximal mechanism and concluded that self-deception is used to minimize anxiety. This may be true enough as an understanding of the proximal mechanism or motivation; it requires the use of the evolutionary perspective to provide a framework for searching for how the (proximal) design of the human psyche serves adaptive (ultimate) functions. Trivers' understanding of the link between self-deception and other-deception was first brought to an understanding of psychoanalysis by Slavin (1985,

1990) in his conception of repression as a hiding of aspects of the self in social environments (in which they would be maladaptive) by storing them in the unconscious so that they can be used later when needed (cf. Slavin & Kriegman, 1992).

However, what is the mechanism for knowing when to bring the repressed forward into a potentially new environment where it may be adaptive? How do individuals know when an environment has changed enough that a repressed part of their personalities may now be adaptive if allowed some degree of expression? The answer seems to be that repression is not an impenetrable, fixed barrier. Rather, it seems to be fluid and, to varying degrees, semi-permeable. This is consistent with Freud's (1926/1959) introduction of the need for constant efforts to maintain the repression of material that continues to push to enter consciousness. It is then continually rerepressed if the danger (signal anxiety) is still present. There are times when the personality is more loosely organized, when self-structures are less cohesive, and the repressed has easier access to expression: adolescence, mourning, drug-induced states, group contagion, and war or crisis. Note that some of these experiences suggest that the times are changing. In such circumstances, it can be adaptive to have access to parts of the personality that were better left repressed in the old environment (Slavin & Kriegman, 1992).

Psychoanalysis itself can be viewed as a changed environment in which it may be safe to allow derepression in order to experiment with bringing out aspects of the personality that may now be useful. This is another way of saying that the old adaptation to the family may no longer be adaptive and that the analytic relationship provides a context for regressive experimentation with new (or older, repressed) ways of being (Slavin & Kriegman, 1992). In such a context, there may indeed be resistance to experiencing parts of the self that were traumatically rejected in one's childhood or that were simply experienced as being dangerous or maladaptive. There may be a role for a form of "confrontation" by the analyst in which the existence of unconscious motives is suggested. When such motives are pressing for expression—at which times such motives and beliefs may be close to entering consciousness and may achieve some degree of disguised expression—well-timed and formulated interpretations may enable the repressed to enter consciousness, where its presence may help to explain and provide mastery over difficult problems.[33] The reentry of repressed memories, knowledge, affects, and motivations also may provide for an expanded repertoire of adaptive behaviors and more flexible (adaptive) ways of organizing experience (Stolorow & Atwood, 1992).

In contrast to the aforementioned misattribution of unconscious intent—the clinical misattribution of intent to ultimate functions that are actually brought about by proximal mechanisms that operate without the individual's conscious or unconscious awareness of their ultimate aims—this type of interpretation focused on repressed material that does exist in some potentially direct form in the patient's unconscious.[34] Helping to bring the latter into consciousness can be useful to patients; with this latter type of interpretation, the impact on the patient can be markedly different from the interpretations discussed earlier that are experienced as either abusive or simply miss the mark.

Who Am I? An Evolutionary Perspective

Another way to understand the interrelationship between proximal mechanisms and distal (ultimate) aims comes from considering the meaning of the word *I*. Kohut's (1971, 1977) attempt to formulate an experience-near conception of the "self" comes close to the meaning most people intend when they use the word *I*: The center of experience and the source of initiative and action. In this sense in ordinary speaking, one does not say, "I beat my heart" or "I grow my hair" or "I heal my wounds."[35] *I* refers to the experiencing and acting agent, the one who makes meanings, has intentions, wishes, needs, ambitions, values, and goals and, on these bases, acts. Because the processes involved in hair growth, for example, are unconscious bodily events, people can never directly influence them by their thoughts, feelings, or intentions.[36] And, in the normal use of language, people say, "My hair grows" or "My heart beats" or "My wounds heal."

However, from another way of thinking about the meaning of the word *I*, this can be thought of as a misperception. In this view, *I* refers to the entire human organism. And, in this sense, I do beat my heart, grow my hair, and heal my wounds. It is in this sense that it is meaningful to say individuals' aims are the adaptive (ultimate) aims of the human organisms that they are. If an analyst is careful to distinguish between the two meanings of *I* (the experiencing and acting intentional agent vs. the entire organism), then statements about motives that refer to the design and aims of the entire organism can be meaningful.

This leads to markedly different interpretations that include several meanings: for example, the proximal meanings of self psychology (i.e., environmental failure, threat, and need to protect or enhance the self) and classical analytic thought (i.e., internal conflict between one's social motivations and motivations to promote one's own interests even if it is at the expense of others[37]), as well as the ultimate aims that the organism as a whole was designed to achieve without any direct conscious or unconscious motive or intention. An interpretation that does not confuse proximal and distal mechanisms—or the aims of the "experiencing *I*" of intention and initiative (whose unconscious motives can become conscious) and the total "organismic *I*" that, in addition, pursues genetic self-interest in myriad ways forever unavailable to direct conscious experience (e.g., motives and behavioral tendencies that were ultimately designed to achieve functional aims without conscious or unconscious intentions to achieve those aims)—can provide several levels of valuable meaning to a patient. An interpretation[38] of this sort might run along the following lines when dealing with a common problem that many clinicians have faced (again, borderline rage):

> Your acting and feeling self is simply trying (intentionally aiming) to protect your existence, which you sense is threatened. Thus, you are motivated by your fear to loudly and angrily state the threat and speak out against how I am affecting you. The reason for this is that—as an evolved organism functioning to achieve adaptive, healthy (life-preserving and -enhancing) ends— you were designed to make sure that threats are recognized and the dangers are not ignored by either you or others. Your fury and rage are a legitimate attempt to protect yourself. Others— who, including myself, are also evolved organisms designed to maximize *their* success—do not want to hear about the danger to you if paying attention to it is more costly to them than ignoring it. Thus, they resist hearing the validity of what you are

saying, say you are exaggerating, and try to get you to keep quiet.[39]

You do, in fact, experience the threat as being greater than others believe it is. This is due to a bias: You have a natural inclination to make sure that others cannot minimize the problem and ignore it while it is often in their interests to minimize it. Thus, it is unlikely that either party can see the situation as the other sees it and likely that both tend to bias their perception toward their own interests. A significant part of the process that shapes your view of the situation—in a manner that others call *biased* or *distorted*—operates outside of your awareness, is automatic, and is built into mental processes that you have no access to. In fact, in many situations, you would not act effectively to protect your own interests if you believed that what you are reacting to might not be real; your experience of the world is usually exactly the way you say it is. If I (or others) say it is not so or that you are exaggerating, you feel like I (or you) must be crazy for you see (experience) it exactly as you are saying.

Furthermore, when you sense that the threat may be even more dangerous if it is ignored, this compels you to yell louder and then you do make what others experience as extreme statements (e.g., "You hate me and always have," "I hate you and wish you were dead," etc.). Although such extreme statements may feel necessary to ensure that your safety is not given short shrift, they, in turn, lead people to label you as "disturbed" or "sick" and then to use such labels to dismiss your urgent cries as the distorted statements of someone who is "mentally ill." This tends to panic you into speaking even louder and making even more extreme statements. A vicious cycle ensues that can get out of hand and has been the source of enormous problems in your life.

Kohut's insistence in placing the self at the center of psychoanalytic theory has made self psychology less prone to the confusion of distal and proximal mechanisms because self psychological interventions are almost always focused on proximal mechanisms (i.e., the patient's experience). One should also remember that Freud did not use a term like *the ego*, which is a hypothetical, metapsychological construct. In German, Freud's term was *das Ich*, meaning *the I*. As much as Freud was enamored with the development of metapsychology, he did not initially set out to understand the metapsychological, experience-distant predicament of a reified psychological construct called *an* ego. He was trying to understand "the Is" experience of being-in-the-world. It was James Strachey, in his translation of Freud's work into English, who used the terms *ego* and *id* and helped make psychoanalysis more experience-distant with a superficially more objective, scientific, and medicalized (Latinized) aura.[40] To the extent that psychoanalysis has always been an attempt to understand the full meaning of "the Is" experience of being in the world, psychoanalysis is coterminous with the essence of self psychology. In this sense, Freud was the first self psychologist or, as Kohut claimed, his focus on the introspective and empathic understanding of self-experience was merely a return to the essential roots of psychoanalysis. Unfortunately, self psychology avoids the confusion between distal and proximal causes by minimizing the importance of both endogenous motives (such as drives) and inherent, inevitable conflict (and thus bias and distortion) in the human psyche or interpersonal relationships. Using the evolutionary distinction between distal and proximal processes, one can avoid throwing out the "baby" (i.e., endogenous motives and interpersonal and intrapsychic conflict) with the "dirty bathwater" (i.e., the confusion of ultimate aims with patients' unconscious intentions; also see Kriegman, 1996a; Kriegman & Slavin, 1990; Slavin & Kriegman, 1992).

An Overview of Possible Outcomes to Interpreting the Unconscious

In Exhibit 6.1, I illustrate the possibilities for an interpretation intended to undo deceptions and self-deceptions and bring unconscious material into consciousness. Of course, real-life events do not fall neatly into one category: They can fall in the gray area in between, or one aspect of the meaning of an interpretation can fall in one category and another part of the same interpretation can be in another. To provide an overview, I consider the category that best fits an interpretation as its proper category. I examine eight possible main outcomes dependent on three conditions: (a) whether the interpretation is productive and useful, (b) the truth state of the interpretation, and (c) the degree of self-deception and repression involved. In each of these cases, I also offer a crude estimate of their frequency derived from my clinical impressions, discussions with others, and reading of the literature.

When Interpretation Succeeds

Looking first at the instances in which confrontation and interpretation lead to useful, productive outcomes, one can see that the interpretation's truth state can be divided into two possible categories: The interpretation is true (the analyst is correct) or it is false (the analyst is wrong).[41] As I note, it is possible for an interpretation to lead to productive results even if it is essentially wrong. The dimension regarding self-deception and repression also can be divided into two categories: No self-deception is involved or repression is active. Consider the first outcome (I.A.1) in Exhibit 6.1 in which the interpretation is accurate and there is no self-deception or repression operating in the patient.

In I.A.1, patients are consciously trying to deceive analysts (to lie), to hide known aspects of the self, or to avoid awareness of facts and feelings that are available to consciousness. In this situation, one can have the most frequent generally positive outcome of an interpretation or confrontation when analysts correct patients whom they sense are hiding or denying something. Many analysts feel that this is not a true interpretation because no unconscious material is brought to consciousness. However, it is a confrontation in that what a patient says is contradicted (even if this is done gently) by the analyst who suggests an alternative reality.[42] This can include simple statements such as "You say you're not angry with me, yet you look upset and sound distressed. Do you feel safe enough to tell me how you really feel?" Or, Freud's insistence (Breuer & Freud, 1895/1955) that his patient follow the fundamental rule: "I no longer accepted her declaration that nothing had occurred to her, but assured her that something *must* have occurred to her . . . and that she was concealing it" (p. 154). If done gently, despite the anxiety they raise, such confrontations may be experienced by patients more as an encouragement or a clarification. Such confrontation is fairly common, and it is not unusual for it to occur more than once in a single session.

The next set of possible outcomes occur when the interpretation is true and self-deception and repression are active. I further di-

Exhibit 6.1

The Analytic "Yield" of an Interpretation That Seeks to Undo a Deception or Self-Deception and Make the Unconscious Conscious

	Truth state of the interpretation			
	True: Deception is occurring (the analyst is correct)			False: There is no deception (the analyst is wrong)
	No self-deception (no repression)	Self-deception (repression is operating)		No deception or self-deception
The effect of the confrontation or interpretation	A. Deception is conscious and intentional: Lying and misdirection	B. Deception and self-deception are semi-permeably conscious or unconscious	C. Deception and self-deception operate unconsciously	D. There is no deception or self-deception
I. Interpretation works: The confrontation furthers insight and growth	I.A.1. Patients are ultimately willing and able to acknowledge the truth—sometimes only after some degree of struggle. The analytic commitment to the pursuit of truth is confirmed and the idealization of the analyst or analysis is supported (fairly frequent).	I.B.1. Same as I.A.1 but less common. This is the classic or ideal conception of the well-timed interpretation that makes the unconscious conscious.	I.C.1. Patients are able to see the truth (fairly rare) or analysts are able to see II.A.2b (uncommon but increasing in frequency with certain self psychological and interpersonal approaches).	I.D.1. Analysts are able to acknowledge error and negotiation of relationship or analysis proceeds with increased insight into the vicissitudes of how the patients' dynamics interact with interpersonal conflict (fairly uncommon). I.D.2. Adaptive mourning: Patients come to terms with analysts' limits in understanding (a limited degree of this is common).

The effect of the confrontation or interpretation	II. Interpretation fails: The confrontation is counterproductive			
		II.A.2. Patients are unwilling or unable to acknowledge what they know is the truth (fairly common). II.A.2a. The analysis is undermined as patients continue to consciously attempt to deceive the analyst; a chronic struggle can ensue. II.A.2b. The interpretation may be "correct" but it misses the point (e.g., the reason for patients' resistance: fear, danger, mistrust, etc.). Thus, the interpretation is "correct" but "wrong."	II.B.2. Same as II.A.2 (also fairly common), but the analysis is less frequently undermined by conscious deception on patients' parts. A struggle may ensue with damage to patients, the analysis, or both. II.B.3. Possibility of false self-compliance that can deceive patients, analysts, or both into believing the interpretation worked.	II.C.2. Same as II.B.2 (also fairly common), but the analysis is not undermined by conscious deception. A struggle may ensue with damage to patients, the analysis, or both. II.C.3. Fairly common occurrence of some degree of false self-compliance that can deceive patients, analysts, or both into believing the interpretation worked.	II.D.2. Struggle ensues with no resolution and possible serious damage to the patient, the analysis, or both (fairly common). II.D.3. Common occurrence of some degree of false self-compliance (in order to avoid II.D.2) that can deceive patients, analysts, or both into believing the interpretation worked.

vided this category into two conditions: The repression is semi-permeable (i.e., ready to break down and allow the nearly conscious material into consciousness) or strong and relatively impermeable. In the former case when the interpretation works, one has the outcome (I.B.1 in Exhibit 6.1) in which a well-timed interpretation can have mutative impact (Strachey, 1934). This is the classical, ideal conception of the well-timed interpretation that makes the unconscious conscious. This is relatively rare, occurring once a week to once every few months depending on how one defines this type of interpretation and other factors regarding the analyst's activities, the particular patient, and the nature of the material.

In the latter case (I.C.1 in Exhibit 6.1), in which the interpretation is correct and repression is fairly solid, the interpretation may crash against a solid wall of resistance. This is a poorly timed interpretation that patients were not ready for and which only rarely leads to true insight about the content of the interpretation. However, such an interpretation can still lead to a beneficial result if, as in Kohut's comment (discussed earlier), the analyst is able to see that the "correct" content of the interpretation may be less important than the patient's active need to resist and maintain the repression. In this case, the analytic work can turn to focus on the analysis of the resistance in a manner that may increase both insight and a patient's sense of safety as the danger is recognized and acknowledged as more important than the analyst's "truth." In my experience, this is uncommon but becoming more frequent with the increasing influence of certain self psychological and interpersonal approaches.

The last possible outcome in which there is a beneficial effect of an interpretation (I.D.1 in Exhibit 6.1) occurs when analysts are wrong and no repression is involved.[43] In this case, the benefit that can accrue to a patient occurs if the analyst is able to see the error and refocus on the patient's experience of the mistake. Patients may then gain greater mastery and understanding of the vicissitudes of how their personal dynamics operate in situations of interpersonal conflict or in situations in which they must negotiate to obtain the understanding they need. The analysis also can be furthered by the increasing safety patients may come to feel in a relationship in which their voice can be heard, their truth respected, and their sense of reality validated. This also seems to be uncommon but increasing in frequency because analysis is increasingly seen as a two-person process that needs to be understood in intersubjective (Stolorow et al., 1987), interpersonal terms (Hoffman, 1983, 1991), a process that requires negotiation (Kriegman, 1996c; Slavin & Kriegman, 1992, in press).

A related gain can come from analysts' *inability* to understand patients' experience. In this case (I.D.2 in Exhibit 6.1), patients must come to terms with the fact that the longed-for understanding (or selfobject response) will never be available from their analysts. This is not always an obstacle to treatment; indeed, it can be the centerpiece of a truly therapeutic engagement. For example, after a long analysis, Ms. D. realized that her deepest longings for an empathic understanding of certain aspects of her experience could not be obtained. The analyst repeatedly made irrelevant—sometimes painfully irrelevant—interpretations based on a theoretical perspective that had no meaning to D., and in her experience, it was the analyst's repetitive return to the same perspective that blocked the longed-for understanding. Because the empathic failure was not traumatic, a transmuting internalization (Kohut, 1971)—in which the longed-for selfobject response (and the function for the self of the selfobject) was replaced by adaptive mourning—occurred as D. realized she could live and move forward in life without remaining in treatment waiting for the type of response she longed for but never received from her mother. In this particular case, after obtaining independent consultation, the patient made the interpretation of her longing, her analyst's failure, and her sad need to end the analysis while the analyst continued to issue the same interpretation. Each repetition by the analyst led to a deeper and sadder mourning in which D. finally entered a highly productive termination phase (lasting more than a year) while the analyst continued to interpret her action as "resistance" to further needed treatment.

This type of growth parallels Dr. Spock's (Spock & Rothenberg, 1985) recommendation to stop going in to soothe a baby who has begun to develop and is ready to consolidate the ability to self-soothe and sleep through the night. Almost universally, on the first night when parents implement this recommendation, the infant sobs and sobs before finally giving up in exhaustion. The second night usually has a small fraction of the first night's sobbing. By the third night, most babies seem to engage in some form of self-soothing (e.g., rhythmic motion or thumb sucking) without seeming to be in any pain at all. It is only through painful mourning and finally giving up on the unavailable, sought-for response that the realization that one is all right and can go forward and find some way to self-soothe can come into being. Likewise, some empathic failures—even if unacknowledged or denied by analysts—can occasionally lead to productive results, and, to some degree, this is probably an unspoken benefit of many treatments. However, I believe it is rare that patients can make the interpretation while the analysts deny its truth, as occurred in the case just noted.[44]

When Interpretation Fails

Consider the outcomes in which the interpretations or confrontations are counterproductive, sometimes damaging to the analytic process and destructive to patients. The first outcome (II.A.2 in Exhibit 6.1) occurs when patients are actively hiding or denying something that they know to be true and analysts insist on presenting what they sense is, in fact, true. The analysis can become permanently undermined and a chronic struggle can ensue if patients feel a need to continue to hide the truth from analysts. An atmosphere of mistrust and suspicion develops and any real analytic work becomes impossible. Although extreme cases in which the analysis is terminated do not appear to be common, they also are not rare, in my experience. This may indeed account for many failed analyses. However, more common than the extreme is some degree of II.A.2 in Exhibit 6.1. Fairly frequently, patients in analysis have a sense that their analyst has responded in a manner that makes them feel that it is not really safe to reveal certain things. In a sense, the interpretation was "correct" but "wrong" because it completely missed the salient point: The patient's fear, shame, guilt, and anxiety were ignored in an interpretation that tried to push forward the analyst's agenda, the analyst's identity and sense of reality, without respecting the patient's needs and vulnerabilities.

In cases in which the interpretation fails and semipermeable repression is active (II.B.2 and II.B.3 in Exhibit 6.1), there are outcomes similar to II.A.2. However, when the content of the interpretation does not become conscious, patients are less likely to engage in active, conscious deception. Patients may attempt to maintain a sense of relatedness and connection to analysts through false self-compliance (II.B.3) that can deceive patients, analysts, or both into believing that the interpretation worked. In my experience, this type of compliance is fairly common (see also II.C.3 and II.D.3). I frequently encounter patients who mouth interpretations that may be true but have a hollow feel to them; they sound as if they are lines, somebody else's words.

When the repression is fairly solid, there is no conscious attempt by patients to deceive analysts (II.C.2 and II.C.3 in Exhibit 6.1). However, a damaging struggle may ensue that can undermine the viability of the analysis as patients find the analysts' interpretation to be threatening or just incomprehensible. There is a fairly strong risk of some degree of false self-compliance (II.C.3) to avoid such a struggle and to preserve the analysis. Such outcomes are not rare and are the most frequent result of a poorly timed but "correct" interpretation.

Finally, there are negative outcomes that result when analysts' interpretations are simply wrong. If analysts persist in presenting the interpretations and are unable to acknowledge the errors and respond appropriately, serious damage to patients or the analyses or both is fairly common (II.D.2 in Exhibit 6.1). To avoid II.D.2, it is not uncommon for patients to engage in some degree of false self-compliance that again can deceive analysts, patients, or both into believing that the interpretation was useful (II.D.3).[45]

Empathy Versus Objectivity and Science

Consistent—in spirit if not in detail—with this overview of the limited utility and major problems inherent in analytic interpretation, confrontation, and authority, the self psychologists and the intersubjectivists have struggled to devise a solution: How can one avoid the abuses of analytic authority while bringing analysts' learning, understanding, and wisdom to the aid of suffering patients? How do trained, learned experts remain empathically attuned to their patients' subjectivities while trying to help them creatively and adaptively reorganize their experience along new lines, using new organizing principles that do not originate within their experiential worlds? The solutions these analysts have developed provide another clue to a deeper understanding of the human psyche and the relational world in which it must function.

The intersubjectivists (e.g., Stolorow, Atwood, Brandchaft, Orange) have tried to move psychoanalysis away from the scientific worldview with its quest for objectivity and truth. Their call is for analysts to "hold our theories lightly" (Orange, 1995, p. 52) in a world where there are as many truths as there are perspectives or experiential worlds. The intersubjectivists want analysts to realize that one's "truth" is a reification of one way of organizing experience. Such a view—consistent with the postmodernist spirit—does call for a move away from scientific empiricism toward hermeneutic interpretation based on internal coherence, aesthetic concerns, and pragmatic[46] utility.

Kohut (1980), by contrast, remained committed to psychoanalysis as one of the natural sciences even though he frequently discussed the major changes occurring in the philosophy of science in relation to psychoanalytic theory. Using 19th-century scientific objectivity,

> the traditional analyst sees his patient objectively, and seeks to discover discrete mechanisms of a mental apparatus; the self psychologist [using 20th-century scientific objectivity] acknowledges his own impact on the field he is observing, and using empathic contact with the patient, is able to broaden his perspective beyond this mechanistic view. (Shane, 1985, p. 69)

Kohut's solution to the problem of analytic authority was not to reject the search for objective, empirical, scientific truth.[47] Rather, he emphasized empathy as the field-defining tool because he was aware of the biasing but inevitable impact of theory on observation (Goldberg, 1985); only an empiricist's commitment to remaining true to the data obtained through empathic observation could help analysts guard against the inevitable biases introduced by their theories and personal subjectivities. In contrast to Orange's (1995) call to hold theory (truth) lightly, Kohut's solution was to hold the analyst's agenda lightly. This is the essence of the most frequently quoted of Kohut's comments (presented earlier). Kohut was not questioning his truth as truth. Rather, he was questioning his need to pursue his scientific truth instead of putting his analytic agenda aside in favor of searching for the subjective meaning of what his patient was trying to articulate (cf. Friedman, 1992; Kriegman, 1996a).

I would suggest that both of these approaches are major improvements over the traditional analytic approach with its naive realism, its objectivity hubris, and its dangerous potential for analytic abuse. However, both approaches fail in both theory and practice; they both must fail. That is, from the evolutionary perspective, the very need for such responses to analytic authority is rooted in the inevitable conflicts of interest that characterize the relational world. Analysts simply do not hold their theories lightly.[48] And they do not want to give up their agendas for their patients. Of course, sometimes analysts must struggle to do what they do not want to do. This is only ethical. However, the very fact that it is a struggle and they need an ethical sense to help guide them indicates that they can only partially succeed. Analysts, like all humans, have been "designed" to hold to their truths and agendas and resist those of others. In a conflictual relational world, where another's views may be inimical to one's interests, versions of truth and control over the agenda are matters of major importance to all the participants in any conversation.

Although the self psychologists and intersubjectivists have made a major advance, I would suggest that only by returning to the reality of interpersonal conflict, a reality that was overemphasized in the classical theory (Kriegman, 1988, 1990) that these theorists have largely rejected, can analysts achieve a deeper understanding of the clinical phenomena. In this evolutionary view, these solutions to the problem of analytic authority—that analysts need to hold their truths or agendas lightly—are recast in terms of the inevitable negotiations of conflict that characterize all human relationships, including psychoanalysis. From an evolutionary psychoanalytic perspective, negotiations of conflicts of interest, conflicts that are often represented as clashing truths and agendas, are central to the analytic process (Kriegman, 1996c; Slavin & Kriegman, 1992, in press).

Summary and Conclusions: Toward an Epistemology for Analytic Interpretation

In this chapter I have attempted to address the problem of how to maintain a commitment to the scientific approach and to the empathic stance simultaneously. There is a tendency to use a simple solution that consists of trying to separate introspective from extrospective knowledge. Only patients know their own internal states and there are two separate worlds: the intersubjectively verifiable (the domain of the extrospective sciences) and the private world of experience and meaning (the domain of the psychoanalytic field). For many modern analytic writers, "Never the twain shall (or should) meet." In self psychology, there is a tendency to say, "The customer is always right." However, both clinical experience and controlled studies force analysts to acknowledge that their patients, like all people, are often being deceptive and self-deceptive (Kriegman, 1996a, 1996c). Thus, there are times when analysts know something that their patients do not know or are unwilling to acknowledge. And, of course, the more traditional analytic approaches are built on the concepts of deception, self-deception, and resistance; for such approaches, it is the essential function of, the traditional definition of, an analyst as one who makes interpretations that confront the patient's worldview with an alternative against which the patient resists.

So far, I have explored the difficulty analysts seem to be having maintaining a commitment to the field-defining empathic stance without sacrificing a scientific attitude and their clear and distinct sense that in significant ways patients distort, deceive, and self-deceive. Can analysts maintain the gains achieved by self psychology in reducing the tendency to force patients to acquiesce to analysts' worldviews and simultaneously retain those aspects of classical analysis that capture the human tendency to distort and deceive? Can analysts remain committed to an understanding of unconscious mental processes—and the clinical goal of increasing insight and self-awareness—while guarding against the natural human bias that would have them lay claim to the superiority of analysts' understanding?

If you have made it this far, then you know that this presentation of an evolutionary perspective on these issues of analytic authority, interpretation, confrontation, and the unconscious is complicated. It does not offer the simple vision of self psychology in which the only truth analysts must deal with is the patient's experiential world. Nor does it offer the simplicity of the classical view in which trained analysts can function as the arbiters of truth. Nor does it offer a way out of making choices between these views by saying there is no truth that analysts must struggle to find because they create their own truths together with their patients. No, this is a complicated perspective. However, people live in a complicated world in which they do in fact create the truths they discover; both are true. As self psychology would have it, patients' experiences are indeed sacrosanct. By the very definition of what comprises psychoanalytic data about the subject being investigated (the patient's experienced complex mental states) and the observational tools analysts use (empathic understanding of patients' communications about their experience), patients must be the ultimate arbiters of the truth about their experiential world, and because the treatment is for the patient, not the therapist, the elucidation, validation, and actualization of patients' aims and goals within their experiential worlds must be the analyst's agenda. However, as the classical perspective reminds us, patients come to treatment because they need a therapist's reality because they sense that their realities—their grasp and way of organizing their often confusing and internally inconsistent experiential worlds— are missing something or are "off the mark."

Using this complicated perspective, I have suggested a cautious evaluation of interpretative confrontations. If this evaluation has any validity, the one fairly common category in which interpretive confrontations are likely to be true and to work is the one that many analysts would claim is not a true interpretation; it is more of a clarification (I.A.1 in Exhibit 6.1). The other positive outcomes are all infrequent (except the common but limited benefit of I.D.2, which operates *despite* the efforts of the analyst) and, by my estimation, are less frequent than the negative outcomes.

In this context, I can join with those who decry the use of the notion of scientific objectivity to support analysts' tendencies to make confrontative interpretations without awareness of the full extent of their potential destructive impact. However, I do not see the problem as being either the act of confrontation per se or the use of an objectivist epistemology. In fact, the view I am presenting is developed within a fully empiricist commitment to testing these ideas to see what is actually true. Rather than joining those who reject both confrontations and objectivity, I believe that the very skepticism with which we must confront analysts' interpretations is completely consistent with a scientific worldview. It remains an empirical question, but at least the data from my clinical observations suggest that confrontations are not useful or are destructive far more often than they are useful. This suggests that, rather than eschewing all notions of objectivity, interpretations, and all confrontation, one ought to indeed be careful and judicious in making confrontative interpretations. Analysts can reuse Freud's (1912/ 1958) metaphor of the analyst as surgeon: Like surgery, which has both the power to cure and to destroy, confrontative interpretations (even if offered gently and compassionately) may best be used sparingly and with great respect for the real danger involved. And, because it may not always be the wisest move to let a surgeon decide whether surgery is the best treatment, before offering an interpretation it may be helpful and ethically necessary to ask, "Whose interests are being served?"

At this point, I offer a tentative answer to the question of why our outstanding success in dealing with the nonhuman world has not been repeated in our attempt to deal with ourselves. We are designed to perceive reality fairly clearly and without distortion when it is in our best interest to do so (e.g., when we attempt to gain mastery over the nonhuman world). When we are dealing with ourselves in a social context—and this also includes some of our perceptions of, and social presentations of, ideas and "facts" about the nonhuman world—we are designed to have a biased, distorted view that promotes our own agenda and self-interest most effectively. Such biases hold true for both patients and analysts. The assumption that people can straightforwardly design social, clinical, medical, and scientific theories that function solely for the best interests of others or for some pure abstract motive such as the pursuit of Truth and that well-analyzed analysts can use their theory objectively is naive, indeed. However, with care and safeguards, psychoanalytic insights, interpretations, and even confrontations can prove extremely valuable.

The safeguards, as I have suggested, are primarily the empirical approach coupled with a clear acknowledgment of the field-defining empathic and introspective stance in the context of an evolutionary-psychoanalytic understanding of universal tendencies toward deception, self-deception, and bias. Although the very theory I am presenting suggests that such a scientific theory itself is—as all theories and ideas are—far from objectively unbiased, our best protection against bias is to turn to the empirical evidence and, using the knowledge that bias is ubiquitous and inevitable, to attempt to be as cognizant as possible of such biases and their impact.

I believe that the current antiscientific trends in psychoanalytic thought (and other social arenas) are based, in large part, on the accurate perception of the misuses that characterize many, if not most, human claims to authority. However, this fact cries out for empirical safeguards. As can be seen in Kriegman (1996c) and Slavin and Kriegman (in press), one can fully acknowledge the need to struggle with the inequities of the roles of analyst and patient without invoking a call to abandon science. One can be highly sensitive to the omnipresent danger of abuse in relationships of markedly unequal power (and the need to guard against such abuse) without rejecting the scientific approach with its related concepts of empirical observation, objectivity (and its corollary of biased and distorted subjectivity), intersubjective verifiability, causation, and prediction. In fact, it is precisely the need to guard against the biasing influences and ideas of others that leads to the notion that the human tendency to empirically test ideas may be an innate, inborn human protection (Kriegman, 1996a). Without the sophistication of modern science, all cultures and societies have developed the colloquial equivalent of the empiricist sentiment found in the declaration, "I'm from Missouri, show me!" The point of such universal sentiments is that it is a natural human tendency to proclaim in some form "Whatever your status or claim to authority may be, I want to see for myself; I want to examine the data myself."

The lost respect that a revised and revitalized psychoanalysis is poised to regain must not be thrown away again by calls to abandon a scientific attitude. New ideas have developed as analysts have empirically tested, expanded, and corrected earlier notions that just did not fit the facts. Analysts can take up the call for humility and an acknowledgment of their fallibility (Orange, 1995) from within a scientific worldview without rejecting the empirical approach of natural science for psychoanalysis.

Finally, with an evolutionary-psychoanalytic understanding of how hard it is to see ourselves accurately and with insights into the biases that lead us to color our self-knowledge, we may now be able to take up the challenge of the 17th century and shine the enlightenment into the dark recesses of our psyches. Hopefully, we can now begin to match our successful understanding of the non-human world with wisdom that leads to effective action when dealing with ourselves.

And we better hurry.

Notes

1. This is subjectivist in the sense that the truth of a proposition was determined by the cleverness with which the individual, starting with "establishing truths," then used syllogistic, deductive logic to produce a belief. The syllogistic combination of abstract Aristotelian ideas with interpretations of passages from the Bible and church dogma was almost entirely a reflection of the mind of the one producing the argument. The argument was thus subjective in that it was influenced little by any observation of the world.
2. So powerful was this vision that the church eventually had to accommodate and acknowledge its truths. For example, in a remarkably "rapid" about-face, the church rescinded its denunciation of Galileo and, 3.5 centuries after he was forced under threat of death by torture to recant his theories (and then had to spend the rest of his life in house imprisonment), pardoned him. It was not until "the year of our Lord" 1992 that the church finally accepted the legitimacy of Galileo's claim that Copernicus was right: The earth goes around the sun. The dominance of the empiricist perspective in scientific fields of knowledge was only attained with great difficulty and remains under siege today.
3. Geha's (1993) rejection of truth and objectivity is an extreme (and clear) example of this trend. He forcefully rejected objectivity and the notion that anything "true" can ever be known: All that exists are creations of the human psyche and therefore all is fiction. Yet, a careful

reading of Geha suggests that he was being provocative in arguing for a position that appears to be intentionally phrased in extreme terms. Geha does seem to believe in truth; he forcefully rejected a *correspondence* view of reality—which in its crudest, naive realist terms assumes that unclouded, careful human perception can create an objectively accurate experience in the subject that corresponds nearly perfectly to an external reality that exists (as perceived by the observer) independent of the observer—and the notion that the analyst has a clearer view of Truth than the patient. He ultimately presented criteria for establishing "truth" (e.g., coherence and aesthetics). Yet, I would argue that this is a mistaken direction for psychoanalysis because more than coherence and beauty are involved in establishing what is.

Even if one accepts the British empiricists' (Locke, Berkeley, and Hume) limiting of knowledge to that which can be known subjectively, as Locke argued, there must be something (even if it is unknowable) that exists beyond human subjectivity (Kriegman, 1996a). Support for this Lockean position—in contrast to Hume, whose thoroughgoing skepticism prevented the assumption of the existence of anything beyond experience—can be found in the natural response to Geha (1993), who suggested that psychoanalytic truths are really fictions that "are the fruits of imagination and they grow only within the gardens of the psyche" (p. 214). Even if one agrees that the human mind molds, shapes, and colors the world as our psyches structure and "create" our experiences—and thus the only reality that can be known is a subjective construction—there is certainly something beyond the "gardens of the psyche." Some fruits grown in human psychic gardens bear little resemblance to others (are not intersubjectively verifiable), have little or no predictive utility, and conflict with other knowledge of the world. There appears to be something unknowable beyond our psyches that contributes a reliability and structure to our experience. This reliability and structure can be known, described, and used to make predictions.

Orange (1995) clearly rejected empiricist approaches to knowledge —and, like Geha, forcefully rejected a correspondence view of what can be known—while trying to retain a moderate realism that both Robert Stolorow (personal communication, 1995) and George Atwood (personal communication, 1995) felt they could embrace as their earlier positions (Atwood & Stolorow, 1984; Stolorow & Atwood, 1994) continued to develop and evolve. Yet there still is a problem with this view in that "a realist believes there is something . . . to be more fully known, discovered, or articulated" (Orange, 1995, p. 61). In Orange's (1995) view, some facts are "made" (constructed, interpreted, organized) and others are "given" like something that "smacks one in the face like a 40-mile-an-hour wind" (p. 87). Apparently, people must face aspects of an external reality in what Orange called a "pragmatic" epistemology. Truth emerges as "one perspective on a larger reality" (Orange, 1995, p. 62). Although the use of the words "emergent truth" (p. 62), and William James' bastardization of Charles Sanders Peirce's "pragmatism" (cf. Kriegman, 1996a, p. 87n) protects Orange from the objectivism and the correspondence view of reality that she was trying to avoid, from where does the truth emerge? If it emerges simply as a construction of the human psyche (individually or in community), then it is relativism, which she rejected. If it emerges from an interaction between human psyches and some reality outside of people, then she was slipping into correspondence thinking, or at least the notion that there is a partially knowable reality out there and truth emerges at least in part from human perception of it. In her epistemology—which she called *perspectival realism*—what is a "perspective"? A perspective on or of what? (In contrast to Geha's and Orange's views, see Kriegman, 1996a, for a presentation of an epistemology in which a subjectivist, noncorrespondence view of reality is integrated with the empiricist *Weltanschauung* of science.)

4. I am aware that some modern philosophers would unabashedly embrace such a claim, as I believe Geha would. In a sense, this would be progress for me: If all natural sciences are merely hermeneutic constructions of coherent, aesthetically pleasing meanings arising from one's examination of nature's text, then the supposed distinction between scientific empiricism and the psychoanalytic creation of narratives of meaning is lost and one can once again embrace the scientific method—although in this model analysts would have to claim that they are creating fictional scientific narratives, of course—for psychoanalysis.

5. The list is endless. Although few psychoanalysts could provide a credible explanation for more than one or two of these common devices, some readers might be able to "explain" all of them. (This can probably be done by a much higher percentage of readers of this book than of a random selection of psychoanalysts.) But how far could the explanations go? Although I can "explain" them all, I still have trouble with simple things like electric motors: When electricity (whatever that is) travels (however it does that) through windings of wire, how does it "cause" a magnetic field (whatever that is), and how can an immaterial field of no mass cause mass to move? That is, I can describe some of the activities and materials needed to create the mechanism along with some basic theory to provide a satisfying answer to the problem (i.e., to give myself and others a sense that we "know" how a thing works). However, these explanations are not really answers in that they inevitably lead to more fundamental questions about which we are ignorant. This, of course, is simply the way of science: The goal is, using Occam's razor, to create theories with the fewest unexplained postulates (the fewest "moving parts") that can account for the greatest number of observations. Thus, one postulate,

gravity, can be used with one universal set of equations to explain why the planets follow their elliptical orbits around the sun, how fast a ball will fall, and why the tides occur. The problem that has been developing is that in our scrutiny of the fundamental forces (gravity, electromagnetic, and the strong and weak nuclear forces), in our attempt to reduce them further to some more basic unifying essential elements, we have been creating theories that become virtually unintelligible. (See Kriegman, 1996a, for documentation and a fuller discussion of the implications of this trend.) Thus, science has progressed to the point where the constructs it uses are as distant from human experience as angels dancing on the head of a pin.

6. See Hawking (1988) and the discussion of that work in Kriegman (1996a, pp. 97–98, 104–105).

7. Where some may argue that success has occurred in our understanding and dealing with human problems (e.g., in the treatment of mental illness, management of the economy, organizational dynamics and management, and others), the success is both equivocal and far from spectacular.

8. The extreme barbarity of the 20th century is true only in absolute numbers, not proportions or ratios. Contrary to the received wisdom, the empirical evidence overwhelmingly documents the greater "murderousness" (relative to population size) of prestate ("uncivilized") societies (see Keeley, 1996). Yet as the terrible world wars and ongoing worldwide violence of the 20th century attest, this relative (proportionate) decrease in destructiveness appears to be a result of changes in the structure of societies and the way war is conducted, not an increase in knowledge, understanding, and wisdom.

9. It may be that many of the major psychotherapeutic approaches have clinical validity that potentially can be empirically demonstrated and shown to support the specific theory guiding the approach. Therapeutic schools may have attracted adherents whose particular personalities interact with the particular problems of particular patients (generally the type of patient around whom the theory was designed) to produce the actual (empirically demonstrable) results predicted by the particular theory. Rather than clinicians' theories producing self-confirming clinical data through a process of selective reinforcement of patients' verbal responses—a self-fulfilling prophecy controlled by therapists' expectations and actions—what we may be seeing is a more complex interaction. That is, actual clinical phenomena produced in certain forms of treatment of certain types of patients by certain types of clinicians cause clinicians to tend to gravitate to those theories that best fit their clinical experience. Rather than clinicians shaping the data through selective reinforcement (Masling & Cohen, 1987), the empirical data may be selectively shaping the clinicians.

Although, to a degree, this is how science is supposed to work—the empirical evidence should lead scientists toward theories that it selectively reinforces and away from those that it falsifies—note that in psychotherapeutic work (with the complex interaction effects between therapist, patient, and technique) this could lead to numerous conflicting theories, each with valid empirical evidence. Like the metaphor of the blind men and the elephant, various psychoanalytic schools and other clinical approaches may each have latched onto an aspect of the truth (Slavin & Kriegman, 1992) that has valid, empirical evidence to support it—that is, a specific approach may actually effectively yield the beneficial results predicted by its theory when practiced by certain clinicians with specific types of patients. Note also that clinicians who do not see a necessity for controlled, extraclinical research agree with Masling and Cohen (1987) that the psychoanalytic method is not itself an empirical method (e.g., Mitchell, 1993; Orange, 1995). Rather, they argue for a plurality of "truths" and a need to be able to tolerate ambiguity and confusion: "As psychoanalysis gradually relinquishes its claim to be a natural science and takes its proper place among the realms of human wisdom, the uncertain and the imprecise will find the respect they deserve" (Orange, 1995, p. 124). And Orange (1995), Mitchell (1993), and Spezzano (1993a, 1993b) were more moderate in their deemphasis of extraclinical empiricism than were others such as Geha (1993), Habermas (1971), Atwood and Stolorow (1984), and Stolorow and Atwood (1994). In contrast to those who want to move away from empirical approaches to knowledge, in this chapter I argue that analysts should strive to create and maintain a clinical attitude that retains the empirical method at its core but couples it with humility in the face of their fallibility and the very real limits of their understanding. Analysts need not throw the baby of knowledge based on careful observation and analysis out with the dirty bathwater of scientific hubris and self-aggrandizement.

10. Singer and Singer (1994) noted these concerns and tried to open a dialogue between narrative and clinical approaches and those who hold a more positivist perspective. I agree with them that the perspectives are not inherently opposed, as well as with their sense that integration and dialogue will not be easily attained.

11. Freud (1905/1953) discussed *his loss* that resulted from Dora's premature termination: He was unable to ascertain "when and under what particular influence Dora gave up masturbating" and substituted her hysterical symptoms for masturbatory satisfaction (p. 79). However, he did not even consider the possibility that *Dora's loss* of a needed therapeutic experience may have resulted from his attempt to force her to acquiesce to erroneous or terribly, poorly timed interpretations.

12. Many analysts who would object to the notion that there is any way to determine whether an interpretation—that is profoundly embedded in a specific relational context—is "correct" would agree that this

particular interpretation had a high likelihood of being unhelpful or even hurtful to this particular patient.

13. Although one could dismiss this case as an example of an ethically inappropriate therapeutic relationship—it is the therapist's duty to get a consultation or halt a treatment that is clearly damaging—again, I would note that, at times, about 50% of my practice has consisted of such cases and I have consulted on many others. Although my practice is not a random sample and other therapists may therefore suggest that their experience does not corroborate this view of the extent of the problem, note that in all of these cases numerous other therapists have been consulted. Thus, many analysts have had access to the same data I observed. Yet, although other consultants acknowledged the damage, most did not. Because it is difficult to determine the source of a patient's dysfunction, most analytic therapists assumed that the damage preceded the analysis, the patient's protestations notwithstanding. This was especially so among those analysts who were trained in a more classical perspective and who heard "objectively correct" interpretations being made. Id-resistance and negative therapeutic reactions have even been defined by the patient's failure to improve—or by further regression—after a "correct" interpretation is made (Kriegman & Slavin, 1989). At such points, extremely forceful interpretations have even been characterized as "heroic" and necessary (Corwin, 1973).

However, how does the analyst know if the interpretation was correct if the clinical result—the patient got worse, not better—does not support it? Theory and other analysts will tell us. If one disagrees with the theory, then one is resisting and needs analysis to come to see the truth. Such dogmatic thinking has prompted the accusation that psychoanalysis has left the scientific method behind and has become more of a religion with nonfalsifiable beliefs. As I note in a moment, a relatively large group of analysts (who can be roughly grouped under the rubric of self psychology) have shared the concern about how allegiance to a theory that claims that objectivity resides in an analyzed therapist who uses a scientific clinical theory can lead to abuse of patients.

14. She was Melanie Klein's daughter and a psychiatrist-analyst herself.

15. For a detailed account of a psychoanalytic failure (focused on an autobiographical account of a failed training analysis), see Strupp (1982). Strupp, Hadley, and Gomes-Schwartz (1977) offered one of the more thorough discussions of the general problem of negative effects in psychotherapy.

16. He even acknowledged that all confrontations (which, to some degree, means all interpretations) must—despite whatever usefulness they may have—involve a degree of countertransference acting out (Myerson, 1973, p. 30).

17. Although these issues stand out clearly in the analytic perspective of

self psychology, the same arguments can be applied to similar debates between (and within) other analytic perspectives. Teicholz (in press) noted that, in response to concerns about hierarchical authority, some postmodern analytic writers seem to reject empathy as well as objectivity. The rejection of empathy is a bit harder to understand, but it seems to be related to questioning the sense that one can know anything, including another's experience, with any degree of certainty. For example, Renik (1993) wanted to replace both empathy and interpretation with "authentic engagement." This rejection of empathy also has been directly linked to concerns about authority as "Loewald and Kohut . . . are now seen by [certain postmodern theorists] as having given up *interpretive authority*, only to replace it with *patronizing provision*" (Teicholz, in press).

18. In these deconstructionist views, analogous to the classical system of dream interpretation, the superficial or "manifest content" of a set of ideas is the realm in which misguided arguments occur as to what is "true." The deeper or "latent content" is where the real meaning of a belief can be found. Interestingly, in another similarity to classical interpretation, the latent meaning (i.e., whose interests are being promoted) seems to have a direct correlation with classical drive interpretations; the underlying interests (the real meaning of a belief system) are usually seen to be the pursuit by a minority of the lion's share of power (money, political status, control over police forces, etc.) and pleasure (sex, food, creature comforts of shelter, clothing, and freedom from unpleasant labor, etc.).

19. The translation of this word is usually *the city*.

20. Specifically, I have proposed a general epistemology for psychoanalysis (one of the introspective sciences) consistent with the epistemological assumptions used for the extrospective sciences (Kriegman, 1996a). In this epistemological view, objectivity and truth are defined as those collections of ideas, including both facts (actual experiences) and notions about how the facts are related to one another (e.g., notions of cause and effect), that maximize the ability to predict future experiences of the world (future observable facts). The most satisfying explanation consistent with this predictive ability constitutes a large part of our natural (innate) sense of "truth." In this view, truth is never absolute: We can only make probability statements based on past experience. Although some may have a high level of confidence—we can, for all intents and purposes, act as if they are simply true—every belief in this system is subject to future confirmation or disconfirmation. It is in this manner that it is an empirical epistemology. Authority, wish, and agenda may color and shape our empirical attempts to ascertain truth. However, to the degree that they do so, they distort ideas and take us away from more objective knowledge. Only the highest authority—empirical observation—can legitimately lay claim to our allegiance because knowledge based on careful study of our experi-

ences of the world tends to have much greater, lasting predictive utility than authority, wish, and biased agendas.

Note that certain forms of explanation inherently satisfy and others do not. Occam's razor was shaving arguments to their simplest terms long before William of Occam. That is, there are probably forms of arguments that "ring" true in important ways and the human psyche is innately sensitive to such aspects of the presentations others make. To stay with the case of Occam's razor, people ignorant of the named principle can be heard to exclaim "You're trying to complicate the matter" and other such protests against obfuscating complexity used to promote the speaker's agenda. I believe that such ideas can be found in all cultures, in all languages, at all times. If belief systems are designed to be used to promote the agendas of individuals, then there must be protective ways of evaluating ideas—which are also built into the human psyche—to prevent people from being bamboozled.

The fact that people are frequently fooled by their attraction to simple (but highly misleading) ideas such as political promises (e.g., the height of the silliness that the close shaving of ideas can lead to is exemplified by the often incredibly simplistic, soundbite-sized slogan) cannot be used to argue against such a protective mechanism having been built into the human psyche. In fact, the opposite is true. Nature has innumerable "arms races." For example, butterflies develop fascinating camouflage and birds then develop greater visual acuity. Therefore, butterflies develop better camouflage and birds develop better visual acuity and so on. If people developed a tendency to evaluate arguments on the basis of simplicity (without superfluous "moving parts"), then surely someone (e.g., politicians) will come along and develop the fine art of persuasion by using simplicity and the removal of ostensibly obfuscating complexity to profit from the selling of the silliest of simplistic ideas.

Despite such pitfalls, the tendency to be satisfied by ideas of certain forms (e.g., Occam's simplicity and Descartes' notions of "clear and distinct" ideas) probably was designed by selective pressures that promoted effective ways of knowing and organizing knowledge of the world. Thus, the satisfying sense of an explanation is related to its utility to the listener even though promoters can use the principles of satisfaction to advance ends that are often inimical to the listener's agenda. The protection? Empiricism. The human sense of what is true should be ideas that both are satisfactory in form (e.g., Geha's [1993] coherence and aesthetics) and meet empirical standards (i.e., meet the need to have evidence that can be trusted). In fact, I have argued (Kriegman, 1996a) that the empirical tendency itself is thus structured into the human psyche.

Yet, it must be noted that religion stands in stark contrast to the scientific attitude that I claim is embodied in the human psyche. Religion knows of no experimentation. It is accepted on faith. It cannot be proved or disproved. Therefore, one could argue that the human psyche is not structured to operate along empirical lines. There appear to be certain aspects of social, group, and religious behavior that fly in the face of any essential scientific attitude that may have been structured into the human mind. Although this is not the place to deal with theories of religious beliefs, I obviously must acknowledge that there are many unscientific tendencies in the human psyche, including many beliefs that are superstitious, religious, and clearly irrational. Suffice it to say, it appears that under certain conditions, an abandonment of the objective, empirical attitude also has been selected for and that under certain conditions humans clearly behave in a most unscientific manner.

Yet, the same individuals can still accurately predict certain social behaviors. The most fanatically religious individuals can still accumulate data, organize it, and make accurate predictions about machinery, mechanical events, and interpersonal occurrences and predictions of human behavior. Effective religious leaders can be and are "scientific" in their study and discovery of the best methods for influencing others' beliefs. That is, the scientific attitude, which is forgone in superstitious and religious beliefs, is not lost to the religious individual in a large number of crucial actions and interactions with his or her environment. There is an Arab tale of a man traveling with Mohammed. As they stopped for the night, the man asked Mohammed, "Should I tether my camel or trust in God?" Mohammed replied, "Trust in God *and* tether your camel" (Lippman, 1990).

The fact that there are unscientific cognitive tendencies does not mean that there has not been strong selective pressure for a scientific, empirical attitude. There are clearly strong altruistic tendencies that have been selected for within the human psyche along with clear selfish tendencies (Kriegman, 1988, 1990; Kriegman & Slavin, 1990). Both are necessary for maximizing inclusive fitness (i.e., for the most successful survival and replication). The argument that natural selection has created altruism or that natural selection has created selfishness should not be used to negate the opposite. Opposing, dynamic forces are used in the natural (biological) and artificial (human-made) designs of many homeostatic mechanisms. In fact, the very existence of a divided psyche with strong altruistic and selfish motives appears to reflect the balance the individual must achieve between adaptive, relational needs and necessary egoistic aims (Slavin & Kriegman, 1992). The existence of one of two opposing tendencies in the psyche clearly does not indicate that the other tendency does not exist.

Thus, I am arguing that there were strong selective pressures to create a scientific inquiring mind that has a built-in, fundamental "faith" in something we refer to when we use words such as "objective reality" and "empirical observation" without denying that there are aspects of human experience in which traditional (religious) faith, belief, wish, and fantasy are the overriding factors shaping and structuring human experience.

21. There are many unconscious mental processes—such as the ways in which the brain processes information and forms a 3-D visual world out of the pattern of electrochemical impulses sent to the brain from the retina—that can be included in an analysis of how mental functioning evolved. However, for psychoanalytic discussions, the unconscious processes focused on are those that can at other times exist in consciousness.

22. In another situation, the same woman may indeed have sexual wishes of the type described by classical theory. The point is that the experience created in an observer is an unreliable indicator of the individual's motivations. Is she acting on a conscious or unconscious desire? Or is he projecting his desire? Or is it a mixture of the two? Unlike theories of projective identification and others that recommend the use of countertransference to identify a patient's unconscious (or unstated) motivation, in this view, feelings aroused in the therapist are far more likely to be accurate clues to the therapist's psychic life and, at best, biased indicators of the patient's experience and motives. Although feelings in the therapist may correspond to what is going on in the patient, they may not. This is why sustained empathic inquiry is necessary: Through such a process the analyst's conjectures can be empirically tested against the patient's communicated experience even if that experience can be known only in a limited manner and must be co-constructed in the analytic dialogue.

23. This is remarkably well documented in the Old Testament, where many stories are about the troubles caused by men's reaction to women who were "very fair to look upon." Despite the enormous transformations of modern society, people have not changed all that much.

24. The reciprocations found in friendships and work relationships can be vitally important for survival and reproductive success (Kriegman, 1988, 1990; Trivers, 1971).

25. The danger to the patient is especially marked because the arrangement—even when harmful to the patient—can benefit the analyst directly and indirectly. Such interpretations do not just support the analyst's (who must confront a self-deceived patient) assumption of "wise authority," helping to maintain the patient's dependence on the analyst's superior judgment and wisdom—an arrangement that, when it works, can directly provide an analyst with financial support for many years. In addition, there are less materially tangible benefits; the analyst's self-esteem, sense of worth, value, and identity are all enhanced as the analyst engages in the societally sanctioned role of wise guru: the superior person who has penetrated the difficult secrets of human existence and compassionately offers aid to troubled souls.

Although these are valid experiences—after all, there must be some motive to make someone want to become an analyst, and these benefits to the analyst may be necessary for successful analytic work—when the analyst can benefit from a relationship that is damaging to a patient, there is also a dangerous potential that must be carefully monitored. In my opinion—and I am suggesting that this is also the opinion of many modern analysts and most postmodern analysts—the existing safeguards, while significant, have been woefully inadequate.

26. Sackeim and Gur (1978), in reviewing the research evidence for repression (which they called self-deception), noted that it is important to distinguish "intentional" from "motivated"; that "*intentionality is not* a necessary condition for acts of other deception [or self-deception and that] *motives are* necessary constituents of self-deception" (p. 150, italics added). All actions (including psychological, mental events) must be motivated but the results need not be intended. With acts caused by a direct motive that can be conscious or unconscious, the notion of intention may be appropriate. With acts that result from indirect motives or permanently unconscious processes, intention has no meaning. With acts that result from motives that are thoroughly repressed (but that can, under certain circumstances, become conscious), it is less clear if there is any meaning to saying the act was intentional. If "I" am truly unaware of a motive, what meaning can there be to the claim that "I intended" to act on it? (See the further discussion of the meaning of *I* and intentionality.)

27. The patient often needs to experience the reality of the therapist's struggle with the conflict between the legitimate needs of the patient and those of the therapist that are aroused in treatment in order to use the therapeutic relationship (Kriegman, 1996c; Slavin & Kriegman, in press). Therapists who manage to deal with their countertransference reactions too well may actually deprive their patients of their genuineness (Myerson, 1973). And Havens (1973), in response to this issue, quoted Jaspers (1900/1963), "Nothing happens until the doctor is touched by the patient" (p. 676). Interestingly, Buie and Adler (1973) described a successful "confrontation" in which a reckless, borderline patient was told to call his therapist whenever he was likely to endanger himself. The goal was to *confront* the patient with the analyst's real existence and concern, knowledge of which they believed the patient was avoiding. The intervention was successful, but I would not see this as evidence to support the use of confrontation of aspects of reality that are actively avoided (resisted). Rather, I would suggest that the therapist engaged the patient in an emotionally real manner as he changed the rules of their relationship to protect the patient, an act that palpably demonstrated the patient's effect on the analyst as well as the analyst's caring. The patient had an impact on the analyst's life; the analyst actually invited the patient to intrude into his life.

Thus, the patient had not been avoiding experiencing something that was demonstrably real and that could be used to confront the patient's reality; rather, the patient's "acting out" brought into existence a real demonstration of the analyst's caring—a response that indicated the patient's overwhelming experience was actually being perceived and mattered to the analyst—that the patient could then experience.

28. Note how important in sports is the idea that the team must be "psyched" to win and how hard athletes try to "psych out" their opponents. The home team advantage is well-known.

29. For other examples, see Kriegman (1996a).

30. Note that I do not consider the possibility that the price is really the lowest for which they are willing to sell the car because there is no empirical evidence that such a phenomenon has ever occurred.

31. See the clinical example and discussion of the analysis of proximal mechanisms.

32. In controlled studies, resistance to subliminal messages (psychodynamic activation effects; Bornstein, 1990b) is consistently less than to supraliminal messages. However, lexical priming studies show a clear supraliminal advantage. Masling (1992) noted that this appears to be a paradox in need of a theoretical explanation. Why should studies consistently show subliminal advantage for some (emotional) messages and supraliminal advantage for others (containing information)? The evolutionary view being presented here may help explain this otherwise paradoxical result.

In a conflictual relational world, people should resist influence, not information. If others will often act to influence us in a manner that benefits them (often at our expense), we should have a natural tendency to resist influence. Thus, influence presented supraliminally—even just the awareness that someone is trying to influence them—should raise resistance in the participant. Influences that can get past the conscious defenses (some subliminal stimuli) may be able to influence participants without their being aware that they are being manipulated, thus not raising the tendency to resist being influenced. However, neutral data, which are not being perceived as an attempt to manipulate the participant, should be perceived more accurately if it is perceived supraliminally (usually increased exposure allows for more accurate identification of stimuli; Kriegman & Biederman, 1980). People should have no resistance to neutral percepts (the lexical priming studies): The more accurately people perceive basic information about the world, the more effective their actions and beliefs can be. People should resist perception and influence only when the information is disturbing (nonneutral) or they detect or suspect an attempt to manipulate them on the part of others.

33. Bornstein (1993) discussed the limited empirical, laboratory evidence that making memories conscious may change a participant's current experience of related feelings and phenomena. Interestingly, he ap-

peared to overlook the implications of his own discussion elsewhere (Bornstein, 1992) of subliminal exposure effects that provides one of the only laboratory demonstrations of how making the participant aware of unconscious influences can change conscious experience. Participants were subliminally exposed to stimuli. They could not detect exposure, yet the studies reviewed by Bornstein (1992) all replicated the finding that there is evidence of subliminal awareness of the stimuli: Participants reported "liking" the stimuli that had been presented subliminally (familiar stimuli) more than unfamiliar stimuli. However, when Bornstein and D'Agostino (1990) told participants that they had been exposed to the stimuli, the liking rating dropped down below that of participants who were not so informed. Bornstein's (1992) interpretation is that those who did not know that they had been exposed to the stimuli misattributed their sense of familiarity with the stimulus to liking the stimulus. When they were told what had happened, they made corrections (probably unconsciously, as they had no conscious reason to believe that previous exposure would have any effect on their liking ratings). In fact, they overcorrected and reported liking the stimulus less than a control group subjected to no experimental manipulation. Knowledge of what is affecting people unconsciously—especially knowledge that they potentially are being manipulated—can change conscious experience. This is familiar to all analytic clinicians who have heard patients report a sense of relief, insight, and increased mastery when they become aware that their reactions to their spouses, bosses, children, and so on may have a recurrent pattern of sensitivity that was clearly developed in other relationships. The misattribution of their old feelings to the current situation is made conscious and the patients report being able to correct for the old influence: They report actually feeling differently about the other person in the here and now.

This analysis of Bornstein's findings may appear to be too cognitive for some analysts: Simple cognitive awareness of the source is not likely to affect a person's experience profoundly. Yet, consider two common examples of tactile stimulation. In one case, imagine tickling yourself, trying as hard as possible to duplicate the physical stimulation caused by being tickled by another person. No matter how carefully matched the stimulation is and no matter how much we try to convince ourselves that there should be no difference, it is uncannily different from the experience of actually being tickled for the latter is fundamentally structured by the cognitive awareness that the source is someone else and that we are not controlling it. (Of course, this is even more striking in sexual interactions.) For another example, consider the difference in the experience of being accidentally bumped by another person and intentionally shoved. The actual jarring and physical injury (if any) in both cases can be the same. However, the cognitive attribution dramatically alters the experience. In one case only physical pain; in the other, severely hurt feelings can completely outweigh any physical sensation. All this is due to the attribution or the understanding of the interpersonal dimension of the experience. Interpretation that alters the conceptual scheme in which current relational events are interpreted, that alters the meaning, can dramatically alter conscious experience.

Note that the unconscious experience need not become conscious for this to occur: People can simply believe that unconscious memories may be coloring their experience. Bornstein and D'Agostino's (1990) participants who had not been exposed to the stimuli but who were told they had been also made the "correction," which in their case was a miscorrection. This would seem to indicate that making the unconscious conscious is less relevant than what patients believe is happening. However, one must remember that the participants in the laboratory experiment had no vested interest in the truth (whether they had seen the stimuli), no vested interest in the actual stimuli (whether they liked them or not), and there is no reason to assume that unconscious information was "pressing" to enter consciousness or to exert a powerful influence on them. Because of these factors, the participants had no reason to be concerned that they might have been misinformed. Patients, on the other hand, are likely to change lifelong ways of organizing vitally important affective experience only when they are thoroughly convinced that their current experience is a misattribution of old to new (i.e., when the unconscious colorings and distortions become vividly palpable through the recall of repressed affective memories in a new situation that does not call for the old familiar response). Thus, it is true that simple cognitive interventions often have little clinical impact and the patient must test and struggle within the interpersonal relationship before changing pathogenic beliefs (Slavin & Kriegman, in press; Weiss & Sampson, 1986).

34. Singer and Singer (1994) noted that "it is . . . exciting to see 'hard-nosed' psychology experimentalists increasingly emphasizing unconscious or implicit attitudes, some even contradictory of consciously reported beliefs, the very material that psychodynamic therapists claimed they could infer from treatment sessions" (p. 173). Although some experimental evidence may point to the existence of this type of repressed unconscious material that exists and exerts an influence even though it remains unconscious, the same caveats about psychoanalytic interpretation—the importance of not confusing proximal mechanisms and ultimate causes—should be applied to the conclusions reached by the "hard-nosed" experimentalists.

35. People also do not give the I credit for forming a 3-D image of the world out of the pattern of electrochemical impulses sent to the brain from the retina. That is, in addition to the bodily functions that "just happen" without the sense of the self as active agent, there are innumerable mental processes (information-processing tasks) of which

people do not have a clue. Although they operate outside of consciousness, they are not unconscious in the analytic sense because they can never be available to consciousness.

36. Of course, there are those who hope this is not so. In fact, many bodily processes may be influenced by our thoughts and feelings. However, the influence is always indirect (e.g., there may be some evidence that optimism and good spirits help the immune system to fight bodily infections and hopelessness and despair seem to depress its functioning) because people can have no direct awareness of the processes that immediately govern such bodily events.

37. The selfish, asocial motivations I am referring to were encoded in the classical model in the concept of "drives."

38. I am not suggesting the following as a literal interpretation that one might actually say to a patient. Nor am I even suggesting that the content (e.g., the statements about "evolved organisms") should be said in any direct form. Rather, I am suggesting that the essential, interpersonal, and intrapsychic meaning of the following may be a crucial "interpretation" in the treatment of a particular patient.

39. The extremes that attempts to keep patients quiet can reach can be seen in the treatment of psychotic patients whose chaotic complaints and outcries (symptoms) are used by others as reasons to take extreme measures to "shut them down." Such measures include drugs, electroconvulsive therapy, and lobotomy. It is unclear to what extent the increasingly common use of drugs for virtually all patients (see Kriegman, 1996a, p. 107n) is operating in the self-interest of others besides the patient (Kriegman, 1996b), with evidence of such self-interest being actively suppressed (see Breggin, 1991; Breggin & Breggin, 1994). With more neurotic patients, attempts to quiet their complaints can be pursued by becoming more forceful and insistent that the patient accept the analyst's interpretation. This is discussed more fully later.

40. Consider the different feel of "Where id was, there ego shall be" and "Where it was, there shall I become" (see Mitchell, 1993).

41. To avoid having to rehash an enormously complicated discussion of truth and objectivity (much of which has already been discussed in this chapter and in Kriegman, 1996a), I would suggest that readers use their preferred system for establishing "truth" in following this discussion. For example, one could use empirical research (Masling & Cohen, 1987), conversation (Spezzano, 1993a), hermeneutic coherence (Atwood & Stolorow, 1984), social constructionism (Hoffman, 1991), or even truth as fiction (Geha, 1993). For those systems for establishing truth that require dialogic co-construction—where the following examples have a profound lack of patient–therapist agreement—imagine the creation of a coherent, aesthetically satisfying (even if fictional) narrative of truth created by either party with a subsequent consultant with whom they then follow this discussion using hermeneutic inter-

pretation of the meanings embedded in the text of the analysis as a guide.

42. In support of the notion that all of these interpretations entail some degree of confrontation, consider Buie and Adler (1973), who noted that confrontation may be necessary to get patients to pay attention to aspects of experience that are conscious (I.A.1 in Exhibit 6.1) or about to become conscious (I.B.1 in Exhibit 6.1). Although this can be done gently—they noted that their goal was not to force patients to change—such confrontation still operates in the service of making patients more aware of that of which they wish to remain unaware. They also noted that it sets up interpretations that are likely to be even more strongly resisted.

43. There is no repression in the sense that what the analyst suggested was operating outside of consciousness did not exist. Of course, repression may be operating on other material.

44. Another potential gain from an erroneous interpretation was already suggested in an earlier footnote in which I discussed the limited evidence from controlled studies that demonstrates the effect of making the unconscious conscious. As noted there, a significant change in attribution and interpretation can lead to significant change in psychotherapy. Yet, in Bornstein and D'Agostino's (1990) study, a subject's *erroneous* beliefs that he or she was being manipulated unconsciously (subliminally) led to changes in how the subject felt about the stimulus presented.

   Thus, in some cases, it is likely that a change in what the patient *believes* is unconsciously coloring conscious, present-day experience can alter the patient's experience, whether or not the belief is valid. For example, a patient who believes his reaction to his wife is an overreaction because of the unconscious influence of memories of mistreatment by his mother may successfully restructure his present-day experience and form a more adaptive accommodation to his marriage. The "truth" regarding the degree, if any, to which early experience may be coloring present-day experience may in some cases have less bearing than does the patient's belief. In this sense, the postmodernists—at least those postmodernists who believe that the meanings analysts and patients find in their co-constructed stories are all that really matter—are, to some degree, correct. Yet, again I would suggest that this type of change, even if beneficial, is not the goal of psychoanalysis. Rather, such a mechanism of change may help to explain part of the gain that can be achieved by suggestion.

45. Note that in many of these situations in which interpretation fails, I suggest that a false self-compliance may hide this fact from the analyst and the patient who complies to avoid disrupting the relationship. Contrast this with Corwin (1973), who referred to the act of making a threat of abandonment, which forces the patient to face reality, as a heroic confrontation. In my view, such threats almost always lead to

termination, intractable struggles, false self-compliance, or (in rare cases) to transmuting internalizations (I.D.2 in Exhibit 6.1). Boris (1973) referred to what I call "false compliance" as a "cure" effected through introjection or identification rather than through the increased mastery of understanding. I must acknowledge that all accommodations to the analyst should not be cast with the pejorative connotations of "false self-compliance" (my term) or introjections that are not insightful (Boris's); in some cases, accommodation can represent an adaptation to an other that can be of utility in relationships outside of treatment; accommodations can be moves toward healthy functioning. Welpton (1973) noted the danger of dependent compliance but actually might have described such a process of adaptive accommodation. This necessitates the consideration of another possible benefit from confrontative interpretation that is not included in Exhibit 6.1. In such cases, the accuracy of the interpretation may be irrelevant to the usefulness of the accommodation in furthering effective relating outside of treatment.

Even if the result of a "heroic" confrontation is positive in this manner, I doubt many analysts would see it as analysis. Essentially, the analyst is using threats of punishment and negative reinforcement (e.g., "I insist that you accept my interpretations, my rules, and stop your infantile demands. If you do not, I will continue to forcefully berate you or kick you out of treatment"). Just as a child may repress parts of the self in an adaptive accommodation to a parent, a sufficiently charismatic or authoritative therapist may force an adaptive accommodation on an "acting-out" patient. Beneficial or not, however, this is certainly not psychoanalysis, even though "successful" work may occur along these lines. I have heard stories of well-known analysts who use their authority and charisma in just this manner. These stories could be misrepresentative "sour grapes" tales told by trainees whose imitation of their charismatic mentor's authoritarian limit-setting approach failed. Yet, I see no reason to assume that such a process is never beneficial even if it should more properly be considered a form of relational aversive behavior modification.

Related to such potentially productive, nonanalytic interpretations that force an accommodation to, acquiescence to, or introjection of the analyst's reality are interpretations that are false or even fantastic that offer patients idealized belief systems (religions) with which to organize experience and guide their lives. Psychoanalysis can—and at times does—provide some of the functional benefit offered by religions. This is consistent with Masling and Cohen's (1987) view of the suggestive effect of psychotherapy. However, their identification of the suggestive potential, a major component of a potentially powerful placebo effect, should not be conflated with potentially therapeutic interactions that in research should be compared with such suggestive placebos. That is, if an intensive, interpretive relationship or any other form of treatment is more than suggestion, then such treatment must be tested against suggestive placebo treatment (rather than therapy being compared with being placed on waiting lists or simply having regular contact with a clinician). New psychoactive drugs should be tested against active placebos, placebos that create enough of a tangible, physical side effect for suggestion to reach most of its potential impact (especially when the drug being tested produces tangible physical effects making "blind" tests an illusion that only a mother or drug company could love or believe in). Just so, it would be of interest to see a major treatment modality compared with active "placebo" treatments that include active, believing "therapists."

46. That is, pragmatic in the William James sense of pragmatism, not Peirce's, which is more compatible with the scientific worldview (see Kriegman, 1996a, p. 87n).

47. However, he clearly wanted to challenge Freud's idealization of Truth (Kohut, 1982).

48. As Arnold Goldberg (personal communication, 1997) pointed out, "holding one's theory lightly" is a *theory* itself. My own (empirical) observation at self psychology conferences suggests that it is a tightly held theory at that.

References

Arvidson, R. (1973). Aspects of confrontation. In G. Adler & P. G. Myerson (Eds.), *Confrontation in psychotherapy* (pp. 163–180). Northvale, NJ: Jason Aronson.

Atwood, G., & Stolorow, R. (1984). *Structures of subjectivity: Explorations in psychoanalytic phenomenology.* Hillsdale, NJ: Analytic Press.

Bacon, F. (1620). *Novum organum.*

Bibring, E. (1954). Psychoanalysis and the dynamic psychotherapies. *Journal of the American Psychoanalytic Association, 2,* 745–770.

Boris, H. (1973). Confrontation in the analysis of the transference resistance. In G. Adler & P. G. Myerson (Eds.), *Confrontation in psychotherapy* (pp. 181–206). Northvale, NJ: Jason Aronson.

Bornstein, R. F. (1990a). Subliminal mere exposure and psychodynamic activation effects: Implications for the psychoanalytic theory of conscious and unconscious mental processes. In J. Masling (Ed.), *Empirical studies of psychoanalytic theories* (Vol. 3, pp. 55–88). Hillsdale, NJ: Erlbaum.

Bornstein, R. F. (1990b). Critical importance of stimulus unawareness for the production of subliminal psychodynamic activation effects: A meta-analytic review. *Journal of Clinical Psychology, 46,* 201–210.

Bornstein, R. F. (1992). Subliminal mere exposure effects. In R. F. Bornstein

& T. S. Pittman (Eds.), *Perception without awareness: Cognitive, clinical and social perspectives* (pp. 191–210). New York: Guilford Press.

Bornstein, R. F. (1993). Implicit perception, implicit memory, and the recovery of unconscious material in psychotherapy. *The Journal of Nervous and Mental Disease, 181,* 337–344.

Bornstein, R. F., & D'Agostino, P. R. (1990, August). *Limiting conditions on the exposure effect: Boredom and attributional discounting.* Paper presented at the 98th Annual Convention of the American Psychological Association, Boston.

Bornstein, R. F., & Masling, J. M. (1994). From the consulting room to the laboratory: Clinical evidence, empirical evidence, and the heuristic value of object relations theory. In J. M. Masling & R. F. Bornstein (Eds.), *Empirical studies of psychoanalytic theories: Vol. 5. Empirical perspectives on object relations therapy* (pp. xv–xxvi). Washington, DC: American Psychological Association.

Brandchaft, B. (1983). The negativism of the negative therapeutic reaction and the psychology of the self. In A. Goldberg (Ed.), *The future of psychoanalysis* (pp. 327–359). Madison, CT: International Universities Press.

Breggin, P. R. (1991). *Toxic psychiatry.* New York: St. Martin's Press.

Breggin, P. R., & Breggin, G. R. (1994). *Talking back to Prozac.* New York: St. Martin's Press.

Breuer, J., & Freud, S. (1955). Studies on hysteria. In J. Strachey (Ed. and Trans.), *The standard edition of the complete psychological works of Sigmund Freud* (Vol. 2, pp. 1–305). London: Hogarth Press. (Original work published 1895)

Buie, D. H., & Adler, G. (1973). The uses of confrontation in the psychotherapy of borderline patients. In G. Adler & P. G. Myerson (Eds.), *Confrontation in psychotherapy* (pp. 123–146). Northvale, NJ: Jason Aronson.

Buss, D. M. (1992). Mate preference mechanisms: Consequences for partner choice and intrasexual competition. In J. H. Barkow, L. Cosmides, & J. Tooby (Eds.), *The adapted mind* (pp. 249–266). New York: Oxford University Press.

Buss, D. M. (1995). Psychological sex differences: Origins through natural selection. *American Psychologist, 50,* 164–168.

Corwin, H. A. (1973). Therapeutic confrontation from routine to heroic. In G. Adler & P. G. Myerson (Eds.), *Confrontation in psychotherapy* (pp. 67–96). Northvale, NJ: Jason Aronson.

Elder, G. H. (1969). Appearance and education in marriage mobility. *American Sociological Review, 34,* 519–533.

Eysenck, H. J. (1972). The experimental study of Freudian concepts. *Bulletin of the British Psychological Society, 25,* 261–274.

Fisher, H. E. (1992). *Anatomy of love: The natural history of monogamy, adultery, and divorce.* New York: Norton.

Freud, S. (1953). Fragment of an analysis of a case of hysteria. In J. Strachey (Ed. and Trans.), *The standard edition of the complete psychological works of Sigmund Freud* (Vol. 7, pp. 3–124). London: Hogarth Press. (Original work published 1905)

Freud, S. (1955). A difficulty in the path of psycho-analysis. In J. Strachey (Ed. and Trans.), *The standard edition of the complete psychological works of Sigmund Freud* (Vol. 17, pp. 136–144). London: Hogarth Press. (Original work published 1917)

Freud, S. (1955). Group psychology and the analysis of the ego. In J. Strachey (Ed. and Trans.), *The standard edition of the complete psychological works of Sigmund Freud* (Vol. 18, pp. 65–143). London: Hogarth Press. (Original work published 1921)

Freud, S. (1957). On narcissism: An introduction. In J. Strachey (Ed. and Trans.), *The standard edition of the complete psychological works of Sigmund Freud* (Vol. 14, pp. 67–102). London: Hogarth Press. (Original work published 1914)

Freud, S. (1957a). Instincts and their vicissitudes. In J. Strachey (Ed. and Trans.), *The standard edition of the complete psychological works of Sigmund Freud* (Vol. 14, pp. 117–140). London: Hogarth Press. (Original work published 1915)

Freud, S. (1957b). Thoughts for the times on war and death. In J. Strachey (Ed. and Trans.), *The standard edition of the complete psychological works of Sigmund Freud* (Vol. 14, pp. 273–302). London: Hogarth Press. (Original work published 1915)

Freud, S. (1958). Recommendations to physicians practicing psycho-analysis. In J. Strachey (Ed. and Trans.), *The standard edition of the complete psychological works of Sigmund Freud* (Vol. 12, pp. 11–120). London: Hogarth Press. (Original work published 1912)

Freud, S. (1959). Inhibitions, symptoms, and anxiety. In J. Strachey (Ed. and Trans.), *The standard edition of the complete psychological works of Sigmund Freud* (Vol. 20, pp. 75–175). London: Hogarth Press. (Original work published 1926)

Freud, S. (1961). Beyond the pleasure principle. In J. Strachey (Ed. and Trans.), *The standard edition of the complete psychological works of Sigmund Freud* (Vol. 19, pp. 3–64). London: Hogarth Press. (Original work published 1920)

Freud, S. (1961). The ego and the id. In J. Strachey (Ed. and Trans.), *The standard edition of the complete psychological works of Sigmund Freud* (Vol. 19, pp. 1–66). London: Hogarth Press. (Original work published 1923)

Freud, S. (1961). The economic problem of masochism. In J. Strachey (Ed. and Trans.), *The standard edition of the complete psychological works of Sigmund Freud* (Vol. 19, pp. 155–170). London: Hogarth Press. (Original work published 1924)

Freud, S. (1961). Civilization and its discontents. In J. Strachey (Ed. and Trans.), *The standard edition of the complete psychological works of Sigmund Freud* (Vol. 21, pp. 59–145). London: Hogarth Press. (Original work published 1930)

Freud, S. (1964). New introductory lectures on psycho-analysis. In J. Strachey (Ed. and Trans.), *The standard edition of the complete psychological works of Sigmund Freud* (Vol. 22, pp. 1–182). London: Hogarth Press. (Original work published 1933)

Freud, S. (1964). Analysis terminable and interminable. In J. Strachey (Ed. and Trans.), *The standard edition of the complete psychological works of Sigmund Freud* (Vol. 23, pp. 216–254). London: Hogarth Press. (Original work published 1937)

Friedman, L. (1992, October). Discussion of Evelyne Schwaber's paper, "Psychoanalytic theory and its relation to clinical work." Scientific Meeting of the Psychoanalytic Society of New England, East.

Geha, R. E. (1993). Transferred fictions. *Psychoanalytic Dialogues, 3,* 209–243.

Glover, E. (1955). *The technique of psychoanalysis.* Madison, CT: International Universities Press.

Glover, E. (1956). *On the early development of mind.* Madison, CT: International Universities Press.

Goldberg, A. (1985). The definition and role of interpretation. In A. Goldberg (Ed.), *Progress in self psychology* (Vol. 1, pp. 62–65). New York: Guilford Press.

Greenson, R. (1967). *The technique and practice of psychoanalysis.* New York: International Universities Press.

Habermas, J. (1971). *Knowledge and human interests* (J. J. Shapiro, Trans.). London: Heinemann.

Havens, L. L. (1973). The place of confrontation in modern psychotherapy. In G. Adler & P. G. Myerson (Eds.), *Confrontation in psychotherapy* (pp. 225–248). Northvale, NJ: Jason Aronson.

Hawking, S. W. (1988). *A brief history of time.* New York: Bantam Books.

Herman, H. (1993, March). Question: How often do men think about sex? *Ladies Home Journal,* pp. 96–99.

Hoffman, I. (1983). The patient as interpreter of the analyst's experience. *Contemporary Psychoanalysis, 19,* 389–442.

Hoffman, I. (1991). Toward a social constructivist view of the psychoanalytic situation. *Psychoanalytic Dialogues, 1,* 74–105.

Holt, R. R. (1989). *Freud reappraised.* New York: Guilford Press.

Jaspers, K. (1963). *General psychopathology.* Chicago: University of Chicago Press. (Original work published 1900)

Keeley, L. H. (1996). *War before civilization: The myth of the peaceful savage.* New York: Oxford University Press.

Klein, M. (1975). Notes on some schizoid mechanisms. In *Envy and gratitude and other works.* New York: Delacorte Press. (Original work published 1946)

Kohut, H. (1959). Introspection, empathy, and psycho-analysis. *Journal of the American Psychoanalytic Association, 7,* 459–483.

Kohut, H. (1971). *The analysis of the self.* Madison, CT: International Universities Press.

Kohut, H. (1972). Thoughts on narcissism and narcissistic rage. *Psychoanalytic Study of the Child, 27,* 360–400.

Kohut, H. (1977). *The restoration of the self.* Madison, CT: International Universities Press.

Kohut, H. (1980). Reflections on advances in self psychology. In A. Goldberg (Ed.), *Advances in self psychology* (pp. 473–554). Madison, CT: International Universities Press.

Kohut, H. (1982). Introspection, empathy, and the semi-circle of mental health. *International Journal of PsychoAnalysis, 63,* 395–407.

Kohut, H. (1984). *How does analysis cure?* Chicago: University of Chicago Press.

Kriegman, D. (1988). Self psychology from the perspective of evolutionary biology: Toward a biological foundation for self psychology. In A. Goldberg (Ed.), *Progress in self psychology* (Vol. 3, pp. 253–274). Hillsdale, NJ: Analytic Press.

Kriegman, D. (1990). Compassion and altruism in psychoanalytic theory: An evolutionary analysis of self psychology. *Journal of the American Academy of Psychoanalysis, 18,* 342–367.

Kriegman, D. (1996a). On the existential/subjectivism–scientific/objectivism dialectic in self psychology: A view from evolutionary biology. In A. Goldberg (Ed.), *Progress in self psychology* (Vol. 12, pp. 85–119). Hillsdale, NJ: Analytic Press.

Kriegman, D. (1996b). The effectiveness of medication: The *Consumer Reports* study. *American Psychologist, 51,* 881.

Kriegman, D. (1996c, October). *Using an experience-near understanding of inherent conflict in the relational world in the treatment of a "psychotic" patient.* Paper presented at the 19th Annual Conference on the Psychology of the Self, Washington, DC.

Kriegman, D., & Biederman, I. (1980). How many letters in Bidwell's ghost? An investigation of the upper limits of full report from a brief visual stimulus. *Journal of Perception and Psychophysics, 28,* 82–84.

Kriegman, D., & Kriegman, O. (1997, June 7). *War and the evolution of the human propensity to form nations, cults, and religions.* Paper presented at the Annual Human Behavior and Evolution Society Conference, Tucson, AZ.

Kriegman, D., & Slavin, M. O. (1989). The myth of the repetition compulsion and the negative therapeutic reaction: An evolutionary biological analysis. In A. Goldberg (Ed.), *Progress in self psychology* (Vol. 5, pp. 209–253). Hillsdale, NJ: Analytic Press.

Kriegman, D., & Slavin, M. O. (1990). On the resistance to self psychology: Clues from evolutionary biology. In A. Goldberg (Ed.), *Progress in self psychology* (Vol. 6, pp. 217–250). Hillsdale, NJ: Analytic Press.

Kriegman, D., & Solomon, L. (1985). Psychotherapy and the "new religions": Are they the same? *Cultic Studies Journal, 2,* 2–16.

Lippman, T. W. (1990). *Understanding Islam.* New York: Dutton/Blackstone.

Masling, J. M. (1992). What does it all mean? In R. F. Bornstein & T. S. Pittman (Eds.), *Perception without awareness* (pp. 259–276). New York: Guilford Press.

Masling, J. M., & Cohen, I. S. (1987). Psychotherapy, clinical evidence, and the self-fulfilling prophecy. *Psychoanalytic Psychology, 4*, 65–79.

Masson, J. M. (1984). *The assault on truth: Freud's suppression of the seduction theory.* Boston: Faber & Faber.

Masson, J. M. (1988). *Against therapy: Emotional tyranny and the myth of psychological healing.* New York: Atheneum.

Masson, J. M. (1990). *Final analysis: The making and unmaking of a psychoanalyst.* Reading, MA: Addison-Wesley.

Mitchell, S. A. (1993). *Hope and dread in psychoanalysis.* New York: Basic Books.

Murray, J. (1973). The purpose of confrontation. In G. Adler & P. G. Myerson (Eds.), *Confrontation in psychotherapy* (pp. 49–66). Northvale, NJ: Jason Aronson.

Myerson, P. G. (1973). The meanings of confrontation. In G. Adler & P. G. Myerson (Eds.), *Confrontation in psychotherapy* (pp. 21–38). Northvale, NJ: Jason Aronson.

Nesse, R. M. (1990). The evolutionary functions of repression and the ego defenses. *Journal of the American Academy of Psychoanalysis, 18*, 260–285.

Orange, D. M. (1995). *Emotional understanding: Studies in psychoanalytic epistemology.* New York: Guilford Press.

Ornstein, P. H. (1995). Critical reflections on a comparative analysis of "self psychology and intersubjectivity theory." *Progress in Self Psychology, 11*, 47–78.

Patton, C. J. (1992). Fear of abandonment and binge eating: A subliminal psychodynamic activation investigation. *Journal of Nervous and Mental Disease, 180*, 484–490.

Popper, K. R. (1963). *Conjectures and refutations: The growth of scientific knowledge.* New York: Harper & Row.

Rachman, A. W. (1996a, February). *The confusion of tongues between Sigmund and Anna Freud.* Paper presented at the Eighth Biennial Conference of the Psychoanalytic Society of the New York University Postdoctoral Program.

Rachman, A. W. (1996b, October). *The evolution of the concept of empathy: From Ferenczi to Kohut.* Paper presented at the 19th Annual Conference on the Psychology of the Self, Washington, DC.

Renik, O. (1993). Analytic interaction: Conceptualizing technique in light of the analyst's irreducible subjectivity. *Psychoanalytic Quarterly, 62*, 553–571.

Ricoeur, P. (1970). *Freud and philosophy: An essay on interpretation* (D. Savage, Trans.). New Haven, CT: Yale University Press.

Ridley, M. (1993). *The red queen: Sex and the evolution of human nature.* New York: Macmillan.

Sackeim, H. A., & Gur, R. C. (1978). Self-deception, self-confrontation, and consciousness. In G. E. Schwartz & D. Shapiro (Eds.), *Consciousness and self regulation: Advances in research* (Vol. 2, pp. 139–197). New York: Plenum.

Schmideberg, M. (1970). Psychotherapy with failures of psychoanalysis. *British Journal of Psychiatry, 116,* 195–200.

Segal, H. (1964). *Introduction to the work of Melanie Klein.* New York: Basic Books.

Shane, M. (1985). Summary of Kohut's "The self psychological approach to defense and resistance." *Progress in Self Psychology, 1,* 69–79.

Singer, J. A., & Singer, J. L. (1994). Social-cognitive and narrative perspectives on transference. In J. M. Masling & R. F. Bornstein (Eds.), *Empirical studies of psychoanalytic theories: Vol. 5. Empirical perspectives on object relations theory* (pp. 157–193). Washington, DC: American Psychological Association.

Slavin, M. O. (1985). The origins of psychic conflict and the adaptive function of repression: An evolutionary biological view. *Psychoanalysis and Contemporary Thought, 8,* 407–440.

Slavin, M. O. (1990). The biology of parent-offspring conflict and the dual meaning of repression in psychoanalysis. *Journal of the American Academy of Psychoanalysis, 18,* 307–341.

Slavin, M. O., & Kriegman, D. (1992). *The adaptive design of the human psyche: Psychoanalysis, evolutionary biology, and the therapeutic process.* New York: Guilford Press.

Slavin, M. O., & Kriegman, D. (in press). Why the analyst needs to change: Toward a theory of conflict, negotiation, and mutual influence in the therapeutic process. *Psychoanalytic Dialogues.*

Spence, D. (1982). *Narrative truth and historical truth.* New York: Norton.

Spezzano, C. (1993a). A relational model of inquiry and truth: The place of psychoanalysis in human conversation. *Psychoanalytic Dialogues, 3,* 177–208.

Spezzano, C. (1993b). Illusions of candor: Reply to Sass. *Psychoanalytic Dialogues, 3,* 267–278.

Spock, B., & Rothenberg, M. B. (1985). *Baby and child care.* New York: Pocket Books.

Stocking, M. (1973). Confrontation in psychotherapy: Considerations arising from the psychoanalytic treatment of a child. In G. Adler & P. G. Myerson (Eds.), *Confrontation in psychotherapy* (pp. 319–346). Northvale, NJ: Jason Aronson.

Stolorow, R. (1995). Introduction: Tensions between loyalism and expansionism in self psychology. *Progress in Self Psychology, 11,* xi–xvii.

Stolorow, R., & Atwood, G. (1992). *Contexts of being.* Hillsdale, NJ: Analytic Press.

Stolorow, R., & Atwood, G. (1994). Toward a science of human experience. In R. Stolorow, G. Atwood, & B. Brandchaft (Eds.), *The intersubjective perspective* (pp. 15–30). Northvale, NJ: Jason Aronson.

Stolorow, R., Brandchaft, B., & Atwood, G. (1987). *Psychoanalytic treatment: An intersubjective approach.* Hillsdale, NJ: Analytic Press.

Strachey, J. (1934). The nature of the therapeutic action of psychoanalysis. *International Journal of PsychoAnalysis, 15,* 117–126.

Strupp, H. (1982). Psychoanalytic failure. *Contemporary Psychoanalysis, 18,* 235–250.

Strupp, H., Hadley, S., & Gomes-Schwartz, B. (1977). *Psychotherapy for better or worse: The problem of negative effects.* New York: Jason Aronson.

Teicholz, J. G. (in press). Self and relationship: Kohut, Loewald and the post moderns. In A. Goldberg (Ed.), *Progress in self psychology* (Vol. 13). Hillsdale, NJ: Analytic Press.

Torrey, F. F. (1992). *Freudian fraud: The malignant effect of Freud's theory on American thought and culture.* New York: HarperCollins.

Trivers, R. L. (1971). The evolution of reciprocal altruism. *Quarterly Review of Biology, 46,* 35–57.

Trivers, R. L. (1972). Parental investment and sexual selection. In B. Campbell (Ed.), *Sexual selection and the descent of man, 1871–1971* (pp. 136–179). Chicago: Aldine-Atherton.

Trivers, R. L. (1976). *The selfish gene.* New York: Oxford University Press.

Trivers, R. L. (1985). *Social evolution.* Menlo Park, NJ: Benjamin Cummings.

Wallace, E. R. (1988). What is "truth"? Some philosophical contributions to psychiatric issues. *American Journal of Psychiatry, 145,* 137–147.

Weiss, J., & Sampson, H. (1986). *The psychoanalytic process: Theory, clinical observation, and empirical research.* New York: Guilford Press.

Welpton, D. F. (1973). Confrontation in the therapeutic process. In G. Adler & P. G. Myerson (Eds.), *Confrontation in psychotherapy* (pp. 249–270). Northvale, NJ: Jason Aronson.

Wright, R. (1994, August 15). Our cheating hearts. *Time,* pp. 45–52.

Author Index

Numbers in italics refer to listings in reference sections.

Subject Index

About the Editors

Robert F. **Bornstein** is Professor of Psychology at Gettysburg College. He received his PhD in clinical psychology from the State University of New York at Buffalo in 1986. Bornstein has written many articles on perception without awareness and has published extensively on the antecedents, correlates, and consequences of dependent personality traits. He edited *Perception Without Awareness: Cognitive, Clinical and Social Perspectives* (1992); coedited (with Joseph M. Masling) *Psychoanalytic Perspectives on Psychopathology* (1993), *Empirical Perspectives on Object Relations Theory* (1994), and *Psychoanalytic Perspectives on Developmental Psychology* (1996); and is the author of *The Dependent Personality* (1993), a comprehensive review of the empirical literature on dependency.

Joseph M. Masling is Emeritus Professor of Psychology at the State University of New York (SUNY) at Buffalo. He received his PhD in clinical psychology from Ohio State University in 1952; he was director of clinical training at Syracuse University (1959–1964) and chairperson of the Department of Psychology at SUNY–Buffalo (1969–1972). Masling has written numerous articles on interpersonal and situational variables influencing projective tests and has published widely on the empirical study of psychoanalytic concepts. He edited the first three volumes of the series Empirical Studies of Psychoanalytic Theories (1983, 1986, 1990) and coedited (with Robert F. Bornstein) Volume 4, *Psychoanalytic Perspectives on Psychopathology* (1993), Volume 5, *Empirical Perspectives on Object Relations Theory* (1994), and Volume 6, *Psychoanalytic Perspectives on Developmental Psychology* (1996).